ALL IN COLOR FOR A DIME

Edited by
Dick Lupoff & Don Thompson

Published by

 **krause
publications**

**700 E. State Street • Iola, WI 54990-0001
Telephone: 715/445-2214**

A free catalog of Krause Publications material is available upon request.
The toll-free number for placing orders or obtaining the catalog is (800) 258-0929.
Krause Publications' business phone line is (715) 445-2214
and is available for editorial comment and/or further information.

First Krause Publications edition published 1997.

ISBN: 0-87341-498-5

Printed in the United States of America

THIS BOOK IS DEDICATED TO

Otto O. Binder

CONTENTS

★★★

Color Section follows page 144

HELLO, IT'S US AGAIN!

Nineteen-sixty.

Say it out loud.

Roll it around on your tongue, get the feel of it, the taste and the sound.

Depending on your age, it sounds not much longer ago than yesterday—last week at the most ... Or else it was an ancient eon, somewhere between the beginning of the Paleolithic Era and the end of the Cold War.

We had TV in 1960, and they even gave out Emmys. Program of the Year was a production of *Macbeth* on *The Hallmark Hall of Fame*, if you can believe that. (Maurice Evans, Judith Anderson, and Director George Schaefer also won Emmys for that show.) Outstanding humor series was *The Jack Benny Show*, outstanding variety show was *Astaire Time*, outstanding series actors were Raymond Burr (as Perry Mason, of course) and Barbara Stanwyck (for her own anthology series). And the writing award went to Rod Serling for *The Twilight Zone*.

There, that wasn't so painful, was it?

That was 1960.

Best-selling single records included "Are You Lonesome Tonight?" by Elvis Presley, "Georgia on My Mind" by Ray Charles, "The Twist" by Chubby Checker, "Save the Last Dance for Me" by The Drifters, "Itsy Bitsy Teeny Weeny Yellow Polka Dot Bikini" by Bryan Hyland, and "I'm Sorry" by Brenda Lee.

There was no sign of The Beatles, Rolling Stones, Jefferson Airplane, or Grateful Dead.

Leading Broadway musicals were *Bye Bye Birdie* by Lee Adams, Michael Stewart, and Charles Strouse, *Irma la Douce* by Alexandre Breffort and Marguerite Monnot, and *Camelot* by Alan J. Lerner and Frederick Loewe. And Zero Mostel was riveting in Eugene Ionesco's *Rhinoceros*.

Time magazine named as its "Men of the Year" 15 leading scientists—all Americans, all white, and all male. They included chemist Linus Pauling, physicists Edward Teller and Isidor Isaac Rabi, William Shockley (co-inventor of the transistor), and James Van Allen (he of the famous radiation belt).

The Academy Award for best picture was won by *The Apartment*; best actor was Burt Lancaster for his role in *Elmer Gantry*; best actress was Elizabeth Taylor for *Butterfield 8*. The best foreign language film was Ingmar Bergman's *The Virgin Spring*. Some other memorable films of that year were *Psycho, Spartacus, Sunrise at Campobello, Inherit the Wind*, and *The Time Machine*.

The world stage was dominated by the Cold War. Dwight Eisenhower and Nikita Khrushchev glared at each other across the North Pole, brandishing missiles, variously cheered on or calmed down by Mao Zedong, Charles de Gaulle, and Winston Churchill. Deep in the Soviet Union, Major Yuri Gagarin was training for the flight that would, the following year, make him the first human space traveler.

Vice President Richard M. Nixon and Massachusetts Senator John F. Kennedy campaigned busily for the Presidency of the United States.

It was forever and a day ago—or it was just this morning.

On a much more modest level, the world of comic books had reached a low ebb. The first great era of the comics, the so-called Golden Age, had ended at some vague point in the 1950s. The great demand for cheap, lightweight, easily portable, and easily consumable entertainment reading had spurred the growth of the comics at the end of the Depression and during the years of World War II. By the '50s, television was the coming medium, the millions of GIs and swabbies and jarheads had returned to civilian life, first in 1945 and then again with the end of the Korean War in 1953.

The kids were dancing to rock 'n' roll, and their elders were busy building careers, buying automobiles, and adding to the population.

The superheroes were the great stars of the Golden Age and they very nearly became an extinct species. A few of them hung on, most notably Superman and Batman, but most of the great DC line of heroes were gone. All of the Fawcett heroes were gone. All of the Marvel heroes were gone. And the independents—the Green Lama and Black Terror and Black Cat and Lady Luck and all the rest of them were gone ... gone ... gone.

Just for the record: There was no such thing as comics fandom. Oh, kids still read and saved and traded comics, and there were occasional mentions of comics here and there—more often patronizing than respectful—especially in science-fiction fanzines. There were some abortive attempts, especially among fans of E.C. Comics, to produce some sort of ongoing focal point. But the attempts did not succeed in creating a microcosm of wide proportions. When the outside world bothered to take note of comic books, it was usually to trash them, as in the works of Gershon Legman and Fredric Wertham.

There was no such thing as a comic-book store, either. You bought comics off the rack, where they often found a niche between the few surviving pulp magazines and such slicks as *Newsweek, Pic,* and *Look*.

A few people collected comics, but they did so because they loved them and loved to read and reread them. They did not buy comic books as financial investments. That phenomenon was yet to appear.

But a few people remembered, and, in three widely separated cities, three enterprising amateur publishers were preparing periodicals that would mark the origins of comics fandom as it became known in later years. The first of these magazines to make its debut was a mimeographed journal called *Xero*, and the very first issue of *Xero*, dated September 1960, featured an essay titled "The Big Red Cheese."

This was the first installment in a series called *All in Color for a Dime*, and, once it hit, the world of comics was never again the same. Other magazines, most notably *Comic Art* and *Alter-Ego*, followed in rapid succession. Within a year both DC and Marvel Comics were testing the waters for the return of the superhero and the appearance of a whole new generation of adventurers, and before long the second great age of comics, the Silver Age, had begun.

All in Color for a Dime appeared in book form in 1970, followed by *The Comic-Book Book*. These two volumes were edited by Dick Lupoff and Don Thompson. Out of print for a quarter century, the books have become legendary volumes, the foundation stones upon which scholarship and criticism of the comic book—or funny book or graphic novel or sequential art or whatever resonates with what you love in picture stories—rest. Uncounted readers have begged, bid, threatened, and cajoled for the reissue of these books, and here at last is *All in Color for a Dime*, in a new and improved edition.

The front cover is new. The back cover reproduces the award-winning "package" of the first edition.

With the death of Don Thompson, his role has been assumed by his wife and collaborator of many years, Maggie Thompson. We hope that the new generations of readers who are able to peruse *All in Color for a Dime* for the first time will enjoy the volume as much as the older generation, who will surely welcome it back as an old friend.

Upon rereading these eleven essays—as well as the introduction to the original *All in Color for a Dime*—certain observations are inevitable. First is the wide variety of attitude and style among the authors. Each had his own perspective, and, like *Time*'s Men of the Year for 1960, all were white, male, and American.

Some of them wrote very well and went on to significant literary achievements. Others were, to put it gently, perhaps not quite so polished in their prose and in due course sought career opportunities elsewhere. And all of them were young. Very young. They were filled with the enthusiastic energy—and sometimes the excesses—that go with that territory. The world of comics has grown a lot since then.

Research has added immeasurably to the facts these authors presented. Some errors were surely made in their essays, and far more information has been unearthed. For example, some of the judgments, assessments, and usages that were made decades ago have become laughable. Note the references to prices of collectible comics. (The price quoted on the color reproduction of the cover of *Marvel Comics #1*—"$250 and more"—seemed pretty high for something that originally sold for 10¢. But it can now sell for more than *350 times* that $250 price tag.)

And when you read (or reread) the introduction to the original *All in Color for a Dime*, you may notice the mention of ten essays by ten authors. Yes, but there were eleven.

Why?

Well, one author missed his deadline, received an extension and missed his deadline again, until it was time to turn in the manuscript to the publisher. The introduction was locked in place by then. And then the author, en route from Los Angeles to London by way of New York, completed his work while eight miles high over the middle of the continent. He used a lightweight portable typewriter, the 1960s version of a laptop computer. He dropped off his manuscript at the airport and continued on his way.

And that, gentle reader, is the story of the eleventh chapter.

Incidentally, due to a production error, the art for the essay on George Carlson was originally illustrated with a tailpiece by another artist. While we tried in almost every case to maintain rigid adherence to republishing what was released in the original edition, no matter what, we have replaced the erroneous art with Carlson work (and added a bonus color page of Carlson art, to boot). But the old "wrong" art, in case you are curious about it, is also included. (See at right.)

If all goes well, we hope to follow this new/old *All in Color for a Dime* with a new edition of *The Comic-Book Book* and with a third volume (and possibly more) that Don, Maggie, and Dick had been planning at the time of Don's death.

Dick Lupoff
Maggie Thompson
January 1997

INTRODUCTION TO

ALL IN COLOR FOR A DIME

by DICK LUPOFF & DON THOMPSON

WHAT shapes a people? Is it the geography and climate of their country? The political system under which they live? Is it economics, religion, war? Or is it the culture in which they are immersed from birth onward . . . especially the culture in which they are immersed during childhood?

For at least a quarter century, the comic book was the dominant element in the culture of American children—they read them, reread them, collected them, traded them. During that same period, especially during World War II, when servicemen with limited off-duty time hungered for cheap and quickly readable material it achieved great (although less publicized) popularity as reading matter for adults.

In the past few years, television has threatened the preeminent position of the comic, but the slim, colorful pamphlet (really a more appropriate word than book, but the latter is the indelibly accepted term) has fought back to a new revival in popularity.

Comic book characters have become part of the myth-structure of much of the world: not only is Superman more widely known than Paul Bunyan, but even Clark Kent has achieved the same stature. Words, images, ideas, narrative and expressive techniques have all moved from the four-color page and invaded every aspect of our language and society.

Surveys have shown that from 90 percent to 99 percent of American children read comics. That's more than watch television, go to the movies, or read "real" books, except under pressure. Several comics series have achieved circulation in excess of a million copies per issue. Even among the less successful titles, circulation in the hundreds of thousands is the norm, and a sales figure of less than six figures is grounds for discontinuing the comic.

Comic books have been published in a wide variety of sizes and formats ranging from tabloid newspaper size down to tiny things no bigger than a postage stamp. The standard page is just over ten inches high by seven wide. The standard page count was originally 64 plus covers, although extra-thick comics with up to several hundred pages have been published at premium prices. Some years after the comics became solidly established, the page count dropped to 48 plus covers, and later to 32, today's standard. Today, comics seldom run more than 64 pages, at a cost of 25¢. A line of "80-Page Giants" was recently cut back to 64 pages.

Comics have been published in black-and-white, monochrome, and full-color (four-color) processes, the last now being standard. They have been published on a variety of paper stocks but the standard is a rather nondurable newsprint, except for the covers, which are printed on higher grade, slick paper. A few comics have used the cheap inside stock for covers as well; these are most noteworthy for their lack of durability.

Some deluxe comics have been published in hard covers, and a few of the thicker ones have been side-stitched to obtain flat spines. But the overwhelming majority are made in a single printer's signature and bound with staples driven through the cover at the spine and locked at the centerfold.

Prices have ranged from 5¢ to 50¢, with giveaways at the lowest end of the scale and super-fancy editions at the top. For many years, the standard price for comics was a dime—until inflation knocked that out. Now, the 32-page comic costs 15¢, after hovering briefly at a plateau of 12¢—and the 64-page comic that once sold for a dime now costs 25¢.

Surprisingly, in the face of the comic book's tremendous popularity, people who write about the arts and literature have for many years paid little attention to comic books. Not so the comic strip. As early as 1942, Martin Sheridan's *Comics and Their Creators* provided a book-length treatment of the newspaper comics. Sheridan treated literally scores of comic features to a few pages of description, career sketches of their creators, and sample panels. But he had little interest in full-length comic books. In fact, only because Superman appeared as a newspaper feature as well as a comic book was he included in Sheridan's volume.

Coulton Waugh's *The Comics* (1947) offered a superior history and analysis of the strips. Waugh was himself a comic strip cartoonist (he did *Dickie Dare* for several years, then turned it over to his wife), and he wrote with both love and perception. But, again, the emphasis of his book was overwhelmingly on comic strips. He devoted only one chapter to comic books and, although it is truly an excellent one, there is only a limited amount that can be crammed into a score of pages.

Almost all of the later books have followed the same pattern. Becker's *Comic Art in America,* Abel and White's *The Funnies,* Couperie and Horn's *A History of the Comic Strip,* Perry and Aldridge's *Penguin Book of Comics* . . . all have either avoided the comic book completely or have treated it as a minor offshoot of the comic strip. Certainly the strip existed first, and certainly the comic book is an outgrowth of it, but the offspring has outgrown its parent, and deserves attention in its own right.

There have, however been several sociological studies of the comic book. In 1949, Gershon Legman placed heavy emphasis on comic books in his *Love and Death, A Study in Censorship.* In 1954, Dr. Fredric Wertham published *Seduction of the Innocent,* a book devoted entirely to comic books. And, in 1955, Geoffrey Wagner made them the topic of a section in *Parade of Pleasure,* "A Study of Popular Iconography in the U.S.A."

Legman, Wertham and Wagner compete in their merciless castigation of the comics, heaping blazing coals upon them for their excesses of violence and gore, their often unwholesome treatment of sex, and their frequently low level of writing and drawing. Wertham, in particular, laid at the doorstep of comics publishers every social ill from functional illiteracy and sexual perversion to torture, murder and suicide.

Showing that most juvenile delinquents read comics, Wertham "proved" that comics cause juvenile delinquency. It would be equally easy to prove that most nuclear physicists read comics as children, and therefore reading comics causes people to become nuclear physicists.

It's true that there has been bad material published in comic books, some bad because it was objectionable, some bad only because it wasn't well executed—merely weakly written or crudely drawn. To this extent, we must yield to men like Legman, Wertham, and Wagner. But to condemn the comics totally on the basis of bad examples is as wrong as condemning all novels because there are bad novels or all restaurants because you have had slow service or an unsatisfactory mousse at one. There have been good comics and bad ones, and children who have read them have gone on to be both axe murderers and Rhodes scholars, and to fail to distinguish between good and bad is to practice the kind of thinking that condemns a whole race to slavery or the ovens.

In 1965, Jules Feiffer produced *The Great Comic Book Heroes,* the first book devoted to comic books, and especially to their chief mainstay, the costumed adventure heroes, that did not strive to condemn and destroy its topic. The Feiffer book is a lovely volume, containing more than a hundred color pages of reprints of early comic book stories. However; it is, after all, primarily a reprint album of those stories.

Although several histories of the comic book are presently being written, and will be published shortly, the genesis of the present volume gives it, we believe, a claim of priority. This book began to grow in 1960, with the publication of the first of a series of articles collectively titled *All in Color for a Dime,* which appeared in an obscure (and long defunct) magazine called *Xero.*

The format of the articles was essentially similar—each author, as his turn came around, dredged up memories of his own favorite childhood comic hero, and reinforced them with the aid of decades-old comic books, much less expensive to obtain in the days before the explosions of camp and pop culture turned them into premium-priced collectors' items.

Each author was asked to be a three-headed monster, one head being that of a misty-eyed nostalgic, another that of a bibliographically inclined research scholar, and the third that of a social-literary-artistic critic. All of the authors succeeded, although the emphasis naturally varies from piece to piece—some are mostly critical, some are mostly nostalgic. You will not find too much emphasis on "pure" factual scholarship here, as we're mostly interested in recreating and assessing "those thrilling days of yesteryear" (to borrow a ringing phrase from another nostalgic medium). While names, dates, and volume-and-issue numbers of publications do appear in these pages, they're not really what the book is about.

There were ten articles in the original series, running from 1960 through 1963, and even in those days several men saw the series as a potential book. Three in particular—Earl Kemp, Terry Carr, and Henry Morrison—contributed their efforts to bringing the articles into a more durable, collected form. It has taken a long time for their efforts to reach fruition but, as so often happens, perseverance has won its reward.

This book, however, is a far cry from a simple reprint of the original series of magazine articles. Several of the original articles have been dropped, either because their authors did not wish them perpetuated or because we considered them too trivial or narrow in interest. *All* the chapters retained have been rewritten and expanded. And several others have been written specifically for this book.

Almost all of the authors are professional writers and editors—newspapermen, novelists, screenwriters, magazine editors—but only one of them (Roy Thomas) is primarily in the comic book industry. The authors span a broad spectrum in American letters, having written an aggregate book shelf of several dozen books, hundreds of short stories and magazine articles, news copy, films, and radio and television shows. We would suggest, without too strong a touch of *hubris,* that they represent an above-average level of intelligence, education, and social usefulness.

Yet every one of them read comic books as a child—in fact, *loved* comic books as a child—and every one of them retains his interest in and affection for the comics and their heroes. To apply Dr. Wertham's logic again, one can infer that boys who read comic books grow up to be writers or editors.

And, indeed, it is likely that they do! We present here ten case studies to prove the proposition, a good score for this kind of game.

You will find this book heavily (although not exclusively) weighted toward the costumed adventure hero: Superman, Batman, Captain Marvel, Sub-Mariner, Human Torch, Captain America, Flash, Green Lantern, Spy Smasher, Bulletman, and quite a few more. There are others here, too, such as Popeye and Star Pirate, but the emphasis is on superheroes.

These figures often lived other lives and pursued other careers than those portrayed on the comic book page. A good many of them appeared first in comic strips, then migrated to comic books via the early, reprint-oriented series, and finally achieved the distinction of having new stories written and drawn about them especially for the comic books. Others traveled backward along the same route—beginning in the comic books and then jumping to daily or Sunday newspaper comics pages.

Others transferred to comic books from (or from comic books to) many other media. For example, the Shadow started life in pulp magazines and on radio, and has since appeared on the screen, on phonograph records, in hardbound and paperback books, and in two completely separate (and very different) comic book series. Flash Gordon began as a newspaper comic strip, was adapted to movies, a pulp magazine, at least one hardcover "novel," has appeared in reprint and original comics in several series from several publishers and, most recently, in a lush hardcover reprint album of early newspaper strips. Buck Rogers began as a character in a novel in *Amazing Stories,* then found his way to screen, newspaper page, and comic books.

Edgar Rice Burroughs' Tarzan went from pulp magazine to newspaper serialization (of the text), to book form, to comic strip, to comic book, with a long series of motion picture and television versions paralleling the printed page. There have been radio and phonograph record versions, too. Several of Burroughs' lesser-known heroes—John Carter of Mars, David Innes of Pellucidar, and even Tarzan's son Korak—have appeared in comic books.

Not all comic books are devoted to costumed adventurers or to heroic figures, and the variety of features that has appeared is staggering: westerns, romances, detective stories, tales of magic, war stories, aviation stories, jungle adventures, realistic dramas, funny animals, teen-age comedies, sports stories, true-fact comics, medical and psychoanalytic stories (yes!), Bible stories, political biographies, movie and television tie-ins, adaptations of books, historical fiction, horror stories, science fiction, etc.

And that list is not exhaustive. It doesn't even consider such unlikely hybrids as *War Romances, War Horror, Space Detective* and even (we swear) *Space Western.*

Yet the comic book and costumed hero are synonymous in the public mind and, even though it is not a rigorously and literally accurate identification, it is *essentially* correct. While the newspaper comic page is largely the property of adults, the comic book is the property of children. Not that kids don't read newspaper comics or their elders comic books. But strips are written and published for the people who buy newspapers—adults—and comic books are slanted toward and produced for the people who buy them—kids.

There *is* a chicken-and-egg dilemma here. Kids buy comics because they feature superheroes and comics feature superheroes because kids buy them. Adults like their far-fetched adventurers, too, whether they follow Dick Tracy or Steve Canyon, James Bond or Buz Sawyer, but they like them in plain clothes.

But for children there is an ineffable appeal in the *costumed* adventure hero. Even super powers, while desirable, are not vital. For every Superman there has been a Batman, for every Human Torch a Captain America, and for every Bulletman a Mister Scarlet. This is because of an essential difference between the mentality of a child and that of an adult. The adult recognizes the essential absurdity of a self-appointed do-gooder parading through the streets in fuchsia tights and an all-seeing eye blazoned on his chest, a cape of scarlet satin trailing behind. The adult has grown too worldly, knows that such things do not happen, will not accept them, even in fantasy.

The child, however, knows only that the people around him do not do the wild and thrilling things that he sees in his comics. But his hero, in tights and cape, escapes the bonds, the role-playing, that the conventional clothing the everyday world imposes upon ordinary men and women. Not everyone loses sight of this truth, and the modern bohemian (like the bohemian of every era) discards the conventional clothing of mundane society.

This book will provide fairly thorough portrayals of about two dozen comics heroes, and fleeting glimpses of perhaps a hundred more. We hope you will enjoy encountering (or re-encountering) the Blue Bolt, Sub-Zero Man, Ibis the Invincible, Commando Yank, Nyoka the Jungle Girl, Jungle Jim, Hour-Man, Johnny Thunder, the Boy Commandos, the Girl Commandos, the Young Allies, Reed Richards, Eugene the Jeep, Alice the Goon, Mr. Mind, Dr. Sivana, the Red Comet, Gale Allen, Funnyman, Dick Grayson, and all the rest.

A few years ago, an enthusiastic comic book fan attempted to list *all* the superheroes and other costumed adventurers who had ever appeared. He worked till exhausted, and when he gave up, he had accumulated more than *eight thousand* names, and the end was nowhere in sight. We can only guess at the final number. So if your own favorite hero of the past (or present) is omitted, forgive us—the book is lengthy as it stands; to be more comprehensive would inflate it beyond all bounds.

It's certain that we will never be able to give thorough coverage to all the comic heroes, but we hope there will be a sequel to this book—another volume in which a crew of three-headed monsters will attempt to do justice to . . . well, we shall see.

INTRODUCTION TO

THE SPAWN OF M. C. GAINES

For anyone born since, oh, let's say, the mid-1930s, comic books have "always" been around. The cornerstone of comics has been the costumed adventure hero; the most prominent and durable of those are Superman and Batman. Of course "always" has its limits, and a little research quickly shows that Superman dates only from 1938, Batman is even younger, and the modern comic book—despite earlier avatars—dates only from the era of the New Deal.

Ted White was born the same year as Superman. He claims no unusual powers as a result of this, merely pointing out the fact that as a boy he was a fanatic comic book reader and collector, and at one time achieved some fame, and local newspaper coverage, as "the boy with 10,000 comic books."

On reaching manhood, Ted entered on a literary career. He began, surprisingly, as a music critic, then became a science fiction writer and editor. He is currently Managing Editor of *Amazing Stories* and *Fantastic* magazine. Although his literary output has been mainly in the area of science fiction, his interest in comics has endured. He has been a script writer on several TV cartoon series, and is the author of a paperback novelization of the comics hero, Captain America, *The Great Gold Steal,* published by Bantam Books.

In this opening chapter he traces the machinations that led up to the publication of the first Superman and Batman adventures, and traces the careers of those heroes and their creators. It is a fascinating story, although perhaps not as pretty or as pat as a comic book adventure.

CHAPTER 1

THE SPAWN OF M. C. GAINES

by TED WHITE

★★

It's a story which has grown into modern myth—a myth which in some respects equals and parallels the myth of Superman himself—the story of how two boys, Jerome Siegel and Joe Shuster, fresh out of high school, sold their dream comic strip and achieved world fame.

As science fiction fans, Siegel and Shuster had published an early science fiction fan magazine, the title of which was, not so surprisingly, *Science Fiction*. It was a mimeographed publication and appeared in the early 1930s. In many respects, including the poor paper on which it was published, it resembled more closely fan magazines being published by s.f. and comics fans now than it did most of its contemporaries. Most of the material was written by Siegel, and all the illustrations were by Shuster.

As the myth has it, while still in high school, science fiction fans Siegel and Shuster dreamed up their science fictional superman: a man come to Earth from another planet, metabolically adapted for a greater gravity and far harsher environmental pressures than ours. Here on Earth, the superman would find his powers vastly multiplied, just as we would find ours greater on, for instance, the Moon.

According to the story, sample art and scripts for *Superman* were drawn and prepared for submission as early as 1935. M. C. Gaines remembered seeing it while he was associated with the Dell line of comics, but could not find a place for either the original concept or the crude rendering, in books that were then given over entirely to Sunday comics reprints.

The tale of *Superman*'s round of rejections is very much like the story of the best seller rejected by 26 publishers before finding its home with the 27th—perhaps not entirely true, but certainly too colorful to ignore in the retelling. In any case, the team of Siegel & Shuster had sold some half dozen other original strips before finding a home for their baby Superman.

Let's backtrack for a minute, though. To understand the peculiar success story of *Superman,* one must have some understanding of comics publishing in the 1930s.

Newspaper comics were born around the turn of the century, and it was inevitable that someone, sooner or later, would begin collecting the daily and Sunday newspaper strips into book and booklet form. This began in the 1920s, with a variety of nonstandardized sizes and formats. On my shelf of oddities there is a five-by-seven "book" of *Little Orphan Annie* sitting next to a ten-by-ten collection of *Mutt & Jeff,* both products of the late twenties, and both printed in black and white.

In the early thirties, while young Siegel and Shuster were daydreaming in math or science class over their *Superman* or their fan magazine, a man named M. C. Gaines created the comic book.

It was called *Funnies on Parade,* and it was the prototype for the successful *Famous Funnies:* it measured (approximately) seven by ten inches, was printed in color on newsprint, and was devoted exclusively to reprints of the popular Sunday comics features of the time, usually reprinting a complete Sunday feature on each page.

Gaines had simply taken the dimensions in which the Sunday comics were printed, and proportionately reduced them so that his book could be printed on the same color presses and use material prepared for Sunday comics publication. It was less a master stroke than eminent common sense.

Funnies on Parade was a trial balloon. It was followed by *Century of Comics* (so named because it contained 100 pages; it was a dime store giveaway and had no price on it), and one or two other one-shots, including *Famous Funnies.* Apparently both idea and format were a success, because soon *Famous Funnies* was a continuing title and other publishers were coming out with imitations. (*Famous Funnies* outlasted its competition and survived into the mid-fifties, long after the other reprint titles had given up.)

At that time comics were published by newspaper syndicates, by pulp publishers (like Dell), and by distributors. One such distributor was the Independent News Co., whose trademark was an inconspicuous "IND" on the cover of many comics and magazines for a num-

Copyright 1941, Superman, Inc., renewed 1969 by National Periodical Publications, Inc., and reprinted by its permission.

ber of years. Independent owned Detective Comics, Inc., the publisher of *Detective Comics* (not surprisingly), *More Fun Comics* and *Adventure Comics.*

I have found it difficult to pin down M. C. Gaines's movements from company to company in those early years. One might almost suspect he was the Johnny Appleseed of comic books, because he seemed to go from company to company, launching comic book lines at each new place. It appears that he did not stay long with the *Famous Funnies* people, and by 1935 he was with Dell, in time as I mentioned, to see and to reject Superman. By 1938 he was associated with Detective Comics, Inc., although apparently as a publishing partner with a line of his own.

I am not being totally frivolous calling Gaines the Johnny Appleseed of comic books. Gaines was dedicated, *in principle,* to the comic book concept. His fervor was almost religious. At this time, remember, comics as such were not specifically juvenile. Comics were spawned in the newspapers, and presumably were read by the whole family. They were easy to grasp, and yet capable of conveying a considerable quantity of information. "A picture is worth a thousand words" must have been one of Gaines's favorite maxims. It was in this same period that the mass media as a whole were undergoing an entire revolution toward the visual, the pictorial. The year 1936 had witnessed the birth of *Life* magazine and "photo-journalism." Perhaps the linkage of words and pictures represented a new democratic ideal for the time. In any case, Gaines was more than a fast-buck artist looking for an easy way to millions. He was a dedicated man—as we'll see later.

But we are still setting the stage. Gaines had invented the *reprint* comic book: what about the original-material comic?

It's hard to pin down the origins of the "all-new" comics. I suspect the reason was a simple one: in a short time the reprint material was used up and there was nothing left for new titles. Some enterprising publisher made the decision to buy new material, written and drawn especially for the comic books, at first to pad out his reprints (still the headline attractions), and then, later, to replace them.

The early comic book originals were, for the most part, awful. They set out to imitate the reprints, and often a six-page story would have a running head on each page, in imitation of the Sunday reprints, each page of which *required* a running head originally. But surely the artists and writers who produced the new material were far more poorly paid—even if they received the same amount which the creator of reprints were paid. The reprints were earning their big money from newspaper syndication; the new material made what little it did solely from comic book publication. Standards quickly fell, and I think it is significant that even now they have not been entirely regained. Today, in most cases, the comic book is no more than a training ground for newspaper-strip artists.

It must also be said that comic book publishers were, all in all, a thieving, grasping lot. Not to dwell too long upon the point, they were crooks. In many instances, they were men with a good deal of money, recently earned during Prohibition, who were seeking legitimate businesses into which they might safely move. Comics—and pulp magazines—seemed like a good bet. These men had learned their so-called business ethics in a rough school. They applied them across the board in their new businesses.

The first rule was, *Do it cheap.* Find cheap labor, pay cheap prices. Low overhead. Tie up as little money as possible. Take out as much money as possible. The results were predictable—in a few short years the bad drove out the good.

Put in simple terms, most of the work being done for comic books by 1940 was being done by teenage boys, some still in high school, some dropouts. Many were enormously talented, but most came from lower-class backgrounds, were willing to work cheap (the Depression was still being felt), and were easily exploited.

The publishers became millionaires—no comic book writer, editor or artist ever did.

By 1936, Siegel and Shuster were selling strips to *Detective, More Fun* and *Adventure Comics.* These included "Dr. Occult," "Federal Men," and "Radio Squad." Later strips included "Slam Bradley." The art on the early strips was crude. Shuster's work had none of the finesse or quality of an Alex Raymond or a Hal Foster. It was, to speak plainly, amateurish. Siegel's scripts were little better. The plots were rudimentary, the dialogue and captions were in basic English and barely functional at that. Had they never produced *Superman,* I doubt whether anyone would remember them today.

Meanwhile, *Superman* was growing tattered in his trips through editorial offices. Conceived as a comic book original, he had been cut apart, redrawn, repasted, and redone as a daily strip for possible syndication. When, in 1938, M. C. Gaines heard that the publisher of *Detective Comics* wanted to start another title, he recommended *Superman* for it, and the daily strips were again recut, repasted, and reworked back into comic book pages.

The publisher bought it. *Superman* was launched in the first issue of *Action Comics.*

The first four *Superman* stories in *Action Comics* were later reprint-ed in *Superman #1*. In either form it is easy to detect the lines where pasteups occur, to see where panels were extended or added, and even to find different styles of art in adjacent panels. (Later stories, reprint-ed a year or so later from *published* newspaper strips, still carried their ben-day shading over from the black & white medium.)

Judged by current standards, the stories were rudimentary and the art crude. Indeed, National Comics will today not reprint the oldest *Superman* stories in their present reprint titles because they fall be-low acceptable standards. Nevertheless they were full of a raw kind of power which made them an instant success. They were, after all, stories about a *super-man*.

It was 1938, and the country was shuddering its way out from the crippling blow to its economy in 1929. The air was full of talk of war in Europe, and of the mad clown named Hitler. Technocracy was preaching that science could rule the world and end all Man's prob-lems, while the Communists were seeking One World under social-ism in a dictatorship of the proletariat. It was a time of idealism and of shattered ideals. We were down but not out. Our world had crum-bled, but we knew we could build a better one.

We hadn't grown up yet.

Enter Superman.

Born on the planet Krypton, and sent to Earth in a rocket by his father shortly before that planet exploded, Superman landed on Earth while still a baby, was adopted by the Kents, and grew into a super-healthy young man.

But he could not fly. He was vulnerable to gas, to oxygen starva-tion, and to some rays. His skin was tough, but not so tough it couldn't be pierced by "a bursting shell." In his first story, he was described in this fashion:

"As the lad grew older, he learned to his delight that he could hur-dle skyscrapers . . . Leap an eighth of a mile . . . Raise tremendous weights . . . Run faster than a streamline train [which is to say, faster than eighty miles an hour]—And nothing less than a bursting shell could penetrate his skin!"

That last piece of description was over a panel which showed a doctor saying, "What th'—? This is the sixth hypodermic needle I've broken on your skin!" To which Kent replies with a grin, "Try again, Doc!"

"The passing away of his foster parents greatly grieved Clark Kent. But it strengthened a determination that had been growing in

his mind. Clark decided he must turn his titanic strength into channels that would benefit mankind.

"And so was created—

"SUPERMAN—Champion of the oppressed, the physical marvel who had sworn to devote his existence to helping those in need!"

You'll note that Superman was a little more human in those days. Although he could not fly, he could leap "an eighth of a mile," or over a skyscraper, and this was in itself no small novelty in the world of 1938. He could race trains or lift a car, and bullets and knives bounced harmlessly from his skin. It was enough.

(When that page was reprinted in 1960 in the *Giant Superman Annual #2*, billed as "rare, out-of-print scenes from the very first Superman story!", the editors couldn't keep their hands off it. The art appears intact, but the blurb about Superman's skin has been altered to read, ". . . *And not even* a bursting shell could penetrate his skin!" Thus is history rewritten.)

For a man who was setting out to "help those in need," Superman had a remarkably pedestrian mind. For the most part he did not occupy himself with sweeping social change; instead he battled crooks and racketeers, uncovering corruption in low places. One of his favorite tactics was to race ahead of a fleeing car of crooks, and then stop dead in front of it. The car would slam to a stop against Superman's body as if he were a brick wall.

When the crooks came tumbling out of the car, half-stunned, Superman would grab the ringleader and leap into the air with him. There he might simply swing the terrified man about with acrobatic ease. Or he might leave the man clutching fearfully to the top of a telephone pole or the peak of a roof. The object was to frighten the man into subjection. (I'm afraid the Supreme Court would today take a dim view of any confession extracted by these means.) Quite often, as Superman and his captive were falling back to earth, the man would be screaming, "You're gonna kill us!"' or something like that.

It's fortunate for Superman that neither Siegel nor Shuster had absorbed much from their high-school science classes, or, for that matter, from the science fiction of that time. Had the laws of inertia been in force while Superman was standing steadfast before a speeding car, the outcome might often have been quite different. And if Superman had actually had sufficient internal mass to stop a speeding car, I hate to think of the holes he would have kicked in the sidewalks with each of his aerial leaps.

But those were simpler times. And if the comic book had not originally been aimed at a specific age group, it had certainly found one:

the kids. How many kids knew the science that would debunk Superman? *How many kids,* knowing it, *would have cared?*

Superman was a myth-figure: he was our dreams personified, even as he must have been Siegel and Shuster's. Superman was, almost literally, the perfect Boy Scout. We still believed in Boy Scouts then.

Most of the Superman myth was established within the first year of Superman's publication. (He appeared monthly in *Action Comics* as the lead story.) As Clark Kent, he went to work for the *Daily Star* (soon to be the *Daily Planet*) as a reporter. Perry White became his editor, and he quickly found a rival in fellow reporter Lois Lane.

Most of those early stories dwelled, with what I can only describe as a magnificent sense of wonder, upon Superman's physical attributes. (These soon broadened to include an early version of his x-ray vision.) The pages in which Superman did little but outrace trains or cars, leap buildings, or toss crooks around ("Look! The bullets bounce right offa him!") probably outnumbered those in which the plot (if there was one) was materially advanced.

But war was coming. Everyone could see it. In several 1939 and 1940 stories Superman found himself in mythical European countries fighting off invasions of one sort or another. In one of these stories an evil, world-conquering scientist was introduced. His name was Luthor, and he had red hair. The plot of the story in question was probably borrowed from Flash Gordon. Usually Superman, as Clark Kent, would find himself a war correspondent on the scene. When danger threatened, the mufti was doffed and Superman made quick work of the enemy's squadron of airplanes, fleet of tanks, and small army of soldiers. Yeah! Just as we Americans could mop up any *real* trouble.

Then came 1941.

Suddenly, we *were* at war. It must have thrown Superman's publishers into a tizzy. Here was this marvelous man, this superman, who had already demonstrated his ability to handle almost any size war— what were we going to do with him? If he went to war against Hitler, how could we explain the fact that America had not instantly won?

The solution was ingenious. As Clark Kent, Superman went down to his local draft board to enlist. But in his nervous desire to get into the Army, he accidentally employed his x-ray vision during the eye test. Instead of reading the chart before him, he read the one in the room beyond! He was flunked out as a 4-F. The shame—!

Why this should keep Superman *as Superman* out of the war they never explained, but it at least solved the real-life problem. While Captain America, Sub-Mariner, and a host of other superheroes or quasi-super-heroes in the comics went off to war, Superman stayed home to deal with fifth-column saboteurs and war profiteers, and to continue helping little old ladies safely across the streets.

As time went on, Superman lost his early fragility. Rays, gasses, and even bursting shells no longer bothered him. Although he continued to leap into the air in his peculiarly characteristic way, resembling a leap-frog in motion, somehow he had found the power of sustained flight. His relationship with Lois Lane mellowed somewhat, and indeed led briefly to marriage.

(The episode in which Superman and Lois Lane married is one of the most hushed-up in the history of comics. It occurred in the daily Superman newspaper strip, shortly after the war.

(The marriage was intended, by the writer and artist on the strip, to be real, and it lasted for a period of weeks, until someone over at the comic book end happened to discover it. Since the comic book publishers controlled the strip—a reversal of the usual procedure—they dictated an abrupt change. It was explained that it wasn't the same Lois Lane, and that it was all happening on an alien, but parallel, planet, and the marriage was therefore a fraud.

(Since then, Superman and Lois Lane have "married" a number of times, but always in what the editors of the comic books have charmingly called "Imaginary Stories"—stories outside the true, real, mythos—"what-if" stories. But more of these later.)

By the mid-forties Superman was Big Business. Within a year of his first publication, he was selling over a million copies of the titles he appeared in, and he revolutionized the comics industry as a whole. Very quickly everyone was imitating him, usually poorly. Detective Comics, Inc. became Superman-D.C., and sued the first imitator, Will Eisner's *Wonder Man* (a Fox Features comic), out of business. But soon the flood was beyond control, and Superman-D.C. (now National) was reserving its legal guns only for the biggest game. It was ultimately National's lawsuit which drove Fawcett to drop *Captain Marvel,* although I suspect drooping sales were an equal factor.

If Superman was such a hit, surely spin-offs of Superman would do equally well, or so the publishers reasoned. Thus, *Superboy—the Adventures of Superman when he was a Boy.* Although this required considerable revision of the mythos, *Superboy* was introduced soon after the war in *More Fun Comics,* and soon transferred to *Adventure Comics* (*More Fun* was dropped), where he remains today (as part of a "Legion of Super-Heroes").

Early "Superboy" stories tried to be faithful in their fashion. The young Clark Kent wore a miniature Superman costume, but he was concerned with boyish pursuits. One cover showed him shooting marbles with his awed pals; a story in another issue of *Adventure* concerned soap-box racers—a plot closer at heart to those in the boys' books than to comic book superheroes. If Superman was a young man in 1938, then his boyhood must have occurred in the late twenties and early thirties. The earlier artists and writers remembered this; later it was forgotten.

By the mid-fifties, Superboy seemed to live in the present (the cars were all modern, and clothes and plots equally so—every home had television), coexisting with his older self.

By the late fifties, he had time-travel completely under control, and was spending most of his time in the future with that Legion of Super Heroes (about which the less said the better), and had established a high-school enmity with the youthful Luthor (long Superman's nemesis) who had already lost his hair in an unfortunate experiment.

Of course, by then Superman himself was hardly recognizable. He was, we were told, totally invulnerable to *anything* except Kryptonite and—get this!—*magic*.

Kryptonite was introduced in the mid-forties (on his radio program, I believe) because Superman was, even then, becoming too powerful to be easily dealt with by his writers and artists. There was no excitement in a story about a man capable of doing anything required (including traveling in time) to right whatever was wrong within the first two pages of any story. It was decided, therefore, that if gas, rays, or automobiles no longer affected him, perhaps bits of radioactive material from the core of his exploded home planet, Krypton, might diminish his strength.

The early Kryptonite was green. Sometimes its radiation seemed only to strip Superman of his extraordinary powers; on other occasions it seemed to be able to kill him through a cumulative weakening process. In any case, it was always there when Superman was in danger of getting out of his creators' control. Sometime around 1950, Luthor learned to synthesize it, and for a while Kryptonite was as common as old comics under the bed.

In the late fifties Kryptonite mutated into a whole spectrum of materials: Red Kryptonite, Gold Kryptonite, etc., each with its own special powers over Superman. The authors of Superman stories have since gained a good deal of mileage from these convenient new forms.

In addition, they have given us Supergirl (another survivor of Krypton), Superdog, Supercat, and even Superhorse. They have provided a Phantom Zone full of old Kryptonian criminals; a miniaturized Kryptonian city, Kandor, in a bottle (a large-ish bottle, it must be admitted); and even a Fortress of Solitude in the North for Superman's home away from home (this was stolen directly from *Doc Savage* without so much as a by-your-leave). The mythos has become cluttered.

Indeed, if one wants to write a Superman story today, he will find little if anything of the original Siegel-Shuster Superman has survived. His story must fit within the ever more constrictive net woven by the interlocking mythos of Superman, Superboy, Supergirl, the stories in *Superman's Girl-Friend, Lois Lane,* and the stories in *Superman's Pal, Jimmy Olsen,* to say nothing of the shared Superman-Batman adventures in *World's Finest Comics.*

It is not altogether surprising that the best stories published in the last six to eight years have been the *Imaginary Stories.* In these stories the author can depart from the mythos. He can pretend Superman *has* married Lois Lane, and go on from there to see what might happen next. (For a while there was a parallel mythos building around Superman's children by Lois Lane in a series of *Imaginary Stories.*) One of the best of all the stories was "The Day Superman Died." In it, he really did die. Clearly, an "Imaginary Story."

But, what nonsense, really! The proprietors of Superman have virtually painted themselves into a corner with their overwhelming mythos of sub-characters and sub-plot situations. Detail has been piled upon detail until the character and quality of Superman which so endeared him to us have been totally submerged.

Siegel and Shuster are long gone. Shuster apparently stopped drawing Superman in 1939 or 1940. Larry Ivie, a most scholarly Superman-phile, says that he has found the work of at least six other artists in the stories published in that period, and by 1941 or 1942 the style was recognizably different.

The principal artist on these stories was Shuster's assistant, Wayne Boring. Boring drew many of the comic book stories and most of the syndicated newspaper strips throughout the forties and fifties, and still does a story once in a while today.

Shuster did some of the work on the earliest Superboy stories, and penciled for various substandard horror and crime comics in the early fifties. Rumors are that he has lost much of his sight, and his work on the syndicated *Funnyman* (with Siegel, in the late forties) was the last to show his style or carry his name.

Siegel continued to write many of the features that had been started before *Superman,* and to write the early *Spectre* stories for Bernard Baily. But his writing seemed to lose its fire when divorced from *Superman,* and on the other stories he was only a competent hack. In the mid-forties Siegel decided that, although National owned all rights to Superman, and was paying him a comfortable royalty, he had been cheated. He approached M. C. Gaines, and briefly enlisted his support in a legal battle against National. It was at this time that the familiar Siegel & Shuster by-line balloon, which had appeared largely as a courtesy on the *Superman* stories, was dropped. *Funnyman* was to be a comeback for the team, after they lost their lawsuit, but despite a promising start with both newspaper syndication and comic book publication, it failed. Since then Siegel has continued writing comic book stories, some of them, ironically, for *Superman;* others, for lesser features for other publishers. A collection of his stories for the *Archie* comic group's superheroes was issued several years ago as a paperback book titled *High Camp Super Heroes.* In addition he continues developing new comic series concepts, hoping once more to make the kind of hit he did thirty years ago.

And what of M. C. Gaines?

Although Gaines certainly was responsible for *Superman*'s ultimate appearance in print as well as for the very medium in which Superman was published, he was not *Superman*'s publisher. He began his own line of superhero comics, also bearing the Superman-DC imprint, but none of them won him as much success as *Superman* brought his partners. (The best known of Gaines's superheroes were Flash, Green Lantern and Wonder Woman. All are being published today by National.)

In 1941, Gaines, convinced of the importance of comic books, and of the need to fashion the right products for their youthful readership, began publishing *Picture Stories from the Bible.* In 1945 he sold his other titles (the superheroes) to National, and began his own firm, Educational Comics, Inc. There he continued *Picture Stories from the Bible,* adding *Picture Stories of Science, Picture Stories from American History,* and *Picture Stories from World History.*

These "good" comics may have been what Gaines thought the customers *ought* to want, but as has happened so many times in the popular media, they weren't what the customers bought. None made money, and when Gaines was killed in a boating accident a few years later, his business manager quietly folded them. Another Gaines comic, *Fat and Slat* (an imitation of Mutt & Jeff done by Ed Wheelan of *Minute Movies* fame), was converted into *International Crime Patrol,* and EC floundered about among the third-, fourth-, and fifth-rate comics until M. C.'s son, William Gaines, took an interest in the company and launched "New Trend" comics in the early fifties, the best-written and best-illustrated comic books ever produced. This line of comics led to Harvey Kurtzman's brilliant *Mad,* and ultimately to the magazine *Mad* of today. William Gaines sold his company to a Wall Street holding company in the early sixties for a reputedly large sum of money, remained as publisher of *Mad* in the bargain, and has since watched the holding company sell his company (which now publishes only *Mad*) to National in a bizarre sort of full circle. Today, in turn, the Kinney System owns National. . . .

If Superman was the product of youthful dreaming, his partner, Batman, is the product of sharp contrivance. Unlike Siegel & Shuster's *Superman,* Bob Kane's *Batman* was put together in 1939 to meet a need—it was National's own answer to *Superman*'s success, and it is significant that *Batman* shared the honors with *Wonder Man* as the second superhero published.

As I mentioned, National quickly sued *Wonder Man* out of existence; both *Wonder Man* and *Batman* first appeared on the stands the same month.

Bob Kane was a second-rate cartoonist whose sole claim to fame before *Batman* was a series of single-page "funnies" and a poorly drawn adventure strip. (Most of the stories in the new material comic books were adventure strips of varying sorts.)

Batman was not Kane's idea; it was dreamed up in an editorial session. Kane did not write the first story; it was written by either Gardner F. Fox or Bill Finger (reports vary). If Kane even drew the early stories, it was with considerable help from artists like Jack Cole (*Plastic Man*), Jerry Robinson and Bob Wood (*Daredevil*). By the time of its early success, the stories were being drawn by Robinson and his friends. Although Kane's name appeared on every story until the mid-sixties (and the birth of the "New Look" Batman), his sole function was to subcontract the inking and the penciling to other artists—and the subdivision of payments seemed to guarantee substandard art.

Nevertheless, *Batman* was in most respects a better strip than *Superman,* and was a better-conceived character, as well.

In these days of pop art, camp trivia, and lingering memories of the *Batman* television program, it is a little difficult to remember that Batman was originally something of an innovation, and certainly one of the best-realized of the early-forties comics characters.

Properly speaking, Batman was not (and is not) a superhero. He wears a costume, but he is only an ordinary human being: he has no

Copyright 1947, National Comics Publications, Inc., whose name was changed to National Periodical Publications, Inc., and reprinted by its permission.

super powers. As such, he was not the first in comics. National was publishing *The Crimson Avenger* (in *Detective Comics*) before either Superman or Batman first saw print. But *The Crimson Avenger* was basically a copy of *The Shadow,* an already famous pulp and radio character, as was also *The Sandman* (*Adventure Comics*), and the other masked crime-fighters of the period.

But Batman was of a new genre—the *costumed* comic-book hero. Like Superman, he not only had two identities, but when in costume he *appeared* as an awesome figure, quite transcendent over mundane humanity. Masked, his cape spread over his shoulders like two great bat-wings, his costume all greys and blacks, he must have been one of the most potentially frightening heroes in comics.

And this is how he often appeared—avenger-like in the night, sometimes in menacing silhouette, or with his shadow cast before him, twice life size. He *did* things with that cape of his. Superman's flapped behind him like a red bath towel, but Batman's blue-black ribbed cape enfolded him like a cloak, often hiding his muscled body from view.

Batman, like Superman, was an orphan, but his parents were normal Earth humans. The Waynes were coming home from a night out when a crook named Joey Chill shot and killed them. Their son, Bruce, somehow survived and vowed vengeance when he was grown. He studied law, criminology, and forensic science, and he trained his body. He also either inherited a great deal of money or earned a lot fast.

Finally, clad in his smoking jacket, pipe in hand (the very picture of what comic book artists might aspire to be), he speculated on the way in which he would Strike Terror Into The Hearts of the Underworld. A bat flew in the open window, and inspiration struck—he would become The Batman.

And so he did. A pair of grey flannel longjohns, black boots, black gloves, a cowl, mask, and the long, ribbed cape, and he was indeed The Batman.

I have my doubts about the terror such an outfit would strike in the hearts of the underworld, but no doubts at all that for a boy poring over a Batman adventure in *Detective Comics,* this was exciting stuff indeed.

Part of it was in the drawing. After the early awkward illustrations (perhaps actually by Kane), the style evolved into sombre, night-tinged moodiness, replete with great shadows and an implacably stern-visaged Batman. Batman did not toss crooks into the air to frighten them; occasionally he shot them. (He did not, however, often carry a gun. Very few costume heroes in the comics have ever carried guns of the normal, lethal variety.) More often, he found himself in a fight, usually with the odds against him. Sometimes he won; sometimes he did not. (He usually lost in the earlier pages and won in the later pages of a story; it balanced out.)

The writing was important. Not for the actual prose in which the stories were told, but for the use that was made of plots and situations. Batman didn't have Superman's superabundance of muscle—occasionally he had to use his brains. Batman was much more of a detective. (Superman appeared in *Action Comics;* Batman in *Detective Comics;* somehow that did not seem entirely coincidental.) As a result, Batman seemed more at home fighting common hoods, sticking up for the corner shoe-shine boy, or the shopkeeper who wouldn't pay protection. When the war began, you didn't *expect* him to hop the first plane to Europe to put a quick finish to the whole mess.

Batman was human.

It is my firm conviction that the years 1940-46 were *Batman*'s best—in terms of both art and stories. I believe my judgment is unclouded by nostalgia, since I began reading *Batman* comics in the late forties and encountered the earlier stories only much later.

Actually, by the time I became acquainted with The Batman, he had already lost the definite article and was simple, familiar Batman, and had embarked upon a series of science-fictional adventures which were jarringly out of place in his own nocturnal milieu. The slide downhill into the fifties was a quick one. The art deteriorated noticeably, the old plots were replaced by visitors from the future, or aliens from other planets, etc. Even the one "legitimate" use of time travel, Batman's voyages back in time through hypnosis (were they dreams, or were they real?) was abandoned. By the early sixties, alien menaces were Batman's stock in trade.

Then the "New Look" Batman was introduced, not long before he made his TV debut. The titles (*Detective, Batman*) were transferred to another editor, and Carmine Infantino (one of National's major artists at that time) was not only assigned Batman stories, but allowed to sign his name to them. The only costuming change was to place a yellow bullseye around the bat symbol on his chest, and, truthfully, for all the change in art I don't think that the stories were that much better. But the alien menaces *were* shelved, and if Batman had not yet recaptured his old menace and mystery, he was at least functioning as a detective once again.

I've ignored Batman's sidekick thus far, because he deserves treatment on his own.

Robin ("The Boy Wonder") was one of the first—if not *the* first—costumed sidekick, in comics. Ostensibly a boy aerialist with a circus troop, Dick Grayson was orphaned in mysterious circumstances, adopted by Bruce Wayne and trained to be his assistant. (In many respects this "origin" parallels the way in which the Human Torch picked up *his* sidekick, Toro—ah, but it's a small world!)

The notion of giving a superhero a boy sidekick was probably born of a desire to give the comics' youthful readers someone they could identify with. As such, it was a mistake. Boys don't identify with *boys* in mystery-adventure stories; they identify with *men*—especially when one is the real hero of the story. Robin was often excess baggage in Batman's stories, just as were Captain America's Bucky, Green Arrow's Speedy, Aquaman's Aqualad, et al. But for a while, during the first wave of the superhero boom (1940-43), you could hardly find a comic book without a costumed boy sidekick in it. Blame Batman—he started it.

He also caused himself a little extra trouble when Dr. Wertham stated, in *Seduction of the Innocent,* that the relationship between Batman and Robin (which is to say, between Bruce Wayne and his ward, Dick Grayson) was sexually unhealthy. Dr. Wertham was of the certain notion, which became well publicized, that not only was the relationship homosexual, *it was obviously homosexual to the comics' youthful readers!* One shudders to think what the good doctor would have made of the Boy Scout Handbook, with its wholesome enthusiasm for exactly the same sort of "comradeship" between the boy scouts and their counsellors.

It's fashionable today to sneer a little and to chuckle at the Boy Scout image, at the goody-two-shoes approach. It's fashionable to see rampaging homosexual lust in every man's hand on a boy's shoulder, but I wonder if in our cynicism we aren't cutting ourselves off from a part of the innocence of childhood.

I'm certain that Dr. Wertham must have had no knowledge of the ideals and conditioning we had as boys and Boy Scouts. These ideals have permeated boys' books of the last four generations, and their reflection in Batman's fatherly comradeship with Robin was not only innocent, but touchingly inspiring. No boy I ever knew read more than that into Batman's relationship with Robin, and I doubt anything more was intended.

It seems inevitable that if a comic book feature becomes successful, its lead character will accumulate additional supporting characters. Batman also had a butler, Alfred, who began as a roly-poly sort of man, but soon slimmed down into the dignified prototype of an

English servant. Alfred shared the knowledge of Batman's and Robin's civilian identities. (He was also Bruce Wayne's butler.) Alfred was popular enough in the mid-forties to warrant his own featurette in *Batman,* but it lasted only a few years. More recently, the "New Look" killed Alfred off, but, because of demands made by the TV producers, he was brought back to life in a bizarre fashion (he was possessed by an alien spirit).

Another long-time supporting player is Commissioner Gordon. His role has been unswerving—he has served throughout the years as Batman's liaison with the police force, and has personally manned the giant searchlight which for years flashed the Batsignal on the heavens to summon Batman. (In recent years, post-"New Look," a "hotline" phone has taken over this function. One wonders how a line was strung into Bruce Wayne's home without tipping off his identity as Batman. . . .)

There have been a number of girls, none of them lasting more than a few years, despite the valiant attempts of each to become Batman's Lois Lane. Considering what a pest Lois has been to Superman for all these many years, perhaps that's just as well.

But the most memorable supporting characters in Batman's life have been the villains.

He met the Joker in 1940. A fantastic harlequin figure, face chalk-white and rouged like a clown's, the Joker was originally a contract killer, and he and Batman played for keeps with each other. Since the initiation of the Comics Code Authority, however, the Joker has become more of a clown and less of a menace. Like Batman, his best setting was the nocturnal mystery of the 1940s stories.

The second most memorable figure would undoubtedly be the Penguin. A fat figure of a man (and most splendidly portrayed on television by Burgess Meredith), his crimes usually involved birds or umbrellas, or both. He has changed very little through the years, coming on stage in the mid-forties; he now seems to be in semi-retirement.

The Catwoman was originally known only as The Cat, but as she developed during the forties she became Batman's most intriguing opponent. Ruthless and a gang leader, she was also beautiful and romantically intrigued by Batman's square jaw. She reformed in the early fifties, and subsequent adventures have not been quite the same.

The list at this point degenerates into recent repeat villains. Only a few remain from the older days. The best was Two-Face, a demented ex-DA, scarred on one side of his face by acid thrown at him in court, who pitched a half-defaced coin to decide if he would commit a crime. If the defaced side landed upright, he became a criminal; if the clean side turned up, he would refrain from the crime. It was a classic case of split personality, and ultimately he was cured and his face restored by plastic surgery.

The Riddler, exhumed by television to good effect, had appeared only twice, in 1948, in two consecutive issues of *Detective Comics,* before his quite recent revival. I think I can safely say that (in the pages of contemporary comics at least) he would have been better left alone.

In the late fifties and early sixties, Batman, apparently doomed forever to play second fiddle to Superman, had the entire Superman Syndrome wished upon him: a Batdog, a Batwoman, a Batgirl, even an alien pixy, Bat-Mite. "The New Look" scuttled all that, and rightly so, along with a series of "Imaginary Stories" supposedly written by Alfred the butler about the Batman of the future, the grown-up Robin, and Batman's son.

There is something about the Superman and Batman stories of the early forties which, for all their technical crudity, puts them head and shoulders above the slick but empty products of today. Part of it was freshness, newness. Part of it was the youthfulness of the men who created them. And part of it was simply a product of the times. The books were crude, but vital; less realistically rendered, but far more faithful to the idealizations which each character represented. Superman and Batman gave comic books—those which printed new material—their first real commercial viability, and pointed the way for almost three decades of sometimes chancy publishing in the field.

Until 1938, the best comics, and the comics which sold the best, were the reprint publications. Their material was better, and produced to higher standards. Quality, despite the iron-mongers and beer salesmen who publish the comics, has always been what sold comic books.

Superman and Batman changed all that. Each in his own way set standards as yet unexcelled for the field. Each was prototypal. Each also set sales records. Publishers never argue with sales records.

They also set comic books solidly as children's fare: locked the seven-by-ten color-printed newsprint format Gaines devised into a rigid style aimed solely at teenagers and children. So far, all experiments to publish comic books in this format or any similar format for adults have failed. The biggest reason they have failed is public opinion.

The public seems to feel that comics—once the direct competitor of the now-gone adult-oriented pulp magazine—are for kids . . . no matter how many adults sneak-read them. What intelligent, self-respecting man would admit to reading about men who run about in colored tights and capes, Fighting Crime and Righting Wrongs?

Only kids still believe it might be possible.

Perhaps M. C. Gaines would have been happy for at least that much.

INTRODUCTION TO

ME TO YOUR LEADER TAKE

Dick Ellington, a science fiction and comic book fan, has been a labor leader and political activist, served in Military Intelligence in Korea, and is currently Secretary of the Oakland Symphony Orchestra. It is interesting that this combination—science fiction, comics, and music—should describe both of the first two authors in this book. But hardly as strange as the events that transpired in the pages of *Planet Comics.*

Space-tanned and steely eyed rocketeers blasting star trails to distant galaxies . . . giant complex mechanisms shooting sparks and emitting ozone-laden clouds of menacing vapor . . . scantily clad, incredibly proportioned maidens fleeing the clutches of fanged and tentacled monsters intent on performing acts as indescribable as they are unimaginable. . . .

These things seem better suited to the ragged-edged, lurid-covered pulp magazines of a bygone era than to the comics. Yet there was a major sub-class of comic books devoted to space-bound epics that could have easily appeared in the pages of the pulpiest of pulp magazines.

The newspaper comics page long boasted the serialized adventures of Flash Gordon, Buck Rogers, and Brick Bradford, and the comics in the early fifties boasted some truly fine science-fiction stories in the EC line. But in the golden era of the comics, the 1940s, the epitome of comic book space adventure could be found in the pages of *Planet Comics.* The lure of the exotic, the thrill of space itself, the dazzling machines, the terrifying monsters, and certainly the incredible girls were staples in *Planet,* from its first issue to its last.

CHAPTER 2

ME TO YOUR LEADER TAKE

by RICHARD ELLINGTON

★★

Even during my really active comic book buying days (*circa* 1938-44), I had no illusions about the quality of what I was plunking down my dimes for. I realized even at the time that comic books in general were pretty crude items, and toward the last I was even a little ashamed of them and began trying to conceal them from my more intelligent friends.

With this sort of situation, the advent of Fiction House as a major comics publisher in 1940 (actually, the very first Fiction House comics were published somewhat earlier) was quite welcome. Not that these were Adult Comic Books, you understand—far from it. With the possible exception of *Miss Fury,* and a few others, there just "ain't no such thing." But these books were definitely aimed at a teenage audience rather than the little kids, and this fact gave them a glamorous air for me which the other comics just didn't have.

And, of course, at about this time I was beginning to take an active interest in that mysterious Other Sex, and the liberal injections of half-clad, impossibly dimensioned broads that Fiction House dished out was definitely a big part of their attraction.

Starting with the antediluvian bedsheet *Jumbo,* by 1940 Fiction House also had *Jungle, Fight,* and *Planet* on the stands. Later they added *Wings* and *Rangers* (of Freedom) to the line. Oddly enough, at the time I regularly read them all except *Planet,* probably because I had already discovered *Amazing Stories* and *Fantastic Adventures,* and neatly bypassed the science-fiction comic book stage. I guess it's just as well, because those first issues of *Planet* were as abysmal as comic books could be, and they could be really bad.

Unlike most comic book publishers, Fiction House never relied on central characters for a drawing card, relying instead on a definite theme and style for their line and letting these dominate the characters. From the popularity the books enjoyed, the publishers were obviously right in this policy, and never varied much from it. Not that there weren't popular and long-lived characters—the Rangers of Freedom, Sheena, Captain Wings, and a few others lasted quite well—but they never achieved the prominence of the Big Red Cheese, Superman, Batman, et al. . . . The publishers would not allow it.

Fiction House realized, well ahead of their competitors, that there was a big audience in the older teen-young adult market, and capitalized on this quite successfully by merrily ladling out liberal dollops of their own peculiar ideas on sex.

Not that there was anything as blunt as actual copulation in the strips. Quite the contrary, in fact. The morals of the heroes were so far above reproach as to make one suspect their manhood, and the villains of course were always frustrated in their evil aims—albeit in the nick of time. The Fiction House idea of sex—and remember that it was financially successful—was to show as many half-clad females per page as possible, and they needled the mags up with liberal doses of bondage and torture.

You could pick up any Fiction House mag of the forties or fifties and be sure of finding liberal helpings of partially clothed, amazingly proportioned females being tied up, beaten, tortured, and threatened with various Fates Worse Than Death. To say nothing of a little cozy female-to-female contact, *à la* Wonder Woman, just to liven things up. Something for everyone!

Let's pick up a random copy of a Fiction House comic and examine it. I'll use *Jumbo* No. 141 for November, 1950, because it's at hand. The lead story featured Sheena, Queen of the Jungle, replete with long blonde hair, clad in her spotted bathing suit and a few bangles. For added interest there was an equally statuesque brunette in a two-piece fur bathing suit and bangles. Both were liberally man-handled several times and tied up once each. A plot line? Don't be silly.

The Ghost Gallery featured a showgirl in appropriately scanty costume who was killed at the end.

Next came the Hawk, who, incidentally, was also quite a long-lived character. His female accomplice, Velvet, sported shorts and an off-the-shoulder blouse, with the usual blond hair and dimensions. I doubt this costume would really have gone over very well in the historical era in which it was set, libertine pirates or no. Velvet got tied up several times.

Long Bow, an American backwoodsy affair, featured a brunette clad neatly in buckskins (remind me to discuss leather fetishism some time). The end piece was another Sheena, this time featuring what I suppose the artist considered to be Negro women clad in clever little form-fitting crocodile costumes. This strip was remarkable in that Sheena was not tied up even once.

I have no objections to the vicarious gratification of the various fetishisms so prevalent in modern society, but unfortunately that's all Fiction House had to offer. Although aimed at an older audience, their stories were on a par—a low one—with everything else on the market. They showed little imagination and thought, and monstrous technical inaccuracies, and were redeemed only in part by an occasional piece of really superior art.

Planet was, at first, an exception to the rule in that it featured very little of this kind of sex, but it was worse than the other comic books of the line in other ways. Looking over those early issues of *Planet* I am appalled at how bad they were. Only the covers were even moderately competent in the way of art, and significantly, they were the part of the book that stayed pretty much the same throughout the years. They were typical boy-babe-bem (bug-eyed monster) affairs, indistinguishable from their counterparts in the pulp magazine *Planet* stories. The interior art was clumsy and crude, the story lines monotonous beyond belief and with no thought behind them. And the technical work was just non-existent.

With a few minor exceptions, the first eleven issues of *Planet* contained nothing very memorable. About all they did was to establish a few characters and an idea. . . and even the characters were far from steady items, changing constantly from issue to issue. With a maximum of seven strips per issue, a total of eighteen different strips (plus a few one-shot features) appeared in the first eleven issues.

The variety of artists was almost as great, but this seemed to be the rule at Fiction House and it didn't change after the eleventh issue.

Planet did have one redeeming feature, though. In the rest of the Fiction House line, the bylines were usually beefed up with a military rank—particularly in *Wings* and *Rangers of Freedom*. Captain this and Major that spent their spare hours writing strips. But at *Planet* apparently promotions were slow so the ranks were omitted.

Let's take a closer look at the first issue. Surely the lead item should have been something a little better than the rest. In this case, it was Flint Baker, who progressed through a number of metamorphoses under a variety of artists and was eventually demoted to sharing a strip with Reef Ryan some years later, the two of them constituting The Space Rangers. This first one was credited to Dick Briefer (who later drew *Frankenstein*), and was an average example of the low quality in *Planet* at the time.

As with most *Planet* strips, the time was indeterminate but in the first strip it could probably be pinned down to the near future. This particular story was titled *Flint Baker and the One-Eyed Monster Men of Mars*. The title page was a single panel showing a meaningless array of futuristic machinery, and the brief and confusing explanatory note: "When Fletcher Baker's scientist father died, Fletcher was left with the task of completing his rocket ship, to be sent to Mars. Now it is finished, and is ready for magic ((?)) flight!"

Baker favored a wide-collared trenchcoat and ascot scarf on Earth, but in space he changed to a more futuristic outfit.

In this first story an attempt was made to begin a story line. For reasons never explained (it was certainly not because of the danger of space flight), Baker picked for the crew of his rocketship three prisoners from a state prison: Grant, Godwin, and Parks, all ex-mechanics.

After taking off without incident in Briefer's idea of a space ship, a torpedo-shaped affair with lots of chrome and ornaments, they discovered Mimi Wilson of the New York *Globe* hiding in the provision room. Briefer didn't have the knack for drawing sexy girls, but she was obviously supposed to be a blonde version of Lois Lane.

En route to Mars, the three ex-convicts told of their "crimes." They each had one third of a page, and the stories are candidates for a special Banality Award.

"I'm Harry Parks. My fireman on my locomotive was drunk. He wanted to run the engine himself. He whipped out a gun and threatened me! A shovel put him to sleep for good. Fate was against me, and I was sent up for murder!"

"I'm Phil Godwin. Some gangster fell in love with my kid sister. She thought she loved him, and refused to listen to me. The crook was rotten through and through. At the wedding I lost my head. . . ." [He shot the bounder.]

"I'm Cliff Grant. Years ago, I worked for a man who was crazy. But he had hypnotic powers and used me to carry out his plots. I was picked up for murder. Later, he was discovered and put in jail. But he escaped."

After "weeks of monotonous traveling," they reached Mars. . . . and landed right next to a battered spaceship which contained a skeleton and a message warning them to keep away from the dark side(!) of Mars.

The canals of Mars were handy super highways, so joining the traffic pattern in a futuristic car our heroes just happened to bring along, they ended up at a "wondrous city," whose inhabitants were humanoid. Baker and his crew were just in time to fight a group of earthmen who had set up a dictatorship on that mysterious dark side of Mars, led by the villainous Sarko, "last of the wicked earthmen." Sarko's staff were one-eyed critters with only a head, a prehensile tail and legs.

In the first attack, Mimi and the Princess of the city (a brunette, for contrast) were kidnapped by the monsters. Baker and the boys took off in hot pursuit for the dark side (*sic*) where they donned black cloaks because, in them ". . . we'll be invisible here on the dark side." Sarko had strapped Mimi and the Princess to his version of a Fiendish Machine. Coincidence now reared its ugly head again. Sarko was the same evil hypnotist who had sent crew member Cliff Grant to prison. After a tussle, Sarko was beaten down. End of strip. Exciting, wasn't it?

Also in the first issue was Auro, Lord of Jupiter, who managed to survive a surprisingly long time, although, as usual, he went through a variety of changes en route. The idea for this one was quite obviously lifted straight out of Edgar Rice Burroughs. Auro was a combination of Tarzan and John Carter.

Auro was the son of a 21st-Century couple (one of the few times where *Planet* bothered to pinpoint an era). While on a cruise in space, their ship was hit by a flaming meteor and crashed on Jupiter. The parents were killed. A kindly old sabre-toothed tiger rescued the boy and raised him, sharing his raw meat. "The tremendous gravitational force of this planet slowly turns his earthly muscles to steel." You figure that out.

When Auro became an adult he conquered the native, apelike creatures, and became their king. From here the story deteriorated into a straight action strip with Auro saving various Earth girls, who conveniently appeared, from assorted villains or alien menaces.

During the story Auro was killed, and then revived by having Dorna, Princess of Jupiter (don't ask where *she* came from) transfer the "spirit" of Chet Edson, a young Earth scientist, into his body. Auro, now clad in fancy space togs, continued to play the hero, with the ghost of Chet Edson hanging around and interfering whenever it was convenient to the story.

Another comparatively long-lived character in the first issue was the Red Comet. He was particularly interesting because, unlike most of *Planet's* central characters, he was possessed of a special power, the ability to increase or decrease his size by twisting a dial on his "intra-atomic space adjuster." His existence was otherwise never explained at all, and he was referred to regularly as "*The* Mystery Man of Space."

Let's look at a typical adventure of the Red Comet from the seventh issue. A space ship landed on an unexplored planet "somewhere in outer space" to do a little exploring. The explorers discovered a race of giants, and their terrified cries brought the Red Comet to the rescue (how he heard their hollering in space wasn't explained). After assuring the explorers that the giants were just harmless clods (they were actually kind of cute), he then made friends with the giants by expanding to their size. It seemed they had a problem. The Stickers, tiny worm-like affairs with unicorn-like horns on their heads, were bedeviling them by—you guessed it— sticking them. Red Comet attacked them but was pinned down. One of the friendly giants came to the rescue by lapping up the Stickers, who promptly stuck holes in his innards. Red Comet reduced himself and his ship to miniature size and flew into the giant's intestines where he proceeded to ray the Stickers down. (Why he hadn't done this before is something we won't worry about.)

So now, "These giants have nothing to fear, but the next adventure of the Red Comet holds terror and peril enough to fill the universe."

The fourth issue contained one really funny item—Kenny Carr of the Martian Lancers. Only one episode appeared and it was obviously a spur-of-the-moment product. Possibly some artist missed a deadline or the editors were just feeling cute that day. The strip was quite obviously a straight Bengal Lancers affair and (also obviously) had been drawn for use in some other mag—possibly *Fight.*

It started with the hero preparing to return to London, having completed his term of enlistment. The colonel and one of Carr's friends schemed to get him to re-enlist by having a couple of fake natives aboard a train drop a word in his hearing about a coming attack. Loyal Carr rushed back to the post and re-enlisted, and, of course the attack *did* come off, and Carr was the hero of the day.

The uniforms were all strictly Indian Service, as were the natives and such place names as Basha and the Eastern Border. Simply by substituting Martian for Bengal in the title and Earth for England in the opening paragraph, the story was fobbed off as a space adventure.

The sixth issue saw the beginning of what could have been a moderately interesting strip: *Crash Barker and his Zoom Sled,* by-lined Charles M. Quinlan. This strip was set in the present time and, while the art was mediocre, the plotting was adequate and more realistic than the norm, and some of the science was quite good. It was also notable for serial stories, something *Planet* had avoided until that time.

The hero was a stunt pilot and inventor, who had the typical girl friend and a big, tough sidekick (named "Wheel" Barrow, yet). The story opened with a crowd jeering Barker's newly invented "zoom sled" which he was about to demonstrate. The taunts from the by-standers included: "Baloney! Take that looney cart back to the comic books!" The jealous son of an airport owner and a sinister group of foreign agents were also introduced.

In the next issue, while Crash wad demonstrating his zoom sled to an awed crowd, the foreign agents invaded the hangar and tried to steal the plans. The airport owner's son, Bart, with the same idea in mind, discovered the mechanic—knocked out. Bart pulled a gun and went for the agents but was shot himself. Barker completed his test flight by landing the ship inside the hangar, where he discovered the body of Bart, and took off again just in time to overtake and shoot down the foreign agents. Whew!

The zoom sled itself was rather a silly looking affair, but it's interesting to note (this was 1940, remember) that on land it traveled without wheels, on compressed air.

The following issue picked up in time directly after this, with Crash receiving a letter from the War Department informing him: "Enclosed find plans of your ridiculous 'Zoom' sled, as you call it. Such a contraption could never fly, float, or run as you claim. Our shelves are already overcrowded with similar hair-brained schemes. Why not try building one of those perpetual motion machines. We believe you would be able to waste your time much better." Crash and his friends got a hearty laugh out of this and remarked that they were glad they hadn't submitted plans for Crash's new "atmospheric pressure gun." They went out the next day and casually captured a band of pirates operating from a plane—just to test the gun.

Apparently the idea didn't catch on well enough, because the next issue featured a new artist and a new strip, called *Crash Parker*. He had unaccountably become, overnight, an "interplanetary flyer" and was now off with the rest of the herd, fighting monsters on other worlds.

This same issue saw the beginning of Cosmo Corrigan, the first attempt at (intentional) humor in *Planet* and pretty weak all around. He was titled Cosmic Corrigan in the next issue and then back to Cosmo in the next. That brings us up to the twelfth issue, and he was dropped altogether right there.

With the twelfth issue, Gene Fawcette took over as editor, and radical changes began to take place, although many of the characters remained. The artists were completely replaced by a new crew, more attention was paid to the stories, and the magazine's policy was pulled into line with the rest of the Fiction House group—in other words, more sex was added.

The improvement continued through Paul Payne's term as editor and became even more pronounced when J. F. Byrne took over. The basic theme still involved the brawny hero (often undistinguished by any special powers), the leggy girl, and the alien menace, but the way it was handled was altered radically.

There had been a few feeble attempts at letter columns in the early issues, but one of the later editors, probably Payne, was responsible for the initiation of a *real* letter column: the Vizigraph. This wasn't a bad item at all, and was quite honestly handled. They initiated the idea of making the staff responsible for answering the various challenges thrown by the readers at the more blatant technical flaws, and this went a long way toward eliminating them.

The Vizigraph and the contemporary changes in the magazine certainly indicate that *Planet*'s readers were becoming a lot more intelligent. Some of the complaints were quite sound.

A couple of examples are indicative and certainly reminiscent of the Sarge Saturn type of pulp letter column.

From No. 46:

> At last! A Vizigraph! Now I can tell you what I like and dislike. I'm starting with—you guessed it—the cover! Now the art work is swell, but sizzling comet-tails, can't you change the ideas? I mean the eternal triangle—the guy, gal, and the goon, usually called a bem or bug-eyed monster. It's positively boring. I noticed you had a space-scene (the first one) on issue No. 43, but on issue No. 44 you went back to the same old stuff with a purple octopus (which owns a face), holding an oversized bubble which contains a girl, while the hero dashes to the rescue.
>
> One other thing. In the strip "Life on Other Worlds" it was stated that Pluto was next. But I found Callisto was. Yeeps. Where'd the space go? I'd better blast off.
>
> John Grossman
> Des Moines, Iowa

And on the technical end try this little exchange from No. 49:

> Dear Sirs:
> Your theory on the possibility of Earth once being a colony of Venus is all very interesting, but has one serious flaw. When the Venusian colonists transplanted their supposedly well-developed brain into an anthropoid ape, the author assumed that the offspring of the biped would have large brains

too. This is one of the chief fallacies of pseudo-evolutionists, for it is a fundamental principle that acquired characteristics do not reappear in the offspring. For example, if you cut the tails off two rats and mate them, the offspring will still have tails.

Also, it is not unusual for man and apes, both belonging to the same family, to be so different. The domesticated housecat and the man-eating tigers of Bengal are of the same family, and there is certainly a world of difference between them.

I don't see why so much comment is aroused by the Voltamen in Lost World as to their language. It is sublimely obvious to anyone studying Latin that their slang is nothing more than Latin translated into English, but kept in the same form with the verb at the end and the other parts of the sentence placed accordingly. To add to this, almost direct Latin derivatives, such as Video station, etc. are to be found in the Latin lingua.

William Maye
Detroit, Michigan

Dear Mr. Maye:
The article does not claim that the immediate offspring of the apes with transplanted brains also had the identical brains of their parents. It states that this branch of the ape family was the one from which present day man evolved. Children born of apes with highly developed brains would have a markedly different environment from ordinary ape children. Their entire training and education at the hands of such creatures would leave them tremendously superior animals at adulthood. Such a head start toward civilization was given the type of ape used by the colonists from Venus and thus he evolved through millions of years into modern man. The process was not instantaneous.

Sincerely,
H. McLeod Kensington, Ph.D.

I hope Maye was properly put in his place.

Apparently *Planet* was determined to have one humorous strip, for the 13th issue saw the beginning of *Norge Benson,* which at times was really quite amusing. It featured a teenage boy in a vaguely arctic situation, aided by a pet polar bear, a reindeer, and some friendly penguins. The antagonists were a group of villainous penguins, led by Slug, who wore a slouch hat and smoked a pipe. Actually, it was pure fantasy rather than science fiction, even by *Planet's* elastic standards, and apparently wasn't too popular, because it gradually shifted its emphasis until it was really just another action strip with only the polar bear, Frosty, retained as comic relief.

Gale Allen (at times accompanied by a Women's Space Battalion, Girl Squadron, and Girl Patrol) started in the fourth issue with bad art and worse plotting, but managed to pick up, a little at a time, over the next few issues. The strip was consistently credited to Fred Nelson, but the drastic improvements evident in the artwork indicate a shift in artists somewhere along the line. By No. 11 it was obviously popular enough to be retained in the big shakeup of No. 12, though, of course, with a new artist. The idea of a female lead was undoubtedly a main attraction, and the sex element picked up steadily from No. 12 on.

Let's look at a day in the life of this Average Space Miss as she was handled by Douglas McKee in issue No. 32. From a rather plain, tough, short-haired military lady, she had evolved into a lush-figured, mostly unclad, long-haired blonde. She and her Girl Squadron (more of a chorus line than anything else) were investigating the disappearance of ships along the spaceways. They spotted wreckers towing salvage and paused to inquire at the salvage planet. Of course, there were the pirates, lizard-like humanoids, who proceeded to capture the unarmed girls with a net. The pirates were apparently running a slave business on the side and tossed the girls into a prison, where Gale made contact with a handsome male Earthman who was also a prisoner. He was also a whiz of a scientist and immediately rigged a cutting torch out of Gale's planochrono (wristwatch) and cut them loose. We then had the typical last big battle and destruction of the pirates. In other words, the same old jazz but with *lots* of pretty women.

No. 12 also introduced the popular *Star Pirate*. This was originally credited to "Leonardo Vinci" but as usual was tossed merrily from hand to hand for more beefing up. Star was technically a pirate, and on occasion he actually engaged in some mild piracy. But, of course, he had been driven into his life of crime by the evil interplanetary smugglers.

He went through various sidekicks, including a distinctly fishy-looking Martian and a humanoid cyclops identified as a "Trodelyte," or Trody for short, though it was never clear whether this was his name or his race.

Although Star Pirate always acted in typically heroic fashion, I think it was the air of somewhat illicit behavior that made him so popular. He had a black ship called variously the *Revenge* and the *Vengeance,* and was always at least a little at odds with the law.

By issue No. 32, the "Robin Hood of Space" (they were being honest about it by then) took on space gangsters who were trying to take over a legitimate space run. Star was approached by a Space Patrol officer who grudgingly asked his help: "Pirate, this is unofficial . . . I've never approved of your methods, but you do get things done, and that's what's important now."

Star and Gura, his Martian friend, took off but they were too late—another commercial liner had already been destroyed and the pirates were fleeing. Star halted his ship in mid-space to search for survivors. Technically things went completely to pot here. For a space suit, Star sported a little glass helmet. Aboard the ship the "windows" (*sic*) were busted out all over the place, yet Star ran across a man without a space suit who was "slowly dying" (*sic*).

It was Blandow, owner of the shipping company. He gave Star some trinkets to take to his daughter Lara, who was (naturally) another gorgeous lovely in two-piece bathing suit. She mistook Star for another of the gangsters and put him down. Stung by this, Star hired out with the rival shipping firm he was sure was behind the raids in an effort to help the girl. There was a big space-epic finale space battle and a big kiss for Star from the girl.

One of the more interesting strips in *Planet* was *Mars, God of War.* I'm a little vague as to whether he sprang into being full-fledged or was originally a villain in another strip. Whatever his origin, the strip used the interesting idea of an evil central character with a variety of nondescript heroes thwarting his evil plans. *Planet* had tried it briefly in the first issue with *Quorak, Super Pirate,* but dropped it immediately. This was a gimmick several publishers tried at different times with varying degrees of success. Offhand, I can think of the *Claw, Frankenstein* at one stage of his highly colored comic career, *Landor, Maker of Monsters,* and (if you want to stretch things to admit a creature of equivocal morality) *The Heap.*

Mars was cast as a spirit with powers that seemed to vary at the whim of the artist. Normally, he worked by entering the body of a person and influencing or controlling that person's actions for his own evil ends. Eventually it was decided to drop him, and in issue No. 35 they pulled a really cute ploy that is worth relating in detail.

Mars had launched a series of conflicts on Earth, culminating in an anti-intellectual riot that left civilization on Earth mostly destroyed. But—and I quote—"Long years ago, a scientist foresaw this coming madness . . . and so he mysteriously disappeared. The same day, two infants were stolen from plexiplastic cribs. Exiling himself to the moon, Dr. Kort built a laboratory to house all culture of the decaying universe . . . There also, he reared the two children, instilling in their eager minds the knowledge their fathers scorned! And now comes MARS—"

The scientist was just completing the hypno-sleep education of the young man and woman, when Mars discovered them. Kort gave each of the young people a powerful robot which was tuned to function at their mental commands. Mars took over the boy's robot and attempted to kill Mysta, the girl. But she and the scientist destroyed the robot, angering the boy—"Why did it have to be *my* robot?"

Mars, sensing the discord, merged his will with the boy's. He then destroyed the laboratory and killed the scientist, but Mysta sensed his presence and killed the boy. Mars fled, but swore to return, leaving us with "A slender girl, alone against the universe's most evil force . . . the God of War! She is a living temple of Man's essential goodness, is his last hope! CAN MARS STILL WIN?"

And there you have, slick as a whistle, a brand-new strip called *Mysta of the Moon*. Mars was around in the background in the next issue and was then eased out of the strip, leaving another under-clothed, well-built heroine. They tried a variety of costumes and hairdos on Mysta, and the Vizigraph emitted outraged howls when they tried putting *more* clothes on her.

Issue No. 43 saw the beginning of still another strip: *Futura,* by John Douglas. It was exceptionally well drawn and the story interest was well above average. In addition, though there was a sub-plot complete in each issue, the main story had a definite serial continuity from issue to issue with some really good character development.

The story opened on a dark street of Titan, a 21st-Century Earth city. Marcia Reynolds, attractive and partially undressed as per *Planet* stylebook, was on her way home from work. She felt she was being followed, but a police check on the "radiascreen" showed nothing. Obviously, the cops said, she was imagining things. She agreed, for (in her own words) ". . . maybe he's right . . . Why should anybody waylay a second-grade technical secretary? No money, no family . . . only a norm-plus rating in intelligence quota, energo-efficiency and mating potential . . . Who'd be after me?"

Of course, an invisible creature then smashed the window of her room and dragged her off into space on a strange ship. The creature became visible inside the ship, a muscular, satyr-like humanoid, a semi-automaton with a bony chin and pointed ears. "Spehny," he croaked, "Terr bell gree, pojek surr-val . . . hee-hee-hee!" Meaning, "Specimen nine from Terra Belt Green for Project Survival!" The translation was provided by the creature's master, a dwarfed creature with an oversized cranium.

He took the controls. "Now home!" he said, "and if you find our methods ruthless, Specimen Nine, it is because our needs are desperate . . ." They landed at the city of Cymradia on the planet of Cymrad, and it was apparent the girl was to be used for an experiment of some kind. "The life of our Cymrad race at stake. . . strong new flesh and blood is needed to feed and house our treasures of the mind."

As the story developed we were told that the Cymrads were possessed of mighty, immortal brains, but their bodies were weak and there were now very few of them physically alive. These few, under the leadership of Mentor, their leader, were experimenting with various subjects kidnapped from around the universe in order to determine which species possessed the necessary qualities to serve as host-bodies for the Cymrad brains.

Marcia, along with life-forms from a dozen worlds, was tested thoroughly and found to have the potential they desired. She was classified and given the lab name of Futura.

In the dungeons with the other prisoners, she was soon the center of a group planning escape, but the Cymrads were watching her every move, pleased that she had leadership potential. Mentor devised a test of courage for her and set the scene to give her a chance to escape. The strip ended with her heading out in a stolen flier into the purple mists of Cymrad.

Futura had been underestimated, though, and managed to get through the purple mists to Sargazzo, land of the Aborotes, where with the aid of Jarl Nord, who wore a powerful ring, she became the leader of the Aborotes and led them against the Cymrads. By about the third or fourth strip, the story had solidified, and at the end of one of them Futura confronted Mentor on the visiscreen and informed him, "Futura by *your* naming, Mentor—and by that name I'll conquer you. Take warning, Big Head—this tower is ours and not until I lead my Aborotes to Cymradia will I return to earth as Marcia Reynolds."

This established the pattern for subsequent adventures, which were quite well thought out. Some of the ideas showed real imagination. In one issue, for instance, she encountered, practically simultaneously, several species of giant insects, a Tyrannosaurus-like beast, a living tree which fought the beast to save her, and a race of strange beings that were part human and part moth. Certainly this was well above the run-of-the-mill *Planet* strip.

There were many other strips, of course, but for the most part they were gray mediocrities best quickly forgotten. However, I've saved for dessert the most popular and undoubtedly the best strip *Planet* ever produced—*Lost World.*

Lost World alone was worth the 10¢ to me any time and can stand comparison with almost any strip around for interest, imagination, and originality.

The strip was credited to Thorncliffe Herrick and stayed in his able hands throughout its life. I don't recall any other strips by him, certainly none in *Planet,* but he did quite a few of the little two-page stories which *Planet* ran.

According to the Day Index, "Herrick" was actually a house name, and one of the writers whose works appeared under it in *Planet Comics* was Jerome Bixby. Bixby is now a screenwriter, credited with the story for *Fantastic Voyage*.

The setting of the strip was an Earth of the not-too-far-distant future, devastated and with most of the inhabitants killed. The devastators were the Voltamen, surely among the best-known Alien Menaces, and definitely one of the best characterized. Of course, they were typically cloddish villains in their actions, but they had, if not individually, then certainly as a race, real character. They were humanoid, of a pale green complexion with long vertical wrinkles in their faces, practically no lips, fangs, and pug noses. As befitted their ultraregimented culture, they wore uniforms of shapeless dark-green blouses and spike-topped helmets obviously patterned after those of the German army in World War I.

At first they spoke rather plainly, but later they developed a highly distinctive speech pattern (see explanation by William Maye in the Vizigraph) that excited all sorts of pro and con comment from readers. Many identified it correctly as Latin phrasing, thus: "We the switch pull." "The earthling it is!" "No—not fair is! Revenge my right is!" Sounds silly, maybe, but it lent them a definite air of authenticity which most *Planet* menaces didn't have.

The hero was Hunt Bowman, a typically magnificent specimen with no special powers except the usual charmed life and some aptitude with a bow and arrow. No explanation was offered as to why he kept using these primitive weapons when so many others were easily available to him. He was accompanied by the usual semi-clothed, over-developed, long-legged blonde. Her name was Lyssa, and while she was never referred to directly as Hunt's woman, she was obviously, from several hints dropped, a bit more than a Personal Friend of His.

For some time these two were pretty much alone, but later, in one of the better episodes, they discovered three teenagers—two boys and a girl—in suspended animation in a laboratory. They had been placed there by their father, a Brilliant Scientist, and were revived by Bowman. In the following scenes one of the boys was killed off by the Voltamen, but the other, apparently inheriting his great surgical skill from his father, transferred the dead boy's brain to the body of a dead Voltaman, giving the "earthies" a rather unusual ally who paused every now and then when the strip bogged down to meditate and sigh a little over the cruel fate that had stuck him in this awful body.

At about this time, Herrick abandoned the aimless wandering of the group and developed the theme of Bowman and his little gang uniting the remaining handfuls of Earthmen to fight the Voltamen, with the hope of eventually freeing the Earth.

The art was excellent, certainly a cut above most of the rest of *Planet,* and the story lines, while repetitious, were enlivened by an occasional excellent one—and even the poorer ones had fascinating detail, showing a really imaginative hand at work. Chases through subway tunnels, battles in Central Park, lookouts in the Empire State Building; all this lent a definite extra something to the strip.

It was issue No. 36 that introduced the three teenagers, and in No. 37 Herrick followed this up with a trip to Volta, the invaders' home world. As the strip opened the four heroes were captured, but Bruce, in the Voltaman body, saved them, and Bowman said with determination, "First gather up their blasters—we must learn Voltan science. Somehow—I don't know how—we've got to rid the lost world of the Voltamen . . . We must contact other Earthmen . . . weld them—and us—into a powerful force! Well, let's start with those blasters . . ."

They followed this up by raying down a Volta patrol in front of the New York Public Library on 42nd Street and taking over their space ship, which Bruce's Voltaman body was instinctively able to pilot. They took off, but were boarded by a Volta inspection patrol. The others hid and Bruce greeted the inspectors nervously, only to have them fall on their knees at the sight of him. Another happy coincidence—Bruce's body was that of Prince Guth of Volta. The patrol informed him he must return to Volta, before his father, the King, died of grief.

They headed for Volta, where Bruce-Guth greeted his father. The hiding earthmen were discovered, but Bruce weasled out of it when his father exclaimed, "Then they are a gift for me, son? You recalled my experiments on humans!" Later, in typical hairbreadth style, they escaped.

With this and several other issues we had a close look at the home world of the Voltamen and at their regimented, dictatorial society. We were also informed that the rest of the solar system had been conquered, and one issue featured a combined revolt of the slaves from various planets.

But let's follow the crew through a typical adventure. In issue No. 49, the opening paragraph ran:

It was a fiendish devil-kingdom from the outer void that spawned those loathsome Voltans, and spewed them forth in monster spaceships against

the other sky-worlds. So Earth lay shattered and devastated from their awesome blows. Yet some few Earthling survivors with immortal courage
united in resistance. HUNT BOWMAN was their leader, and LYSSA, his
faithful companion. And now they stood before the monument at Bunker
Hill. . . .

There was a little moralizing about birthplaces of freedom, and
then Bruce commented: "This cursed body I wear will ever be a
symbol of their cruelty. But come. The outpost is in an old ship,
named the 'Constitution.' The watcher reported Voltamen in the vi-
cinity!"

But the Voltans had already captured the old man who watched
from the "Constitution" and they demanded that he translate papers
they had found on him. He refused and they tied him to the mast and
fired the ship. Hunt arrived in time to cut him loose, but he was dying. He told Bowman that the paper the Voltans had taken described
the location in the Luray Caverns where a time capsule was buried—
and the capsule contained information on how to make an atomic
bomb.

Hunt, Lyssa, and Bruce headed for Virginia, but meanwhile Volta
scientists had arrived with a new secret weapon called the hypnosphere. Naturally, they landed near the Luray Caverns and deci-
phered the paper giving the location of the capsule. They decided to
test their weapon there, also.

Meanwhile, back in Boston, our three heroes had discovered an
old steam engine, fired it up, and set off highballing it for Virginia.
The Voltan scientists had their hypnosphere set up and had equipped
their troops with special glasses to resist its powers.

"Lever to Gamma adjust now. To twenty million ruds it advance!" ordered the chief scientist.

The machine went into action just as Hunt and Lyssa were about
to dig up the time capsule. Along with a pack of wild dogs, some
other wild creatures, and a stray giant mutated spider, they were
drawn toward the hypnosphere and led inside.

Bruce was also under the influence but fell down a ravine en route
and lay stunned until the machine was shut off. He then freed Hunt
and Lyssa and they took off after the Voltan scientists who were now
in the process of digging up the time capsule themselves.

Hunt grabbed a Voltan flier and aimed it at the cave entrance,
jumping just before the crash. The flier smashed the scientists and
effectively sealed the cave entrance and the atomic secret against all
of them, and Hunt now had possession of the Voltans' hypnosphere.

A few words would be in order here about the tie-ins at Fiction House between their pulps and their comic books.

There were, obviously, *Planet Comics* and *Planet Stories.* The continuing characters in the comic series had no text counterparts in the pulp magazine, although *covers* from the pulp magazine sometimes turned up on the comic book later.

There were *Jungle Comics* and *Jungle Stories,* and there was a pulp devoted exclusively to the adventures of Sheena, the leading heroine of *Jumbo Comics.*

There was a *Wings* pulp and there was *Wings Comics,* and also a *Fight* in each series.

Fiction House had quite a number of specialized comics, other than the "Big Six" which formed the backbone of the line (*Jumbo, Jungle, Planet, Fight, Rangers, Wings*).

There were *Ghost Comics, Indian Comics, Wambi the Jungle Boy, Firehair,* and others. A Fiction House *Movie Comics* adapted various films to the comics format, a device tried at varying times and with various and limited degrees of success by National, Fawcett, and Dell as well.

The Fiction House line is long gone, of course, but several of its titles were reissued years later by the "IW" comic reprint series and are worth looking into if you cannot get copies of the originals.

Even with the fantastic changes made by Fawcette, Payne, and Byrne, I would hardly call *Planet* a great comic book. But the improvement it underwent over the years was truly remarkable.

INTRODUCTION TO

THE BIG RED CHEESE

This book started because Captain Marvel is so unforgettable. Richard Lupoff, a college-educated former army officer, was working as a junior executive for a large, well-known concern, and found his thoughts returning to the halcyon days when the greatest superhero of them all blundered his way through adventures which the kids read for story and adults read for their deliberate humor.

In the early sixties, Dick published a science fiction fan magazine called *Xero*. For the first issue, he wrote an article about the long-remembered captain. Response from his readers was enthusiastic, and a coterie of comics fans was formed.

Shortly after, a full-blown comics fandom appeared and it is still going strong though Dick has disavowed any responsibility. The popularity of *Xero's* comic book articles helped Dick (and wife Pat) win the Hugo award for the best fan magazine three years later.

When not writing prize-winning industrial films, Dick continues to write freelance material. His first book was the non-fiction *Edgar Rice Burroughs: Master of Adventure* (1965; revised edition, 1968). His novels include *One Million Centuries* (1967), *With the Bentfin Boomer Boys on Little Old New Alabama* (1970), and *Up!* (in progress). He's written short stories and non-fiction for many magazines including *Crawdaddy, Fantastic, The Writer, Famous Science Fiction, Castle of Frankenstein, Fantastic Monsters,* and *Dude,* does the script for several underground comic strips drawn by Steve Stiles, and has edited five volumes of the works of Edgar Rice Burroughs for posthumous first editions.

CHAPTER 3

THE BIG RED CHEESE

by DICK LUPOFF

★★★

One balmy winter's day nearly 30 years ago, in the sun-baked village of Venice, Florida, two small boys dressed in tee shirts, short pants, and sneakers wandered into the town drug store. In addition to being Venice's sole pharmacy, the store was the town's main source of beach goods, the local ice cream parlor and short order lunch counter, and the only newsstand this side of distant, metropolitan Sarasota.

The taller of the two children looked to be seven or eight years of age: chubby, jolly, extroverted. The smaller boy was his brother, younger by three years. In general he resembled the older boy, but evidenced a more contemplative and introspective nature. Despite being the younger of the pair, he would more likely remember such a day.

The treasury of the two boys comprised exactly 20¢, entrusted to the more experienced judgment of the older child. It was entrusted wisely. The boy used the coins to purchase a chocolate ice cream cone for himself, a strawberry cone for his brother, and, to be shared by the two children, a copy of the first fat issue of *Whiz Comics.*

The littler boy quickly and sloppily dispatched his strawberry ice cream, gave away the dry bisquity cone, and turned his attention to the colorful world of *Whiz Comics,* where that day he made the acquaintance of a friend and adventuring companion for years to come, whose eventual disappearance from the colored pages of comics was a real loss to many besides that one child. I refer, of course, to the greatest of all comic book heroes, Captain Marvel.

As for remembering that day, the younger boy does—vividly: the sights and odors of that bright day near the Gulf of Mexico, the palmettoes and the scrubby grass that eked uncertain existence from the rocky, sandy Florida soil, the texture and taste of that pink ice cream with its red embedded bits of berry. That 10¢ book of wonders starting with the original story of Captain Marvel. Mostly, I remember Captain Marvel.

His career started with Billy Batson, a poverty-stricken orphan newsboy, hawking his papers on a night-dark street outside a subway kiosk. A dark and mysterious figure beckons to Billy, then disappears into the underground. Billy follows, only to find himself ominously alone in an apparently abandoned subway tunnel.

The tunnel opens eventually into a huge vault; lining the wall of the chamber Billy saw seven gigantic, evil-looking statues representing the traditional seven deadly sins. Passing beyond the shadowy effigies Billy came to an even larger chamber in which stood a great throne carved from a monolithic block of stone. Above it, suspended by the merest thread, hung a huge square-cut block of the same material. Beneath the murderous weight, seated on the throne, was a tall, thin man clad in a simple, floor-length robe. His hair and his long beard were of purest white.

Billy stood awed before the ancient one. The seated figure spoke, and, although the comics were a printed medium, I could hear his voice, cracking and aged but yet carrying the authority of the mighty and the righteous. (For how many years was that printed visage my personal vision of God?) "Billy Batson! I am Shazam, an ancient Egyptian wizard. I have fought evil, but my time is up! You shall succeed me!"

"M-me, sir?" was all that Billy could stammer.

"Yes. You are pure of heart. You have been chosen. Speak my name!"

The boy shouted "Shazam!" A mighty bolt of lightning, a deafening bass peal of thunder, filled the chamber. The frightened child was gone. In his place stool a veritable giant of a man. Clad in a tight-fitting red costume and white cape, the symbol of the lightning that heralded him blazoned upon his chest, the world's mightiest mortal, Captain Marvel, had been born.

He was a huge, massively built figure, covered with bulging muscles. He had thick black hair, heavy eyebrows, a powerful mouth above a broad, cleft chin. A golden sash encircled his waist and his boots were of the same hue. Sleeve trimmings reminiscent of those worn by naval officers decorated his cuffs, and gold workings like those of a naval officer's cape rimmed his own.

No sooner had the heroic figure appeared than a final strand supporting the stone gave way. It crashed to the throne, filling the space between the graven arms. Of Shazam there was nothing left. In a moment a cloud arose, assuming the shape of the dead ancient, risen from his own dust.

"Shazam!" shouted Captain Marvel. Instead of Billy Batson's boyish falsetto it was an heroic voice that pronounced the name of the wizard. Again the thunder and lightning, and in an instant Captain Marvel had disappeared to the limbo from which he had been called, replaced once more by the child, Billy Batson.

"Go now," solemnly intoned the shade of the wizard. "Fight the forces of evil. When you have need of the powers at my command, you need only speak my name, and you shall be transformed into Captain Marvel, possessor of all the powers of the six gods whose initials form my name: the wisdom of Solomon, the strength of Hercules, the stamina of Atlas, the power of Zeus, the courage of Achilles, the speed of Mercury."

With this speech even the shade of the wizard faded from mortal view. Old Shazam's bland mixing of gods, heroes, and a biblical king did not bother a small reader on the Gulf coast of Florida. Nor did Billy Batson note the anomaly as he slowly retraced his path to the street.

Back on the sidewalk Billy himself thought that he might have been having a dream, so strange and thrilling had been his experiences of the night. The stranger who had gestured mysteriously, the hall of the seven statues, the wizard and his words of power. . . .

But the first time he was faced with the need of Captain Marvel (it involved mere mundane crime, with little to hint at the odd and exotic cases to follow), Billy tested the promise of Shazam and found it a truthful one.

Shortly Billy won employment as boy newscaster for radio station WHIZ. His association there with Sterling Morris continued throughout the published career of Captain Marvel, even into the early days of commercial television in the1950s. Also for that entire period Billy wore a yellow-collared red shirt and blue slacks. Billy lived in a comfortable apartment, alone save for his Negro valet, Steamboat Willie.

Steamboat Willie was the exemplification of the racial stereotype of the era, as popularized in innumerable pulp magazine stories, radio dramas, motion pictures (perhaps there most of all), and other popular media. He had huge fat lips and gigantic popping eyes, dressed flashily, spoke a peculiar illiterate jargon, served faithfully and humbly except when terrified (which he usually was) of menace human or supernatural, and of course he was thoroughly drenched in superstition. Although obviously a grown man in the employ of a half-grown boy, Willie always addressed his employer as "Mist' Billy."

Trying to evaluate the stereotypes of that era, the modern critic is left near to speechless puzzlement. The comic black of the popular arts is of course only the most obvious and extreme case, but few, if any, identifiable groups escaped the establishment of a demeaning "type." There were the standardized caricatured Jew, Irishman, Italian, Indian, Russian, Chinese, Spaniard, Mexican, Swede, and so on through every conceivable national, racial, and religious grouping.

The strange aspect of the matter is that the writers (and artists and actors) who created and perpetuated such types were seldom, if ever, vicious in their intentions. The portrayal of Steamboat Willie was essentially a friendly and sympathetic one! It was simply assumed, as a precondition to the writing and the drawing of the character, that this was the way black people looked and spoke and behaved: As if there were a Platonic ideal Negro, of whom all Negroes were more or less faithful reflections.

There were of course other characters who appeared early in the saga of Captain Marvel, and who won enduring roles in the series. Among the most vivid were the villains, two of whom stand above all the rest: Dr. Sivana and Mr. Mind. And, once the popularity of Captain Marvel had been established, Fawcett Publications saw to it that the popular feature spun off a number of variants of itself, designed to exploit a market of almost unbelievable size.

That first Captain Marvel story in *Whiz Comics* started a series of well over 1,000 stories featuring either Captain Marvel himself or other members of the Marvel Family. *Whiz Comics* itself was a kind of variety book, featuring a cast of running heroes who appeared in one adventure apiece in each issue. In addition to Captain Marvel the lineup included Spy Smasher, a costumed adventurer whose exploits concerned—right—smashing spies; Lance O'Casey, a freelance sailor who plied the South Seas in search of danger and romance; Golden Arrow ("the Robin Hood of the West"); and Ibis the Invincible, an Egyptian prince revived in modern times to do battle with the aid of occult powers.

There was also *Colonel Porterhouse,* an amusing feature about an elderly windbag who amused a pair of children by reading them *Whiz Comics* each month and projecting himself into the role of a selected hero for a lampoon of that hero's current adventure. The Colonel Porterhouse technique was revived with fantastic success by Harvey Kurtzman in *Mad* over a decade later, and in recent years has been revived *again* in such comics as *Not Brand Echh* and *Inferior Five.*

With *Whiz* selling briskly, Fawcett added a companion devoted entirely to the exploits of their big hero: *Captain Marvel Adventures.* Later there was a *Marvel Family Comics* featuring Captain Marvel, Captain Marvel, Jr., and Mary Marvel. There were various lesser Fawcett periodicals featuring the red-suited hero, and two attempts to promote him in text form. One was the *Captain Marvel Story Book,* a shotgun marriage of the comic book and pulp magazine featuring alternate pages of text and illustration.

The other (which appeared in 1941—*very* early in the Marvel cycle), was *Captain Marvel and the Return of the Scorpion.* As for where the Scorpion was returning from, that's another matter, as we shall see later. But this publication was a Dime Action Book, one of four issued by Fawcett as their own entry in the Big Little Book sweepstakes.

Resembling the more famous Whitman series, the Dime Action Books were approximately 4 by 5 inches in dimension, containing 192 pages of alternating picture and text.

There were only four—devoted to Captain Marvel, Spy Smasher, and two other Fawcett heroes, Bulletman and Minute Man. Despite their crude artwork and not very polished writing, these four little books are among the scarcest of collectors' treasures today. An example from *Captain Marvel and the Return of the Scorpion* by Otto O. Binder:

> "Oh, a wise guy!" rasped one bruiser, built like a gorilla. Not quite realizing just whom he was facing, he leaped forward and swung at the crimson figure a haymaker that might have broken the neck of an ordinary man. The blow landed solidly on Captain Marvel's chin. Its only effect was to make the thug yell in pain as his knucklebones were crushed.
>
> "Tit for tat," murmured Captain Marvel and, smiling pleasantly, he shot his fist out at the thug's chin like a steam-driven piston. The thug sailed backwards through the air, landed among his henchmen, and piled them all upon the pavement.

The *Captain Marvel Story Book* came later by some years, and was not restricted to such simple writing. Its format, providing full-page presentation of Beck's drawings (occasionally even a two-page spread), gave Beck an opportunity to shine, and many of the illustrations are among the most memorable of the whole Captain Marvel art canon. A sample of the text from a 1949 *Story Book* titled *Captain Marvel and the Gargoyle Men:*

> Captain Marvel was left to his thoughts. But his thoughts refused to mesh. Intruding upon them was the image of a beautiful woman, a woman such as he had never seen before. Captain Marvel shook his head. He tried to think of his friends, but the image of the woman persisted in superimposing itself upon his thoughts. He even thought of Sivana, but even the unforgettable face of that old villain faded into the beauty of this strange new woman. Abruptly Captain Marvel leaped to his feet.
>
> "I'm going back to see what the gargoyle men are doing," he told Dr. Cuchin. "You'll be safe here until I get back."
>
> With that he sprang into the air and vanished into the distance.

In the publishing industry, ever since the early 1960s, there has been a boom in the publication of heroic adventures. Many of the older heroes have been revived and new ones have been added. A glance at the paperback section of a large bookstore reveals a whole lineup of flamboyant adventurers in and out of fancy dress: Captain Future, Starwolf, Tarzan and many other of Edgar Rice Burroughs' heroes, Conan, the Phantom Detective, Secret Agent X, Dusty Ayres, the Avengers (I refer to the comic characters, but the British television stars are there too), Captain America, Brak the Barbarian, Doc Savage, the Shadow, and so on.

A paperback edition of one or several of the *Captain Marvel Story Books* would not be out of place. Certainly the writing is at least equal to the pulp level of many of the reprints and the newly written books, and the appeal of the character is great. But it has not happened and is not likely to, for reasons we shall shortly see.

Another feature familiar to the readers of *Captain Marvel Adventures* was *Lieutenant Jon Jarl of the Space Patrol*. Almost all comics in the 1940s and early 1950s ran two-page short stories in solid text format. Not that the publishers particularly wanted to, and most of the readers generally skipped over them in reading the pictorial stories, but concern over postal and copyright regulations caused the inclusion of these pieces. (More recently they have been abandoned in favor of letter columns and "news" pages—actually promotional material for the publishers' own products.)

In *Captain Marvel Adventures* a series of these two-page stories was devoted to Binder's creation, Lieutenant Jarl. They were frequently charming little pieces, usually with a clever twist to them, and I suspect that the copyright to them might be cleared, and that they would make a most unusual paperback original. There were about 84 of them. Here's one small quotation from *The World Stealers* (1947):

It was a giant space ship, over a mile long! And from its stern came out a long beam of some amazing radiation that seemed to be *towing* Earth along, like a barge behind a tug.

Jon radioed Headquarters. "Attention! Huge space tug pulling Earth out of its orbit."

The answer came back in a bellow. "Don't you think we know it? Good lord, the whole universe is changing around us as we leave Earth's orbit around the Sun. Stop that ship, Lieutenant! We can't get a cruiser there for hours. Stop that ship!"

"And this," groaned Jon, "is my vacation!"

For little *little* children there was even a funny animal version of Captain Marvel, *Hoppy the Marvel Bunny,* complete with the magical word of Shazam, lightning transformation, red suit, and super powers. Hoppy appeared in Fawcett's *Funny Animals* and in a periodical of his own.

As I have stated elsewhere, it is unfortunate that comic books seldom carried complete and accurate credits in that golden era. Certainly it would be fascinating to know exactly *who* did *what* in the founding days of the Fawcett comics dynasty, but only a tentative picture can be sketched from fragmentary records and memories of events nearly 30 years old.

It does seem fairly certain that Captain Marvel was the brain child of Bill Parker (writer) and C. C. Beck (artist). Parker was a Fawcett wheelhorse who had been drafted from the company's magazine department to help launch the comic line. He found the illustrated adventure strip an uncongenial art form and succeeded, once the Fawcett line of comics was successfully launched, in having himself returned to his former area of work. He devoted himself to such periodicals as *Mechanix Illustrated* until his death some 20 years later.

Beck, on the other hand, found the comics very much to his liking, and remained the chief artist of the Fawcett comics line from the founding days in 1940 until the end of the line in 1953, when he moved to Florida and went into commercial art.

Parker and Beck devised their hero as Captain Thunder and planned to feature him in the projected *Thunder Comics.* Except for the names, "Thunder" was very much "Marvel" and *Thunder Comics* was equally *Whiz Comics.* A first issue of *Thunder Comics* featuring Captain Thunder was prepared as a kind of trial run, but never went beyond the Fawcett offices. (A collector who could produce a copy of *Thunder Comics* today would have a treasure beyond compare. A copy was offered in 1963, but after its purchase had been arranged and payment made, the sale was canceled on the grounds that the magazine had been ruined by water damage. Whether the item ever existed at all, outside the seller's imagination, is unknown.)

Between that practice run on *Thunder Comics* and the issuance of the first *published* issue, the transformation of titles took place. As a result, the *first* issue of *Whiz Comics* was called Number Two. One more woe for collectors and bibliographers.

In addition to Bill Parker and C. C. Beck, quite a few other men played a part in the early days of Fawcett's comics venture. Ralph Daigh was editorial director for the entire Fawcett operation, and Al Allard was art director. Ed Herren served as comics editor until he was drafted in 1943, and later contributed many fine scripts. His successor was Rod Reed. But for most of Fawcett's greatest years, their top comics carried the names of Will Lieberson as executive editor and Wendell Crowley as editor.

The team of Joe Simon and Jack Kirby was called in to launch *Captain Marvel Adventures.* The ground was prepared by a one-shot called *Captain Marvel Thrill Book,* an oversize comic printed in black-and-white (but with full color covers). Then came *Special Edition Comics,* a standard sized comic in full color, devoted entirely to Captain Marvel and his exploits. Finally, *Captain Marvel Adventures* was launched.

Simon and Kirby didn't stay around the Fawcett establishment very long, however, but went on to a seemingly endless stream of comics done separately and in collaboration. Both are still active in the comics industry, sporting a credits list that staggers the imagination. Most enthusiasts would agree, I am sure, that their greatest success was scored with Captain America.

After Bill Parker went back to the model airplanes and the hotrod how-to-do-it set, Otto O. Binder entered the picture as the lead writer for Captain Marvel. Binder was one of three brothers who had already made their mark on the pulp magazine industry. Jack Binder (it's pronounced with a short *i,* by the way) was a pulp illustrator who later did considerable drawing for the comics, including Fawcett's comics.

Earl and Otto Binder were writers, beginning their career under the joint pseudonym of Eando (E-and-O) Binder in 1932. Earl shortly left the team, but Otto kept the established byline as his own, and turned out well over 100 pulp adventures, ranging from short stories to novels, in the years that followed. Some of Binder's most popular stories were series: the Adam Link stories about a sentient robot, the Anton York series about an immortal scientist, and the "via etherline" series tracing the exploration of the solar system.

Binder appeared in *Amazing Stories, Astounding Stories, Wonder Stories, Fantastic Adventures, Weird Tales, Comet, Dynamic Stories,* and so on. Before coming to Fawcett he worked on a number of smaller features for lesser comics publishers. He was brought to Fawcett by the original comics editor, Ed Herren. Binder broke in on some of the secondary Fawcett heroes, then took Captain Marvel in hand and shepherded him for all of the Captain's remaining days.

The popularity of Captain Marvel skyrocketed so spectacularly that Fawcett soon advanced *Captain Marvel Adventures* to a schedule of one issue every three weeks. It fell back to monthly but after World War II it advanced to publication every two weeks, at the peak of the magazine's success.

Peak circulation was well over 2,000,000 copies per issue—a figure never reached by any other comic before or since. In those years before postal regulations required circulation disclosures, publishers were skittish about revealing their sales, but Captain Marvel's chief rival, Superman, is believed to have peaked at 1,600,000 copies. An enviable figure itself, but no match for Fawcett's champion.

Fawcett remained in the superhero business until 1953, although during the last few years the road became increasingly rocky. After some early experiments in which page size went as large as a tabloid newspaper or as small as a Dime Action Book, and prices ranged from 5¢ for standard-size comics of 32 pages plus covers up through 15¢ for the jumbo-sized comics, the Fawcett line, like the rest of the industry, settled on a standard 64-page saddle-stapled product selling for a dime.

A combination of paper shortages—and later, a profit squeeze—forced the reduction of the standard comic, first to 48 pages, then to 32. Costs were rising but the standard price seemed immovable. Simultaneously, the popularity of the costumed adventure hero was waning. By the 1950s Fawcett was flailing about trying to find a new winning formula in the western, sports, horror, adolescent humor, and other fields, but none recaptured the great appeal of the once mighty flying men and women.

There was, of course, one other factor in Fawcett's eventual abandonment of its comics line, which has led to endless discussion and a great deal of misunderstanding. This was the famous lawsuit between National Periodical Publications and Fawcett Publications. It might also be known as Superman versus Captain Marvel.

There is a great deal of argument about who was really the first great adventure hero, or superhero, or costumed hero—who set the style for the hundreds and thousands who have followed. A case can be made for such pulp magazine adventurers as Doc Savage or the Shadow, or for Baroness Orczy's Scarlet Pimpernel, or Cooper's Deerslayer. Those who would stick to panel art cite the Phantom, or even Popeye the Sailor. Classicists may cite Ulysses or Jason, Samson, David, or Gilgamesh.

But there is no denying that Siegel and Shuster's Superman set the style for comic book heroes by combining the vividly colored tights and dual identity of the Phantom with the super powers possessed by heroes of earlier media.

And once Superman's success had been established, the presence of so powerful a rival as Captain Marvel proved intolerable to the holders of the Superman copyright. National instituted a lawsuit against Fawcett charging that Captain Marvel infringed upon the copyright of Superman, and seeking to obtain an order that Fawcett discontinue Captain Marvel and pay damages to National.

On the face of it, National had considerable merit in their case. The similarities of Captain Marvel to Superman were substantial. The powers of the two heroes were similar: great strength, invulnerability to most forms of peril, incredible speed, an ability to leap great distances that quickly turned into the power of outright flight. Certainly the physical appearances of the two were much alike: tall, muscular men with dark hair wearing tight-fitting brightly colored costumes, blazoned with emblems upon the chest, and with a cape and boots. Captain Marvel's costume was red while Superman's was blue, and the golden lightning upon the chest replaced Superman's large monogram; these were small differences.

In both cases the hero possessed a mufti-clad alter ego employed in the news media. Superman's Clark Kent worked as a reporter under editor Perry White of the *Daily Planet.* Captain Marvel's Billy Batson advanced in his first adventure from newsboy to boy radio newscaster working for Sterling Morris of station WHIZ.

Even the arch-villains of the two strips were very much alike. Superman dealt with Ultro, a bullet-headed, mad scientist. (Ultro later gave way to the not-very-different evil genius, Luthor.) Captain Marvel tangled with Thaddeus Bodog Sivana who was billed as the world's maddest scientist (in contrast to the world's mightiest mortal), but who preferred the self-bestowed title of rightful ruler of the universe. And of course Sivana sported a scalp just as bald as Ultro's.

The talents behind both strips emerged from the world of science fiction. Otto Binder's background I have already sketched. Jerry Siegel and Joe Shuster were teenage science fiction fans when Eando Binder was first a familiar byline in the pages of *Amazing Stories* and other pulps. From their homes in Cleveland, Siegel and Shuster began publishing a mimeographed science-fiction fan magazine called simply *Science Fiction,* in 1932. By the third issue (January 1933) they featured a story called "The Reign of the Superman" by the pseudonymous Herbert S. Fine—Siegel and Shuster. Here is a brief excerpt:

> A grin of superiority crossed the Superman's face.
> "I can do four things that no one else of the planet can emulate.
> They are: intercept interplanetary messages, read the mind of anyone I desire, by sheer mental concentration force ideas into people's heads, and throw my vision to any spot in the universe.
> "Furthermore," he added, "during the night my mind has assimilated all the knowledge that exists in the universe . . . I am a veritable God!"

Aside from this early stirring of Superman, the issue contains at least two other portents of things to come. One is a letter from Julius Schwartz, then a science fiction fan, later a highly successful comic book writer and editor in the National stable. The other is a mention of *Interplanetary Police,* a projected newspaper strip by Siegel and Shuster. Somehow the project failed, but very shortly they were on their way with transitional heroes called Dr. Occult and Dr. Mystic, and finally, Superman.

But whatever the background of the two great heroes, and whatever derivation of the one might be traced to the other, there was little or no imitation as the years passed—at least, on the part of the Fawcett crew. Many men contributed scripts to the Marvel saga, including Bill Finger (who pioneered the Green Lantern series for National), Carl Formes (who did many stories for Fawcett), and Bill Woolfolk (better known today for his bestselling novels). Still, Otto Binder was the top Fawcett scripter, turning out some 529 Captain Marvel stories alone—more than all other writers combined.

And Binder points out that he and the other Fawcett regulars, at management direction, studiously *avoided* even looking at National's comics for fear of even unconscious plagiarism!

What final disposition would have been made of the National-Fawcett lawsuit had it reached a final judgment will never be known. As it was the suit dragged on for years, with legendary proceedings in which National's lawyer, Louis Nizer, presented Superman-Captain Marvel scrapbooks as evidence. In response to which Fawcett's lawyers presented similar scrapbooks to show that whatever Superman had done before Captain Marvel, Popeye had done before Superman.

Certainly one by-product of the suit was a reluctance on the part of merchandisers to take on Captain Marvel novelties for fear of being caught in the maelstrom. As a result, Fawcett found itself in the novelty business, merchandising Captain Marvel statuettes, stationery, tie-clips, hats, and other products.

What prevented the suit's ever reaching a definitive judgment was Fawcett's decision in 1953 to abandon its foundering comic book line and concentrate its resources on the far more lucrative areas of its business—areas such as paperback book publishing, how-to-do-it books that had spun off from the successful *Mechanix Illustrated* magazine, and other periodicals such as *True* magazine.

Fawcett settled out of court with National, agreeing to suppress and never revive Captain Marvel and the rest of the Marvel Family, and selling off or abandoning the rest of their features. *Ibis the Invincible* and a few others were taken over by Charlton Publications, but in time they disappeared entirely. At least one Fawcett title, *Hopalong Cassidy,* was taken over by National, but it too disappeared eventually.

And so what was unquestionably the greatest battle ever to take place in the comic books ended not in a landmark decision, but in a quiet, out-of-court settlement!

But to get back to the 1940s, it became unpleasantly clear that the *Superman* feature, after a brilliant initiation and immense commercial success, quickly lost the imaginative spark that had at first been present. Siegel and Shuster discovered to their dismay that they had lost legal title to their creation to the publisher, and the writing and artwork were taken over by a series of hired men doing the bidding of a commercial publisher. A rereading of those Superman stories reveals a kind of literal-minded, almost mechanically grim outlook. The stories might have been written by a machine.

But *Captain Marvel* seldom ceased to be interesting and imaginative, with real suspense, clever gimmicks, legitimate plots, and a delightful air of almost whimsical fantasy to the stories. Perhaps the reason behind this is something that Crowley, Lieberson, and Binder realized, something about supermen (with a lower-case *s*) that too few writers ever grasp.

Whether the writer is a pulp novelist like E. E. Smith chronicling the adventures of a Richard Seaton or a Kimball Kinnison, or "Kenneth Robeson" creating a Doc Savage, or a comic book scripter pitting some tights-clad superadventurer against an arch-criminal or mad scientist, there can be no real suspense in the story of a superhero combatting a merely ordinary villain.

One way out of this dilemma is to face the superhero with a su-pervillain, thus restoring a balance of opposing forces in the story. The temptation then is to make the hero maybe a little bit *more* super than the villain, shortly requiring the ante to be upped again, and again, until a totally incredible battle of the gods results. (For samples of this phenomenon, see some of the adventures of a comics hero called the Spectre.)

An alternate maneuver is somehow to un-super the superhero. I can recall, for example, one incident from those bygone days, when Superman developed amnesia, thereby losing knowledge (and effective use) of his super powers. That incident took place in the radio series. And along the way Superman, of course, acquired an immense slew of super-companions, both villainous and heroic. And, of course, the theme of Kryptonite, that mysterious mineral which, in its varied forms, has such strange and powerful influences upon Superman, has been developed *ad absurdum.*

But I'm writing about Captain Marvel, am I not?

Captain Marvel faced an impressive collection of foes, the two most prominent being Dr. Sivana, whom I mentioned earlier, and Mr. Mind, a mystery villain whose true identity was not revealed until well into the lengthy serial adventure which covered his entire career.

Sivana's origins were somewhat obscure. He seemingly held royal status among the residents of the planet Venus, who were portrayed in the traditional pulp-magazine form of frog-like amphibians. Sivana, however, was wholly human, albeit scrawny, bald, snaggle-toothed, and myopic. In the early days of the series he was portrayed as having two offspring, although a Mrs. Sivana was nowhere in evidence.

In the original Sivana family constellation the son was a tall, muscular, god-like, blond young man named Magnificus. He appeared only briefly, and only in the Venusian sequences of the feature.

Beautia Sivana ("byoo-*tee*-a," not "byoo-shuh," according to Otto Binder) played a large and quite intriguing role. She accompanied her father to earth and appeared in many of the Marvel stories of the 1940s. She too was tall, extremely well formed, and blessed with lush, wavy blond hair. Unlike her villainous father, who was the sworn enemy of Captain Marvel, and who provided Marvel with his most popular epithet, "that big red cheese,'" Beautia had distinctly ambivalent feelings.

She was a loyal daughter, and as dutiful as she could be. Further, at least at the outset, she shared her father's ambitions for universal empire. Unfortunately for her peace of mind, however, once she had seen the mighty figure of Captain Marvel she became hopelessly in-fatuated with him. In one very early story, before the full dimensions of Captain Marvel's invulnerability had been established, Sivana invented a gas gun which would have killed any ordinary man, and which succeeded, at least, in rendering Captain Marvel unconscious. Torn between daughterly loyalty and romantic attachment, Beautia deserted her father and nursed Captain Marvel through his recovery—then returned to Sivana's side.

As for the other side of the relationship, things were even odder. Remember that in one aspect of his existence Billy/Marvel was just a boy. In the early days he was, in fact, rather a *little* boy, although of indeterminate age. To Billy Batson, Beautia Sivana was a grown-up woman of incomparable glamour and charm. Billy was definitely smitten, but with the kind of touching "crush" that a child often has on an adult of either sex.

Metaphysical theses have been written on the exact nature of the transformation that took place when Billy shouted the word *Shazam* and disappeared in favor of Captain Marvel. To be quite fair about it, Billy himself often spoke of "calling on" rather than "changing to" Captain Marvel. And, in at least one story, Billy was seen to cheat on a written examination by *whispering* his word and obtaining a wraith-like presence of the Captain, who provided correct answers to the exam.

But all of this notwithstanding, most aficionados are in agreement that Captain Marvel was Billy Batson's alter ego (and vice versa); that in a metaphysical sense they were the same person in two different embodiments; and that in truth Billy did not so much give way to Captain Marvel as become magically transformed *into* Captain Marvel, retaining even as Captain Marvel, the basic personality and identity of Billy Batson.

If all of this seems a digression, take a moment to consider yourself a small, uninitiated boy, with a crush on a gorgeous mature woman. Now—you are miraculously and instantaneously transformed into a man. Bodily. That gorgeous woman all but flings herself upon you. How do you react? Be honest now—you are flustered, confused, embarrassed, even frightened. And that, raised to the *n*th power, is how Captain Marvel reacted to the advances of women in general and Beautia Sivana in particular.

Oh, it was a strange and wonderful relationship.

In the later years of the series Beautia disappeared, presumably returning to the planet Venus to rejoin her brother Magnificus. The two Sivana offspring were replaced by another pair who had apparently been held in reserve all those years on the cloudy planet. The two new Sivanas were Sivana, Jr., and Georgia Sivana.

Junior was a younger edition of his dad, distinguishable chiefly by his non-baldness and his highly visible argyle socks. Georgia was a female counterpart of her brother: scrawny, angular, ugly, bespectacled, brilliant, and evil; her mental acuity was distinctly an inheritance from daddy.

Dr. Sivana and the later little Sivanas were all scientific wizards, forever dreaming up inventions that would permit them to commit outrageous crimes ranging from astounding thefts to walking through prison walls, from traveling through time and altering history to wrecking the entire world. Captain Marvel for his part was supposedly endowed with the wisdom of Solomon, but he did not always use it. The evil schemes of the Sivanas were constantly being thwarted, of course, but their perpetrators always returned with newer and more novel plots.

The proliferation of superheroes is one of the more interesting aspects of the whole superhero phenomenon. I don't mean only that scores of publishers entered the lists, with literally thousands of would-be champions, but that successful superheroes often fissioned into variations of themselves. Captain Marvel very early gave a kind of odd parthenogenetic birth to three Lieutenants Marvel when it was learned that in addition to the original Shazam-blessed Billy Batson there were three *other* Billy Batsons in the land.

By the magic of superheroic proliferation, these other Batsons— Tall Billy, Fat Billy, and Hill Billy—were also able to turn into red-suited superbeings by pronouncing the magical name simultaneously with the *original,* "Real" Billy. While holding lesser rank than their senior counterpart, they occasionally banded together as the Squadron of Justice.

The artwork that went into the Fawcett comics, most particularly the Captain Marvel feature, was remarkable for its charm. Charles Clarence Beck brought to the comics page a style that combined simplicity with a high level of humor, a sense of color and design that matched perfectly the tongue-in-cheek attitude that pervaded the Marvel feature. Although over the years many artists worked on Captain Marvel and its related strips, Beck's influence never ceased to be felt, and at least occasional glimmerings of the original sprightly conception appeared up to the very end.

The first really important proliferation of the Marvel strip was the introduction of Captain Marvel Jr. Junior was conceived by Ed Herren and usually drawn by Mac Raboy, who later took over the *Flash*

Gordon Sunday feature originated by the late Alex Raymond, and drew it until the time of Raboy's own death.

Captain Marvel Jr. originated in the Captain Marvel lead story in an early issue of *Whiz Comics*. A poor newsboy named Freddy Freeman, apparently mortally injured in an encounter with a supervillain named Captain Nazi, was found by Captain Marvel and carried to the cavern of the wizard Shazam. Marvel summoned the wizard by lighting a brazier, as he had been instructed, and pleaded with him to save the youth by means of supernatural intercession. The wizard decreed instead that the World's Mightiest Mortal share his own powers with the boy.

For what seemed to be his final moments of rallying strength, the boy's eyes flickered open. Standing above him Freddy saw the mighty form of his hero and whispered: "Captain Marvel!" In the now familiar burst of thunder and lightning the broken form of the boy disappeared and was replaced by a tights-clad, colorful figure of strength: Captain Marvel Jr. His costume was identical to that of the senior Captain, except for the substitution of blue for red. In form, however, he retained the size and appearance of a boy—and went off into a series of adventures of his own in *Master Comics* (where he displaced *Minute Man* as the leading feature), and in a later series devoted entirely to himself, as well as the *Marvel Family* series. I should mention, in passing, that the powers of Captain Marvel, although "shared" with Freddy in the form of Junior, simultaneously continued *undiminished* in the Captain's own exploits. Another example of the comics miracle.

Twenty years later Will Lieberson told why Junior's magic expletive was "Captain Marvel" rather than "Shazam." "All those kids were going to read Captain Marvel Jr." he said, "and every time they read a story about Junior we wanted to remind them there was a Captain Marvel *Senior* too, so they wouldn't neglect to buy more Fawcett comics."

The use of "Captain Marvel" as Captain Marvel Jr.'s change-word had certain problems with it, that were sometimes either forgotten or simply ignored by scripters. However, they provided amusing possibilities when remembered. For instance, in any Marvel Family adventure, Junior could not speak Captain Marvel's name in direct address without changing instantly to Freddy. Freddy, when out hawking papers, could not shout a headline including either Captain's name (Senior or Junior) without changing. And Captain Marvel Jr., could not even speak his own name without changing back to Freddy!

Mary Batson turned out to be the long-lost twin sister of Billy, and once *she* was found it turned out that the Shazam powers were in her genes too! Instead of the attributes of Solomon, Hercules, and so on, Mary was provided with a purely feminine pantheon: Selena (grace), Hippolyta (strength), Ariadne (skill), Zephyrus (fleetness), Aurora (beauty), and Minerva (wisdom).

As Mary Marvel she wore a short-skirted feminine adaptation of the lightning suit, but like Freddy Freeman she retained her childish size and form despite her supernatural powers. Once launched from the pad of *Captain Marvel Adventures* Mary was transferred to *Wow Comics* where she superseded Mr. Scarlet (a non-powered costume hero) as top feature. And, in time, there was the customary single-character comic for Mary, and the expected role in the activities of the Marvel Family.

This rollcall of Captain Marvel spinoffs seems to go on and on, but there are just a few more, I promise.

Uncle Marvel—in mufti, Uncle Dudley Batson—was a fat old fraud who simply appointed himself a member of the Marvel Family. He made for himself a standard set of lightning-blazoned red tights plus cape and boots, introduced himself to Mary Batson as a long-lost uncle, and joined in the adventures of the family. He was such a good-hearted bumbling fake that although Billy, Mary, and Freddy promptly saw through him, they tolerated, and even abetted his frauds, all the while pretending to be fooled.

He devised the technique of shouting "Shazam" simultaneously with the others, and in the din and glare of their magical transformations, slipping quickly out of his street clothing to appear in the Marvel uniform he wore beneath. Of course, he could not fly or perform other marvelous acts, but he was frequently taken along by the other Marvels, who studiously failed to notice when he hitched a tow on a trailing cape and who "coincidentally" happened to intercept bullets and other missiles directed at him.

When presented with a direct challenge to his Shazam powers, Dudley pleaded a case of "Shazambago," a debility of advancing years, and played upon the sympathy of some authentic Marvel—usually Mary—for help. He survived financially by running a benevolent agency called Shazam Incorporated, and eked out his living by serving as host of a Marvel Family television show.

On at least one occasion, however, Uncle Dudley truly saved the day. In the very first adventure chronicled in the first issue of *Marvel Family Comics,* issued in 1945, the world was being ravaged by a terrible and mysterious being who looked like a member of the Marvel Family, and who exhibited all their marvelous powers, but whose self-assigned mission was universal conquest or destruction.

Summoning the shade of the wizard, the Marvels were told this story: 5000 years ago in Egypt, Shazam had sought to create a hero who would combine human virtue and superhuman power for the good of mankind. Selecting an Egyptian named Teth-Adam, Shazam had put him through the initiation ceremony by now so familiar to Marvel buffs. The product of the thunder and lightning in ancient Egypt was then dubbed Mighty Adam and commanded to struggle for the right.

Abandoning the role of Teth-Adam, the superhuman Mighty Adam turned his powers to personal benefit instead of charity, and seized the throne of empire. Enraged, the wizard Shazam confronted him, re-dubbed him Black Adam, and banished him to the most distant star in the universe.

Black Adam had spent the centuries speeding back from his interstellar exile, had finally reached the earth, and had resumed his march of tyranny. And now, in the chamber of the wizard, he stood in confrontation with the modern Marvels. Black Adam presented an imposing figure: tall, wiry, muscular, with an evil leer on his thin face. His costume was a proto-Marvel suit, the background color black, the trim in the customary pattern of golden lightning bolt, sash, cuff decorations, and boots. (For some reason Black Adam dispensed with the usual Marvel cape.)

At once a mighty struggle commenced, but despite their numerical superiority the Marvels were unable to overcome Black Adam—for, Atlas, and so on. In steps Uncle Marvel, seemingly attempting to achieve rapprochement with the ancient supervillain: "He's so strong," Dudley told his friends, the Marvels, "let's make him a member of the Marvel Family! After all, he got his powers from old Mazham. I mean . . . Hamshaz. No, I mean Shamhaz . . . er, uh . . ."

"You sputtering old fool," Black Adam interrupted, "You mean *Shazam!*" Thunder! Lightning! In place of the muscular Black Adam stood Teth-Adam, an incredible 5000 years of age.

Before the Egyptian could undo the change by again shouting the word he was silenced by a single blow. Then, the weight of his 50 centuries descending in a moment, he collapsed—into a small heap of dust.

Did I say that was the end of the roll? I lied. There was a Freckles Marvel—a young girl who tried Dudley Batson's trick and appointed herself Mary's chum. And Baby Marvel, a foundling adopted by the Marvel Family and decked out in red-and-gold diapers. But within a single adventure Baby was reclaimed by his mother and left the series.

And there was Levram—that's Marvel spelled backwards. Product of a mad scientist's scheming, he was a sort of reverse-polarity evil reflection of the Captain. And Ibac. Ibac was originally Stinky Printwhistle, a small-time crook who received from Lucifer himself a set of Shazam-like powers.

The letters in Ibac stood for Ivan (the terrible), Borgia (the poisoner), Attila (the Hun), and Caligula (the emperor). Stinky/Ibac changed in a flash of green fire, and even as Ibac he was not too impressive, generally looking like a pro wrestler whose costume comprised only a pair of black leotard bottoms.

Several of Captain Marvel's greatest challenges were spun out for the readers of Fawcett comics in serial form. One very early serial took its theme from the then current World War II—as did many Marvel stories. The war and the war effort were brought up repeatedly, perhaps running second only to the endless recidivisms of the Sivana family, and Hitler, Mussolini, and Hirohito appeared personally, and derogatorily, in many of the comics, as did also such surrogate villains as Captain Nazi, Corporal Hitler Jr. and Nippo.

I mentioned Spy Smasher earlier. Let me say just a bit more about him. He was a non-powered costume hero, sporting a modified version of an aviator's suit, helmet, goggles and cape. He zoomed around the world in the gyro-sub, a unique combination of airplane and submarine, protecting America's interests and fighting her enemies at home and abroad.

For a number of issues of *Whiz Comics* in the early forties the Spy Smasher and Captain Marvel features were combined, and the double-length stories were used to follow the furious struggle between the two. Axis scientists had developed a brain-warping machine and captured Spy Smasher. Using the fiendish device, they had twisted his mental processes so that he became sympathetic to their cause and the mortal enemy of Captain Marvel.

For months he fought the world's mightiest mortal to a standstill, generally using his brainpower to overcome Captain Marvel's obvious physical advantage, and several times he nearly annihilated the big red cheese whom he caught in his vulnerable identity as Billy. (Ah, that vulnerable alter ego of the superbeing—what a blessing to script writers it was!)

In the end, of course, Captain Marvel succeeded in subduing Spy Smasher, capturing the brain-warping apparatus, and restoring Spy Smasher to his usual attitudes.

Unquestionably the greatest comic book serial of all time was "Captain Marvel and the Monster Society of Evil," a cooperative product of the efforts of Lieberson, Crowley, Binder, and Beck. This started in the February 1943 issue of *Captain Marvel Adventures* and ran for 26 consecutive installments, ending in the May 1945 edition.

The Monster Society of Evil was a conglomeration of villainous characters, some lifted from Marvel stock and others concocted especially for the occasion. They included Captain Nazi, Nippo, Ibac, the Japanese scientist Dr. Smashi, Herkimer the crocodile man, a giant orange octopus, and assorted others.

Behind them all, operating from the dark and mysterious Planetoid Punkus, lurked the enigmatic Mr. Mind, shadowy master of the Monster Society of Evil. Chapter after chapter passed with Billy Batson about to freeze to death at the North Pole, or be cooked by cannibals (while bound and gagged, of course), or forced to watch helplessly as an interplanetary Big Bertha is fired that will—well, let's catch the flavor of the message that appears at the end of the chapter:

> But how can even the *world's mightiest mortal* stop a shell a thousand times his size?? One shell already heads for *Russia,* to blast that land to shreds! Another is aimed for *America!* Will Captain Marvel save the two great allies—*Russia and America*—from utter destruction???
> See chapter 12, "*Gsv Ylnyziwnvmg Lu Vzigs!*" Next Month!
> (Use your code-finder to work this out.)

Eventually Mr. Mind was revealed to be—not some fearsome and gigantic foe of humanity, but—a tiny green worm! A typical bit of Binder-Beck Marvelizing. And after the tide had turned in the serial, a series of reverse cliff-hangers were used, in which Mr. Mind was about to be crushed under a careless heel . . . or devoured along with a juicy steak by Herman Goering . . . or otherwise eliminated.

At last, though, Mr. Mind is captured in the station WHIZ building, brought to trial for 186,744 murders, prosecuted personally by Captain Marvel, convicted, and executed. Strange that in that day of slaughter of millions, the imagination could conceive of an archfiend murdering fewer than 200,000 victims. Truth is not only stranger than fiction. It is infinitely more horrifying.

Another serial opponent of Captain Marvel was Oggar, the world's mightiest immortal. This character, got up in a Roman toga, spent his time promoting the Cult of the Curse, a movement designed to make him the object of universal adoration.

His origin was that of an ancient Olympian. The original version of Shazam's name was Shazamo, but when Oggar proved too nasty to take, the wizard had dropped him from the acronym. Oggar had been banished from Olympus, and now he was back to work fresh mischief.

This kind of rewriting of "history" in the comics leaves me with a sense of disquiet. Each time the Superman origin story is republished with new twists and flips to convenience modern revisionists, I yearn for the purity of the original version . . . and every time the Captain Marvel origin sequence was embellished it left me equally annoyed.

Besides, wasn't Shazam in Egypt 5,000 years ago, busy with Teth-Adam?

The serial did have one nice twist, though. Captain Marvel knew that Oggar had *one* fatal weakness but he didn't know what it was, so he kept a little notebook and kept checking off possibilities. And Oggar could perform endlessly varied feats of magic, but each one only once. So *he* kept a notebook.

Time after time, there would stand the two opponents, each flipping pages frantically, searching for a device he hadn't already tried on the other. Simultaneously they would cry: "Ah! I have it!" and go to work on each other.

"Magic force! Take Marvel and—*owwwwww!*"

"Here's what I want to try—biting his finger! That didn't do it! Now I'll try yanking out some of his hair!"

"*Owwwww*"

"Still no good! I'll try twisting his nose!"

"*Owwwww!*"

"Nothing worked! And the rest of the pages are blank! I need more items on my list!"

"You had your fun! Now it's my turn! Magic force—create an unbreakable plastic ball around Marvel!"

Ping!

"Holy Moley! Holy Moley! I can't break out!"

"Of course not, stupid! That's a magic *unbreakable* ball! You won't break out in a million years! Haaaa!"

There was one other major series within the Captain Marvel saga: the adventures of Tawky Tawny, the talking tiger. In this age of the Esso tiger, tiger-paw tires, tiger grooming aids for tigers—or men— Mr. Tawny might fit very well. He was intelligent, articulate, well (if somewhat flashily) dressed, and provided an amusing element in the latter days of the Marvel feature.

But somehow, I never warmed to Mr. Tawny. It may sound strange, but I think it was because he seemed unrealistic. I mean, the whole Marvel sequence was about this little boy who could summon magic lightning to transform him into an invulnerable flying man. *That* I could believe. But a talking tiger? It just didn't fit.

At the very end, with the comics industry faltering and their own reliance on superheroes paying fewer and smaller dividends, the Fawcetts tried various devices to perk up interest. One was the introduction of horror elements: King Kull, and the Red Crusher (a Korean war villain). They even had Mary Marvel leave behind her little-girl looks for a rather nubile appearance. One might, through the power of hindsight, criticize the Fawcett management for not holding on longer—superheroes *did* make a major comeback some years later. But in 1953 it looked like the end of the line, so they entered into that wretched consent agreement, and went out of the hero business.

But Captain Marvel refuses to rest easily. Ever since the demise of the Marvel Family, those Shazam wraiths have reappeared and reappeared, in one form or another. There is a whole generation of men and women who remember the big red cheese and the world's maddest scientist and the rest of the Marvel crew.

There were those fortunate enough to see the Republic movie serial of Captain Marvel, with the magnificent Tom Tyler in the title role and Nigel DeBrulier as the wizard. And—remember "The Return of the Scorpion?" I promised I'd explain that reference. The Scorpion was the masked mystery villain of that film serial, and that's where he returned *from* in the Fawcett Dime Action Book.

When Batman came to television in the person of Adam West and became (briefly) a national craze a few years ago, there was a period of several weeks when you could walk into a theater in Times Square and see the entire Captain Marvel serial—12 chapters in sparkling black and white—in one afternoon or evening.

I could say quite a lot about that serial—about Frank Coghlan Jr's delightful portrayal of a slightly older and much stupider Billy, about the supporting portrayals by Reed Hadley, John Davidson, William Benedict and others. Benedict had only a small role as Billy's pal Whitey, but he was so striking that the character was adopted into the drawn version of the feature and ran until Whitey was drafted into the army.

And the serial just won't stay dead. Just recently I went to the Carnegie Hall Cinema to see *You Are What You Eat* with Tiny Tim, Frank Zappa, Malcolm Boyd, and an all-psychedelic cast. And playing with that film, a curtain-raiser perhaps, was Chapter 1 of the old

Captain Marvel serial. Camp? Of course—no one in the audience took it seriously with its corny lines and hammy acting. But they loved it anyway. Groans, hisses, cheers . . . a delight.

And some of us still have our ancient Captain Marvel paraphernalia: comix cards or stationery or statuettes, or our official Captain Marvel Club membership documents. It cost a dime to join and, in addition to other benefits, members received a personal letter from Captain Marvel himself. And . . . look, you remember that cryptic message in the Monster Society serial? *Gsv Ylnyziwnvmg* and so on? If you were a member of the Captain Marvel Club you could *decode* that message.

I wonder if the wizard Shazam will banish me to the farthest star in the universe if I reveal the Captain Marvel Club code. What the heck, I'll risk Olympian-Egyptian disfavor. Just reverse the alphabet: for *a* read *z,* for *b* read *y* and so on. Now that I've shown you how it's done, you can decode that clue yourself. But you'll have to do it yourself; I won't decode it for you.

There were so *many* enjoyable things about the old Captain Marvel stories, and the other features associated with them, that I'm sure that sometime well into the next century there will still be old codgers around who, reminiscing about their childhood scores of years before, will find random recollections unleashing whole floods of bittersweet nostalgia . . .

A particular series, such as the stories featuring Mr. Atom, a gigantic robot who embodied the awesome power of atomic energy. The first story in the series was a beauty. Credit Bill Woolfolk for that, and forget about *The Beautiful Couple.*

Or *Captain Marvel Battles the Giant Earth Dreamer.* A nutty professor tells Billy Batson that he has discovered the universe is nothing but the figment of a dreaming giant's subconscious—*and the giant is about to wake up!* Take it from there.

Or even a single, beautiful, C. C. Beck panel: Billy Batson visiting a crazy surrealistic world in which things work by a different "logic" than they do in our world. Billy looks into a mirror to comb his hair and sees the back of his own head. Or: Sivana captures Billy and tosses him, bound and gagged (natch!) to a giant carnivorous plant.

Or the fantastic leering menacing *funny* face of Mr. Mind. I was always sorry that he was executed at the end of that serial. Couldn't he have reformed and gone on to . . . .

Did you know that Holy Moley and Shazam are struggling to live on as part of the American language? Not three miles from my home is the Sha-Zam boutique! TV's Gomer Pyle often exclaims *Shazam!* And Captain Marvel turns up in the Beatles' song, "Bungalow Bill."

In 1966 a fly-by-night publisher brought out a new Captain Marvel comic book. Credit lines went to Carl Burgos, the man behind the original Human Torch, and to Roger Elwood, a journeyman literary agent and anthologist. It looked hopeful but it was dreadful. The basic conception was unappealing—Captain Marvel's magic word was *Split,* and upon saying it, he would fly to pieces and zoom off in all directions, here a hand to accomplish one task, there a leg to do another. . . . The writing was bad, the artwork worse, and the feature quickly disappeared again.

In 1967 there was a delightful development that unfortunately did not last long either. An independent publisher set up a new comic book line and hired Will Lieberson to edit, Otto Binder to write, and C. C. Beck to draw! They worked out two features together.

One was Fatman:

> A sensational new fighting hero of *pachyderm* proportions, whose adventures are *overweighted* with thrills as he strikes like a *ton* of bricks. Crooks have *slim* chances as he *tips the scales* against crime at every turn!
>
> But that's not all! Fatman's exploits reach *soaring* heights in *high-speed* action full of *horsepower* punch with *the sky the limit!*
>
> He's Boris Van Bradford, gentle fancier of rare tropical exotics.
>
> He's a Fatman—dreaded nemesis of evil-doers everywhere!
>
> He's a human flying saucer, with powers from other worlds!

And his costume, except for the substitution of a stylized flying saucer for the familiar lightning bolt, was a perfect replica of the old Marvel Family standard—this time in a primary shade of green! There were three fat issues of *Fatman*. A decade and a half of writing science non-fiction and spacing it out with straight-faced comic scripts for Superman, Doctor Solar, and Mighty Samson had not dulled the charm and wit of Binder's writing.

Those same years spent editing *Monsieur* and other esoteric periodicals had not dulled Lieberson's editorial skill.

And Beck's years in commercial art must only have honed his talents, for the drawing in *Fatman* glowed with all the charm and wit and general *joie de vivre* of Beck's mid-forties best.

The other Lieberson-Binder-Beck project was to be called *Captain Shazam,* and that name alone should push your thrill button by now, or you're reading the wrong chapter of this book.

But distribution of the new comics was spotty, financing was not reliable, and just at the worst possible moment the neo-super-hero boom in the industry experienced a moderate depression.

The whole new series disappeared before Captain Shazam had seen a single issue.

It was to weep.

Still, only a few months later yet *another* Captain Marvel appeared, this time from the Timely Comics group that had laid a claim to the word *Marvel* from the first publication of *Marvel Comics* featuring Human Torch and Sub-Mariner back in 1939! Their new Captain Marvel, originally written by editor Stan Lee and drawn by Gene Colan, is an alien spaceman marooned on earth. His real name is Captain Mar-Vell, and while the stories are really rather good, I frankly find it painful to see the blaspheming of the old beloved name.

I suppose that consent agreement between Fawcett and National will keep the *real* Marvel Family in the deep freeze forever. But a whole generation who grew up with those marvelous adventures will never, never forget Billy Batson, Shazam, Freddy and Mary, Sterling Morris, radio station WHIZ, the mad leering Sivanas, or . . .

. . . the Big Red Cheese!

INTRODUCTION TO

THE FIRST (ARF, ARF) SUPERHERO OF THEM ALL

Superman's editors like to point him out as the first of his kind, a justifiable boast. He was the first superhero with a secret identity (not just in comic books, but in all literature), and he started a trend that is still going strong. However, he was neither the first superhero nor the first hero with a secret identity.

Bill Blackbeard (yes, that is his real name) is a San Franciscan with a scholarly approach to the most sadly-neglected branch of American popular art, the comic strip. A freelance writer and editor (his first story appeared in the November, 1943, *Weird Tales*), Bill is the organizer of the nation's first nonprofit enterprise devoted to the preservation, collection, and sequential filing for research and study of newspaper comic art: an undertaking which should have been done regularly over the past 70 years by the libraries and universities but has not. He is now writing a critical history of the comic strip which will sharply separate the (few) sheep from the (many) goats in this once-great but now dying and misused field. The book will include "detailed, page-by-page corrections of the erroneous data and misinformed opinions which have packed most previous and extant volumes, articles, and encyclopedia entries on the comics."

The article which follows came out of Bill's years of painstaking research. For publication in this volume, the article has been abridged; a much fuller version is planned for his book on the age of *Krazy Kat, Boob McNutt, Polly and Her Pals*—and *Thimble Theatre.*

CHAPTER 4

THE FIRST (ARF, ARF) SUPERHERO OF THEM ALL

by BILL BLACKBEARD

★★

It is a sign of the essentially mythic quality of the comic book superheroes that one can rarely imagine their reaction to stimuli not a normal part of their highly stylized world of melodrama. How, for example, can one speculate on the likely response of Superman, Batman, or Hawkman at a freewheeling press conference to so simple a query as: "How does it feel, being a superhero?"

The question is deflating; it automatically makes the hero an oddball. If he says, "I like it fine," he seems a dull goof. If he says he *doesn't* like it or tries to grin and modestly deny the applicability of the term to himself, one wonders why the hell he's wearing that garish union suit and cloak.

Yet one of these three feeble, stereotyped, self-indicting responses, stated with careful dignity and pride, is all we can legitimately imagine from a serious comic superhero—and it is a purely random guess as to who would give each answer.

The only kind of response that would be liberating, human, and reasonable is one that would at once reflect the silliness of the question and the absurdity of the superhero label and function, a reply that is highly unlikely to come from any serious superhero's chiseled lips: "*Superhero?* Wha's a superhero? Does ya get it at the supermarket? Arf, arf!"

To a reader who takes the superheroes with dead seriousness, this is the response of an idiot. To most others, it is probably surprising and amusing. But, most important, it is the imaginable reply of an *individual* human being, functioning in a human world: it is, in fact, a refreshing, barbaric yawp out of the comic pages of 30 years ago.

For the crudely humorous arfer, quoted above in words he—and only he—might have uttered, is the first genuine, unshootable, unpoisonable, door-smashing, house-lifting comic strip superham of them all—Elzie Chrisler Segar's Popeye.

Segar's Popeye is a character compounded of vulgarity and compassion, raw aggression, and protective gentleness, violent waterfront humor and genuine "senskibiliky," thickheaded stubbornness and imaginative leadership, brutal emnity and warm friendship, who can knock out a "horsk" in rage and nurse a baby carefully while it is suffering a fever that makes thermometers pop. He is no paranoid daydream, but a realistic, complex, often wrong but determined man of action who suffers continual agonies of decision, who pursues what he believes to be right far beyond the bounds of cop-interpreted law and order, who has to fight his very way to comprehensibility through the warp and woof of an English language that is often almost too much for him.

Knobby-kneed, swollen-armed, with a face like a shipwreck (as his "sweet-patootie," Olive Oyl, once called it), Popeye, even clad in spangled ballet tights and a stage villain's cloak, would last about as long as Sheldon Mayer's great, fat, clumsy Red Tornado of decades ago. Superhero fans seem to want their idols formed from the same stalwart mold. The gnarly mold that shaped Popeye was properly shattered after his creation, sometime late in 1928 on a sunsplashed drawing board in Santa Monica, California, about a year after Philip Wylie wrote—but had not yet published—the first superman novel, *Gladiator*. (When Wylie's seminal work appeared, in March 1930, Popeye had already been on the comic page for 14 months, and many newspaper readers were well prepared for Wylie's prose account of a superhuman being.)

It was on Thursday, January 17, 1929, that a lumpy and unprepossessing Popeye (seemingly years older than the personable character Segar later perfected) first appeared, but it was not until June 10 of that year that the world realized it was watching the adventures of a man literally incapable of being killed—and Popeye, it turned out, was as surprised as anyone else.

The one-eyed sailor's super-heroics, whether involving his invulnerability to death or his superstrength, were surprisingly few and far between. His superhuman powers became an established part of his character, but were not emphasized.

Of far greater interest to Segar and most of his readers was Popeye's scrappiness and cheerful contempt for most social conventions, including "correck" speech.

Here's the cause of it all. If King Blozo of Nazilia hadn't lost his country's gold reserve, which he was using for a filling in his lower left wisdom tooth, POPEYE might be safe on shore instead of very much at sea, mentally and physically, on a mystery ship! To find the treasure that will put Nazilia back on the gold standard, POPEYE is risking life, limb and sanity. Watch for this funniest of all POPEYE adventures in E. C. Segar's comic strip, THIMBLE THEATRE, begnning June 12. It will be in the Oregon Statesman, of course!

It seems ironically amusing that such a major comic personality, widely enjoyed in his own right, should have been the disinterested and comparatively unobtrusive agency through which the later obsessive concept of superhuman strength was introduced to the comic strips—and to the world of popular art as a whole.

Yet the popularity of Popeye with the public during the heyday of Segar's strip far surpassed anything Superman or any other comic book or strip superhero ever knew. Far more people flocked to movie palaces in the thirties to see the Max Fleischer *Popeye* cartoons (*just* to see them, in many cases, when the semi-feature-length *Popeye* specials were released) than ever went to watch the *Superman* or *Batman* serials.

The same *Popeye* cartoons were for a long time the single most popular children's TV series—until their appeal was ruined by the addition of TV-produced originals which lacked the imagination and fantasy of the earlier Fleischer work. The Segar strip had the widest newspaper subscription of any comic in history until Schulz's *Peanuts* of today; the comic strips of *Superman* and *Batman* (both early and later versions) were small potatoes by comparison.

Popeye's super-"abilikies" (which we will go into later) were, indeed, used so casually (in contrast to the spotlighted bombast of the muscle-bound superheroes) that thousands of fans, literally experts in the limited area of superhero comic art, have ignored or forgotten his pioneering role and have assigned it instead to the egregious Superman of Jerry Siegel and Joe Shuster.

This is, perhaps, just as well, for on a gut-instinctive level, the kids were right about the origin of their passion. The very name of the 1938 comic book character (who, after all *was* the first cloaked and tights-outfitted superhero), the ringing, exciting *Superman,* was in itself the first blunt, undisguised appeal to juvenile fantasy-wishes to get a contrary world firmly in hand and *take charge*.

Old "Blow-Me-Down" Popeye, as he was billed in Castor Oyl's posters promoting his early "s'prise-fights," was reluctant to take charge of anything at all and only did so when goaded by slowly mounting fury, when pushed into accepting authority by the total inability of anyone else in sight to handle things, when impelled by some impractical, Galahadian ideal (such as "pilgrimatin'" a new country), or when Olive Oyl (or some other character) was endangered.

Popeye certainly didn't hover around rooftops looking for nefarious activities to spring down on and *smash*. On the contrary, he preferred to live "simpkly," in an undistinguished house, on the proceeds of his boxing or some recent treasure-hunting expedition.

He stayed with his fantastic array of cronies—Toar, Alice the Goon, Poopdeck Pappy, Eugene the Jeep, and his "adoptik" kid, Swee'Pea, until some "irrikating" problem jabbed at him long enough to provoke him to action.

Before we describe a typical Popeye adventure, let's take a detailed look at the remarkable dramatis personae of the *Popeye* strip. No cartoonist ever populated a comic strip with quite so many striking and memorable personalities (the names of two, Goon and Jeep, became so familiar through popular usage that they have been included in the pages of Webster's and other dictionaries) or so sharply rivalled the great comic novelists in the various subtle ways they were integrated into the picaresque flow of his comic narrative.

The fact is that the young Segar—he was 34 when he conceived Popeye—was fascinated with the absurdities and perversities of human behavior, and no other cartoonist ever portrayed the knobbier variations in temperament and motivation so graphically and unforgettably. Segar liked people, particularly people despised by the public at large. He tended to champion their forlorn stand against the world, without losing sight of the antisocial biases and torments that made them what they were. The depth and seriousness of his understanding are always evident beneath the grand comic sporting on the surface, as in the work of the greatest comic artists.

Popeye, of course, was Segar's most original, most individual personage, but if Popeye had not made Segar's critical fortune, the rotund, mooching J. Wellington Wimpy of the open hand and empty stomach would certainly have done so. And long before Popeye and Wimpy entered the comic strip, Segar's earlier cast of characters was already making a reputation for the cartoonist: Castor Oyl, the irrepressible, pint-sized bum who never took failure as final, blandly cheating and swindling his way to disaster and swaggering eagerly back for more; Olive Oyl, his sister, gawky and bony, but as certain of her charms as a courted ostrich, who—long before the start of her rocky, tatterdemalion affair with Popeye—was sure that Castor's shady activities represented the fullness of life's possibilities and doggedly undertook to aid or follow him despite his disgusted rebuffs; and Ham Gravy, a lean, banana-nosed fall guy, who adored Olive for reasons best known to himself (unless, as was often the case, there was a more attractive girl around) and wasted his time palling around with Castor until the entrance of Popeye ultimately edged him offstage and into one of the dustier corners of Segar's imagination.

Theatre

Olive—of course—and Castor Oyl continued to appear in the strip after Popeye's appearance. Other recurring characters who lent so much to the comic fantasy and rich humanity of the strip were the long-whiskered King Blozo, the melancholy-mad monarch of Nazilia, whose one pleasure in a miserable life was reading American comic strips; the terrible-toothed Oscar, a one-time subject of Blozo's, as aggressively goofy as Jerry Lewis, but rather more amusing because Segar realized that very little of such antics goes a long way and kept Oscar's onstage pratfalls to a minimum; the cadaverous, ghoulish Sea Hag, whose skeleton ship haunted the dark seas of the earth and whose periodic reappearance in Segar's strip provoked letters from outraged parents who said their children were having nightmares as a result; Alice the Goon, the Sea Hag's shadow-skulking subhuman warrior woman, whose broad chest, bulging forearms, furred middle, and grieving, cavern-eyed, rhesus-nosed face gave *adults* nightmares; Toar, the million-year-old caveman, who once drank from "Pool of Never-Die," and whose gargantuan hulk was in the service of the Sea Hag's sister until he, like Alice, abandoned the sea witches to join Popeye's bunch; Eugene the Jeep, the spotted, pot-bellied, two-foot-high creature who could move in and out of the fourth dimension at will and foretell the future with invariable accuracy as he munched his favorite delicacy, five-dollar orchids.

Others included George W. Geezil, the tangle-bearded paranoid, who felt persecuted by the mere proximity of "flies-in-mine-zupe" Wimpy and schemed to murder the cloying moocher by any reasonable means at hand; Roughhouse, the grizzle-lipped waterfront restaurateur, plagued by miserable business and the importunities of Wimpy until he was likely to seize a meat cleaver and clamber over the counter in red-eyed pursuit of the panhandler; Poopdeck Pappy, Popeye's long-lost father, who was the plug-spitting image of his son except for his unshaven chin, black-collared shirt, and tattoo-free arms, but whose nocturnal behavior (when buoyed by cash) could begin with mere antisocialities like pushing ugly women into the river and then galloping (in the tilt of a glass of "fizzly water") to demoniac misuse and destruction of anything or anyone in sight; and Swee'Pea, the bald, mute, nightshirted and intensely personable "infink kid" adopted by Popeye, who would cheerfully break his nursing bottle over the head of anyone mordantly inclined to kitchy-koos.

There was a host of others less spotlighted but quite as sharply realized, who reappeared from time to time over the years. Among them were Olive's long-suffering parents, Cole and Nana Oyl; Mr. Kilph, the maddened and frustrated boxing promoter, obsessed with the idea of somehow getting Popeye demolished in the ring, whose increasingly desperate attempts included backing a gorilla and a robot against Popeye; and Pooky Jones, Poopdeck's short, bewhiskered sea buddy, who helped haunt a ship for the hell of it and aided Poopdeck in his salty affairs with mermaids.

Finally, there were the innumerable bizarre figures who appeared only once in the strip but were often unforgettable, such as the Sea Hag's equally shrewish sister who shared one longing with the Sea Hag—the chance to hear her sister's deathrattle; "Salty" Bill Barnacle, an old, pre-1929 sidekick of Popeye, whose appearance in Roughhouse's one day in 1933 triggered the great ten-month Sunday page adventure of "Plunder Island" (which was, in this author's opinion, the greatest comic strip narrative of all time); Bluto, a mammoth, blood-thirsty rogue who appeared in a 1932 adventure called "The Eighth Sea" (Segar usually gave his story episodes specific names), who became Popeye's permanent opponent in the Paramount movie cartoons, largely because he was the heavy in the comic strip at the time the new film series was shaping up in Hollywood; and many, many others, including a host of unnamed Segar standbys, such as his frantic, pill-prescribing doctors; his brutal and/or stupid cops; his armies of sensibly frightened, peace-loving soldiers; his wily but decent small-town sheriffs; his bemused judges; war-crazed generals; egomaniacal "diktapaters;" money-mad industrialists; and melancholy cartoonists, that would take pages simply to list.

As Coulton Waugh summed it up in *The Comics,* Segar had "comic genius." After considering the gripping, thrilling, unflaggingly funny continuity Segar maintained through more than 750 Sunday pages from 1924 to 1938, and more than 5,800 daily strips from 1920 to 1938, for a rough total of 47,000 panels, it does seem to be just as simple—and just as remarkable—as that.

At an initial glance, there appeared to be very little that was prepossessing or impressive in Segar's style. Mostly, it seemed to be comprised of squiggles and blobs, some of which wore hats and some of which wore smokestacks, with the latter usually subordinate to the former. His characters had dots for eyes, flat ovals (in most cases) for faces, simple peg noses, one-line mouths, and curlicue ears, while their hair was a loop or a half dozen sketchy lines. The backgrounds looked, at first, like something turned out desperately as list-minute pulp art.

Deserted, probably haunted, hiding its alluring hoard of secret gold, the Sunken City of "The Eighth Sea" has frustrated the efforts of thousands of treasure hunters to penetrate its mysteries! Here you see POPEYE, King Blozo and Olive Oyl standing on the brink of another episode of their great new laugh adventure, which will be portrayed with lots of humor, more action, and a minimum of tragedy by E. C. Segar in THIMBLE THEATRE, STARRING POP-EYE. Follow this great comic strip every day in The Oregon States-man for laughs, thrills, mystery and suspense.

But—none of that matters. All you have to do to fall under the spell of the strip is to start reading the old daily or Sunday pages, anywhere between 1920 and 1938, and—very suddenly, very soon—the scrawly characters become invested with delightful life and personality, the backgrounds swell with mystery and terror or dance with sunlit humor, and you are hopelessly caught up in whatever story is under way (or under weigh, in this nautical strip).

If this is not comic genius at work, then there is none in Dickens, Twain, Waugh, Herriman, Chaplin, or W. C. Fields. We have only to acknowledge and enjoy it—as in the daily sequence which ran from December 14, 1936, to April 3, 1937. The story was called "Mystery Melody" and opened on a typically poetic and shuddery note:

It was night at Popeye's house. Olive was visiting, and she and Popeye stood looking across the room at a dejected Poopdeck Pappy. "Acks kind of queer, don't ya think, Olive?" Popeye asked. "Look at him—listenin'—always listenin'." Then Segar threw the title panel at us: a blackly shadowed hillside on which stood a lean, dark silhouette with a gigantic, spread-winged vulture behind it; beyond the hill, a black three-master, afloat on a moonlit sea. "MYSTERY MELODY," read the title, "A Mystery as Deep as the Sea . . ."

"There! There!" Poopdeck cried in a frenzy a night later. "Do ye hear it?" Popeye and Olive looked at each other, unable to hear a sound. "Ssssh—" Poopdeck said, in one of those dramatic series of small dialogue balloons which added so much to the pace of Segar's work, "Ssssh—hear it? Listen. There it is now. Ssh—It's floatin' in off'n the sea!"

The next night, Poopdeck had calmed a little and was seated in front of Popeye. Obviously, he felt it time to explain. "Son," he said, "I wants to tell ye before it's too late that onc't upon a time many years ago I was a kind-hearted swab. I don't mean I was soft—I had me share of fights like all sailormen. But I was hooman then—aye, up to the time I was thirty-seven. I be ninety-nine now."

Poopdeck, it seemed, had proposed marriage to a beautiful girl, then fled when she appeared in her true guise as the Sea Hag, a scrawny, ugly, black-hooded creature of only token femaleness. The Hag had come for him again and not even Toar could fight her—the Hag's vulture (possibly her sister transformed to a bird) lifted his 900-pound carcass and dropped him through Popeye's roof. Pappy was captured by the Hag and put in her castle dungeon. Popeye enlisted Wimpy's aid, but the Hag took Wimpy to her boat for a romantic interlude (Wimpy had once made love to her in exchange for a barrel of hamburgers).

Wimpy was not completely treasonous, however, and used the witch's magic flute to pipe food supplies to the captive Poopdeck. He also piped himself an immense quantity of hamburgers and, at one point, an entire cow.

Popeye located his kidnapped Pappy with the aid of the Jeep, which then unveiled another power, that of mummifying and de-magicking witches. He left the witch stiff as a post, but not dead. She sailed away at the end of the episode.

From his yard overlooking the harbor, Popeye pointed to the sky just above the sea. "Look, Olive," he said, "there goes the bird, hea-din' out to sea—out toward that ship. Hah—it's *her* ship, an' she's puttin' on canvas. The ol' Hag'll sail to another one of her magic castles far away, an' I yam glad she ain't dead."

Popeye's closing "sediments" represented those of most followers of the strip. Segar's superbly malevolent Sea Hag, however, was not seen again after "Mystery Melody," though she had been involved in four previous adventures; her almost certainly scheduled return was forever canceled by Segar's death little more than a year later.

Despite Segar's death, a ragtag, chuckle-headed lot of characters named "Sea Hag," "Popeye," "Wimpy," "Olive Oyl," etc., can still be seen doggedly hanging around the comic books, funny pages, and TV screens almost a third of a century later. Since 1938 these crea-tures have, of course, been the products of other hands and they present a considerable problem in writing about Segar's characters and strip today, for the images in the writer's mind are not likely to be those familiar to most readers under forty.

Segar was ill for a long period in 1937; the strips he was unable to draw then were ghosted by King Features' continuity trouble-shooter, Doc Winner. Recovering for a time, Segar drew several more months of daily and Sunday work on his own—dailies through August 1938, and Sundays through October 9, 1938. After Segar's death, the daily strip was ghosted for a week by Joe Musial, then tak-en over again by Winner for the remainder of 1938.

In 1939, both the daily and Sunday strips were drawn by Bela Zaboly, with Tom Sims on the story. This team worked on the Pop-eye strip through the war years and the late forties, until they were replaced by Ralph Stein for a short period. Then the strip was given over to Bud Sagendorf, who turns it out today.

The failure of Segar's successors to maintain the strip on its pre-vious level of adult appeal, coupled with the contrasting box office success of the Popeye movie cartoons in the forties and their subsequent smash impact on TV, apparently led the King Features executives who controlled the Popeye strip to demand that it be slanted at the same enormous juvenile audience which responded so heartily to the movie cartoons. Sagendorf's potential ability to create and maintain a mature, imaginative strip is not therefore in question; it may simply be that he has no need to engage the interest of grownups in his dutiful concentration on entertaining the kiddies.

Whatever the cause of the extreme simplification and demeaning Segar's strip has received over the past 30 years in comic books, newspaper strips, and movie-TV cartoons, it is obvious that readers under 40 have no choice but to turn to the actual Segar strip if they wish to see *why* it was the most popular strip of its time and (with *Krazy Kat* and the Milton Caniff *Terry and the Pirates*) very possibly one of the three greatest achievements in the art of the comic strip. No prose approximation can do the job; like a stage play or a motion picture, a comic strip must be followed in images as well as words to be properly comprehended, and only the original images, in complete sequence as initially published, will serve.

Here, unfortunately, a particularly absurd situation exists. Unlike virtually any book of popular or academic interest, the run of a comic strip cannot simply be plucked off a library shelf or ordered at a book store; nor, like most widely appreciated pieces of graphic art, can it be looked at in a gallery or found reasonably well reproduced in a number of accessible forms. This seems decidedly unfair.

There are a sizable number of American cartoonists possessed of humorous and narrative gifts that markedly surpass those of some authors still given academic attention, and their equal availability in hard covers should be assured. *The Complete Frank Willard* (20 volumes of *Moon Mullins*) is as logically deserving of library space as the works of John Steinbeck. But since—of course—*all* comic strips have long been condemned out of hand by educators and academics as trash, individual work in the field has never had the critical attention and study individual works of prose fiction have received without question. As a result, if the appetite of an intelligent reader is whetted by a description of a long-lost comic strip, there is virtually no convenient and routine means by which he can sate it.

It can be done—though with difficulty—and done, moreover, outside of private, cherished collections or dealers' showrooms with a high bank-balance admission charge. It can be done by bypassing the derivative books and magazines and going directly to the original place of the strip's publication: the newspapers.

The central library in every sizeable American city maintains a file of back copies of the local papers and often some major out-of-town journals. These vary, depending on the finances available to the library in past decades, from sad, tied monthly bundles of folded papers, yellowed and crumbling and ready to split down the creases when unfolded, through the more usual twenty-pound, bound volumes of papers, to the recent innovation of monthly microfilm reels of entire runs of papers (with available viewing apparatus) on file in a periodical room.

All of this may sound like a bonanza to the comic strip reader and researcher, but it is not. It is very difficult to locate complete runs of *Popeye*. From 1919, when the strip began, to the mid-thirties, the strip ran almost exclusively in Hearst papers. It takes a great deal of effort to locate a city with a source and, once you do (if you do), you will eventually exceed the patience and good nature of the library clerks. You may simply want too much, too often, for their taste. How you handle this, in order not to wear out your welcome or have your purposes in reading the old papers too closely questioned (some libraries flatly forbid any "casual" reading in their newspaper files), is up to you. It may be wise, however great your enthusiasm, to space out your reading, to keep pencil and paper at hand for frequent "notes," and to dress conservatively, even beyond your years if young.

Is it worth it? I think so. I think ferreting out detailed knowledge of one of the greatest comic artists of the century through his buried and ignored work repays all the sweat and frustration involved many times over. But you do have to go through all the trouble to find out that it *is* worth it.

It means bucking all your ingrained notions, based on what you've seen of newspaper comic strips over the past 30 years, to even get started. As you dig you will discover the lost work of other gifted cartoonists as well: Herriman, Starrett, Caniff, Tuthill, Gottfredson, Willard, Johnson, De Beck, Dwiggins, Crane, Gross, Gray—but that of course, is another article—another book, in fact.

There is a mild time-travel effect in digging out the Segar strip (or others) in old newspapers. There is a dusty, archeological atmosphere stirred up as you delve through the yellowed pages that can be very exciting. And once found, the Segar panels themselves, like other great lost strips of the twenties and thirties, prove to be utterly timeless. The laughter with which you read them, the delight with which you pursue the stories and relish the characters are purely contemporary feelings—and the things you learn about the strip are frequently genuinely surprising.

Like its name. You wouldn't get very far if you started through those thousands of newspaper pages looking for a strip called *Popeye*. In fact, you'd never find it. For there is, and has always been, only *one* legitimate name for the Popeye strip, a name as little known since 1930 as Segar's is now. *Thimble Theatre* has been the sole name of the Popeye strip for a full 50 years. True, a few small-town papers actually labelled it *Popeye* when they took on the feature in the early thirties, but they were quickly called on the carpet by King Features and made to substitute the registered name, *Thimble Theatre*. It's a good name, an effective one, and the only sort of name that could adequately cover a strip so amorphous in character and direction in its formative years.

Segar had enormous self-confidence and needed it to sell his *Thimble Theatre* idea. He was born in 1894 in Camptown, Illinois (the town whose racetrack had been celebrated by Stephen Foster a half-century before). Segar was still a young cartoonist knocking around the country when he left a job with no future on the Chicago *American* to go to New York and approach Hearst's King Features Syndicate with his idea for a simply drawn little strip—on the order of Shulz's early *Peanuts*—to deal with a guy, a girl, and a stage villain running through a daily vaudeville-style takeoff on old-time melodrama. The strip was styled to run six to twelve equal-sized small panels, which could be broken up and fitted in among the other comic-page features. It was meant to furnish a quick, easy laugh for people too hurried to read the more elaborate strips with their solidly packed balloons of dialogue.

Although Segar's professional credentials consisted primarily of a stint on the multi-authored *Charlie Chaplin's Comic Capers* in the 1910s (an unfunny strip of a parasitic kind, later to become more popular in Great Britain than in the U.S.A.), Hearst liked his art—attractively uncomplicated, it could be funny as hell, and Hearst decided to take a chance on his novel idea for a strip.

Almost immediately, *Thimble Theatre* appeared on one of the most widely read comic pages in America, Hearst's New York *Evening Journal* of 1919, and never left it as long as Segar lived. (Shortly after *Thimble Theatre* began, Hearst suggested that Segar begin a second strip, to appeal to the harassed suburban commuter who often missed his packed train, to be called *The Five-Fifteen*. Segar's simplistic style looked deceptively easy, and Hearst may have decided, as he chuckled at the daily *Thimble Theatre* jape, that an artist with so easy a row to hoe could certainly be turning out at least one more strip for his money.)

Ham Gravy, his girl Olive Oyl, and the villainous, top-hatted Willy Wormwood were the comics who acted out Segar's first skits in *Thimble Theatre*. At first, these were little pseudo-melodramas, archly tongue-in-cheek, in the manner of Harry Hershfield's *Desperate Desmond* of a decade before; then they shifted, with the early departure of Willy Wormwood, to brief, blackout-style gags in which Olive or Ham jumped backward out of the last panel in dismay at what had happened or been said.

Ham played straight man to Olive but when Olive's brother Castor was introduced after a few months the real central personality and active protagonist of the strip took his bow. Castor, described by Olive as "batty" and "off in the coop," quickly showed that he had earned his kooky reputation by being nervy and individual enough to follow his impulses toward pleasure and profit into highly unusual areas of activity. It is such adventurous behavior that precipitates not only comedy but narrative as well.

The continuing day-to-day story line common to many strips today evolved slowly in *Thimble Theatre*. Anything like that was rare in the comics of the early twenties—although Ed Wheelan was attempting it in his *Minute Movies*—and cartoonists usually linked their strips by moving their characters to new locations for awhile (Mutt and Jeff showed up in Pancho Villa's Mexico in 1911; Maggie and Jiggs travelled to China in 1920) or by providing a provocative theme (as George Herriman did in his early *Family Upstairs* strip, in which an apartment house family, the Dingbats, were driven crazy every day by their always futile efforts to get at least a *peep* at the weird and unseen "family upstairs").

Segar chose the latter method, and in a short time, *Thimble Theatre* became a series of increasingly longer themes, developed in daily punchlined episodes. By 1922, Segar was drawing actual continued stories and getting away with it through a masterful pacing of daily episodes that provided both a laugh and a hooker to bring the reader back for another look the next day.

The technique of developing a theme soon became popular. And once the syndicates discovered that readers would keep buying papers simply to see what *happened* to a favorite character, regardless of whether they were handed a laugh or not, the modern adventure strip was only a short step away (a step taken by Roy Crane in his *Washington Tubbs II* strip of 1926, before most syndicates were quite ready for it).

Castor and Ham spent two years out West in the desert in one Sunday continuity adventure (March 4, 1928 to March 9, 1930— 104 Sunday pages, 1,700 panels). When it ended, Castor's wife (Cylinda Oyl) had divorced him for desertion and Popeye made his first Sunday comic appearance.

Fourteen months after Popeye first appeared on the daily *Thimble Theatre* stage, where he had become a public sensation, it was time for him to throw his Sunday punch. He did it effectively, in a knock-down, drag-out "fisk" fight with Ham Gravy over the alienated affections of Olive Oyl (who had fallen with virginal totality for the one-eyed sailor in Ham's absence).

Popeye was given no formal introduction by Segar, since the cartoonist assumed his readers were already familiar with his new hero from the daily strip. He credited them with enough imagination to understand that the two-year desert trek of Ham and Castor supposedly took place *after* their historic first meeting with Popeye in the January 17, 1929, daily strip, so that Popeye could have made out with the deserted Olive while Ham was gone.

The brief, fierce battle between Popeye and Ham on March 9, 1930—in which Olive herself was mauled unmercifully—climaxed and ended both the desert adventure *and* the long involvement of Ham in the strip. Already dropped as an obviously superfluous character in the daily strip, the lean, long-nosed vaudevillian vanished for good with this last, humiliating drubbing. It must be said in all frankness that he was not, this straightest of straight men, ever missed in the least (*certainly* not by Olive Oyl).

It may seem odd to the modern reader, familiar as he probably is with some of the adolescent conventions of the comic books, to find that Popeye, the first comic superhero, did nothing in the least "super" for months after that first Sunday page.

Popeye's first act of this kind (outside of pretty casually winning some prizefights for Castor, a reasonable thing for a tough sailor to do), was to take one wall of a jail apart on June 25, 1930. After that, he did nothing especially spectacular until January 18, 1931, when he rather violently dismembered a hot dog stand. His next super-stunt, part of a short narrative, was to kayo a gorilla in the ring on July 12 and 19, 1931. He then walloped a hole in a livingroom wall on August 2, 1931, wrecked another jail on January 24, 1932, and defeated a robot in a prizefight on April 24, 1932.

But two years of examples are enough. The pickings are meager and the pattern is clear. Even if we cite Popeye's comparative indestructibility (he cannot be killed, but *can* be battered, crippled, and knocked loopy by sufficiently sizeable or tricky opponents) and mention his more astonishing feats (such as lifting an entire house or stepping out of a stalled "airyplane" only to land on his chin after a fall of "thousings" of feet), it is evident that Segar's Popeye is only incidentally a superhero.

Any comic book superhero, after all, given a Sunday page for a similar two-year spread, would have saved sixteen universes, defeated thirty and a half supervillains, and had his mysteriously created and laundered supercostume replaced a dozen times.

Popeye—human, smelly, capable of disastrous mistakes, able to slug a woman, pursue likely looking chicks with lusty interest, swear a blue streak when "irrikated," able to be cheerfully cynical about almost everything dear to the proper, from patriotism to making money, and with a capacity to look as sloppy as he behaved—was certainly more of an *anti*-superhero than anything else. Yet it was his jaunty character and behavior that wowed the public and made them turn to *Thimble Theatre* first among the comics for a full decade.

Obviously, Popeye's underplayed invulnerability and super-strength could have been dropped (or never introduced) without the least effect on his popularity. His *toughness,* of course—his ability to take and deliver a beating—is quite another matter. The public adored and relished it. This vigorous display of Popeye's fighting competence, as a fundamental part of his character, was surely one of the prime reasons for the mass appreciation of *Thimble Theatre* in the thirties.

If Wimpy rambled into comic verse or Segar wrote of wild, inter-dimensional jungles known only to Jeeps, it may have been boring to some readers, but they still kept a close watch on the strip because of the always-imminent likelihood of yet another lengthy, panel-rocking, balloon-crushing battle between Popeye and some new, mountainous bruiser.

Segar himself obviously cherished these recurrent imbroglios, and a good part of his native genius lay in his ability to consistently render such obsessional violence in drawings that were at once ex-citing and funny. It is little wonder that he quickly came to have a deep affection for the one-eyed character who had so unexpectedly provided his drawing board with endless possibilities for pictorial mayhem—and in the process made him the most popular cartoonist on earth.

Despite the force and fury with which these gripping slugfests were drawn, the incredible fluidity of line encompassing the hur-tling, slamming bodies and fists, and the wry humor of the sideline reactions and comments by other characters, it was not the fights or brutality that made the strip particularly impressive as narrative art. It was, rather, the people of the strip, the basic creations of Segar's mirth and poetry, who made it radiant with their presence, from the leads down to the most transient bit players.

Curiously, the most fully rounded, sensitively conceived and at-tractive character of the whole raucous crowd was not Popeye but the worthless, bumming, swindling, stealing, conniving, cowardly, hamburger-obsessed J. Wellington Wimpy. No central character of any other strip was lower or meaner than Wimpy—even Pete the Tramp, Happy Hooligan, and the Yellow Kid, though shiftless and thieving, had the hearts of gold essential to most popular low char-acters of the period.

Wimpy was only interested in Wimpy—and how the main chance could benefit Wimpy. His attractiveness rested on no virtue of any kind; he was without personal charm, and only the Sea Hag loved him. Yet we smiled on his entrance, guffawed at his behavior, and cherished his every word and gesture. He was literally a treasure of a character, a figure so inherently amusing and poetic that his essen-tial ruthlessness—aimed, after all, at such innocuous ends as a square meal or a stolen kiss—was blunted and made part of his in-nocent appeal.

Not fully realized as a character until almost two and a half years after Popeye appeared in the strip, it was in Wimpy that we found the true culmination of Segar's creative genius. Wimpy was the ultimate achievement of his art, and the most sorely missed comic figure in the genre, after the equally amoral and anarchistic Ignatz Mouse and his immortal inamorata, Krazy Kat.

One of Segar's greatest talents lay in phrase-making, and Wimpy provided him with his richest opportunities. After the great, self-assertive, manifesto of Popeye, echoed since by a million pairs of sympathetic lips, "I yam what I yam, an' tha's all I yam!" Segar's most memorable lines were murmured by Wimpy.

His classic wheedles, delivered and perfected over Roughhouse's fly-blown lunch counter ranged from the optimistic "I'll gladly pay you Tuesday for a hamburger today," through the dodging "Let's you and him fight," to the deceptive "Come on up for a duck dinner; you bring the ducks."

The striking thing about these both brazen and tremulous suggestions, originally created simply to delineate and heighten the essential Wimpiness of Wimpy himself, is that they are widely repeated today by millions who have never heard of Segar and who think of Wimpy as a simple clown for kids. They are now literally part of the language.

This is not surprising. The way a character spoke and framed his thoughts was as important to Segar as the way he was drawn. Certainly this was the case with Popeye. On his initial appearance in *Thimble Theatre*, all of him—not just his face, as Olive specified—resembled a shipwreck. He had the grace of an oyster and the shape of its shell. But there was a light within the squinty, pipe-puffing sailor, and eventually Segar shaped Popeye's battered carcass and face to fit the light and the speech. His one-eyed near-masterpiece became a viable comic unit only after a while, but his dialogue was developed fully in his first adventure.

Everything was funny in that first escapade. It has been retold amusingly enough by Coulton Waugh, in his early, popular history of the strips, *The Comics,* but Waugh, oddly, omitted what is certainly the single most interesting aspect of Popeye's first "superheroic" demonstration of indestructibility: its *external* source.

Popeye, in a days-long battle with a villain named Snork, was shot fifteen times, the last time directly in the chest at point-blank range. He crawled into the hold and lay there all night, passing in and out of comas, rubbing the head of the magic Whiffle Hen (Castor had brought her along because rubbing her head gave a man luck, and Castor used this power to win millions of pazoozies at a gaming casino off the China Coast). In the morning, Popeye reappeared on deck to face Snork again.

It was June 10, 1929, and a superman was born. Castor cried, "Popeye! I thought you were shot!" Ogling him with contempt, Popeye pointed to his riddled chest. "Well, whatcher think these is, button holes?" he asked.

Snork, flabbergasted by Popeye's reappearance, was quickly eliminated by Popeye's fists. Reader reaction brought Popeye back again in August, and he never left the strip again.

Obviously near death each time the Whiffle Hen revived him, Popeye had also rubbed the little creature's head to win at craps before his tussle with Snork. This sequence of events would seem to make Popeye's invulnerability a direct result of the Whiffle Hen's magic. Without any other explanation in the strip to contradict it, the conclusion to be drawn is that Popeye rubbed himself enough luck out of the Whiffle Hen's head to survive not only Snork's bullets, but any number of later shootings, knifings, hangings, and beatings. (To those interested in superhero categories, this data removes Popeye from the company of "natural" super-heroes like Superman and places him with the "magical" ones like Captain Marvel.)

Popeye's superstrength, on the other hand, doesn't seem to be involved. Not made a major point of display during this first adventure, it was later credited by Popeye himself to plain, garden-variety spinach—suggesting that the one-eyed sailor had some miraculous metabolic ability to assimilate the vegetable not just usefully (which is hard enough for most people) but downright dynamically. Relishing the taste, Popeye sometimes devoured enormous quantities of the stuff when he felt particularly challenged in the ring.

By and large, however, spinach was given little emphasis in the strip (unlike the enervating focus of the film cartoons), and the huge statue of Popeye erected by spinach growers in Texas in the thirties was certainly more perseveringly earned by Max Fleischer than by Segar. (It was, of course, essentially a matter of imaginative priorities; Segar was only interested in gimmicks when they offered extensive story or gag possibilities, and spinach was a dead end.)

So much for Popeye's "origins" as a superhero. They are, obviously, not nearly as important to readers familiar with the Segar character as the origins of the average comic book superhero are to *his* devotees. Segar himself, of course, was always interested in giving explanations and sources, on some level of fancy, of the supernormal phenomena in *Thimble Theatre*. A storyteller above all, he carefully elaborated on the source and operation of each of the Jeep's miraculous abilities, accounted exotically for Toar's immense age, specified and localized the Sea Hag's magic, and invented and clothed in history and customs whole fantastic nations such as Goon Valley and the demons of Demonia.

Unlike the work of his successors on the strip, Segar's fantasies have no loose ends, no absurdities for the sake of absurdity. Segar was a master of the little-understood art of rational limitation in fantastic narrative, and this was primarily the thing (aside from his innate creativity and humor) that distinguished his strip from the versions that followed.

Segar, who apparently developed a strong interest in the western, turned a simple flower in the Sunday, May 12, 1935 episode into poetry—and poetry of a particularly ironic kind, in view of Segar's death a short time later. Popeye, Olive, Castor, and Swee'Pea, on their way to Slither Creek to dig for gold, became separated from Wimpy, who had also tagged along. Wimpy, suffering from a desert madness which causes those afflicted to roam around speaking in verse, stumbled across a blossom growing from the eyehole of a steer skull. The quiet moocher had been days without food and was sure his number was up. Fixing his watery eyes on the flower, he swayed and began to recite what might as well be called—

J. WELLINGTON WIMPY'S APOSTROPHE
TO A DESERT DAISY

Oh, flower of death, so frail, so red,
Growing from a thing so dead—
Even as *I* will be quite soon—
Merely bones 'neath sun and moon.

Oh, life—oh, death—so close akin,
Though death can't lose—life can't win;
For death is sure, but life—ah well,
'Tis not for me to break the spell
That binds all things in a mighty plan
That can't be changed by laws of man—

That can't be altered by human tricks,
Or e'en be tilted by politics—
Fate alone can pull the strings
That control all human and earthly things.

It is just so, and so 'twill be,
Till the very end of Eternity—

So I cast my lot along with my kind,
And there'll be nobody above to remind—
To remind the gatekeeper an' pass the tip
That J. W. Wimpy was only a gyp.

But—shall you live? *You*—just a weed!
To scatter forth your worthless seed—
While I, creation's thing supreme,
Pass on to further nature's scheme?

Nay! Nay! Not so! I'll turn about—
I'm Fate today, you lowly sprout—
I'll pull you up, you little cuss—
Hah! Dust do dust the each of us!

Oh, desert daisy, so pure, so sweet,
You grew from soil that once was meat—
Aye, meat of my choice you chose for food.
Oh, why? —Why have I been so rude?

We both crave beef; we're unlike the others—
We're kindred souls; we may be brothers—
But I've killed you, my flower so bright,
Plucked you from your home so white.

Sorrow stills my desert madness,
Wild emotions turn to sadness—
But in my brain there is no lull,
For I picked you from your desert skull—

A skull your throne, whereupon you sat—
And the skull of a cow at that, at that—
And the skull of a lovely cow at that—
And the skull of a *lovely* cow at that—

L'ENVOI (as Mr. Wimpy collapses)
Plop!

INTRODUCTION TO

OK, AXIS, HERE WE COME!

A number of sociologically inclined critics have observed the co-incidence of booms in the comic book business—especially costumed adventure comics—and war. Although comics existed well back into the 1930s, their first great boom coincided with the preliminary rumblings of World War II and the war itself. Indeed, comic book people still speak of the 1940s as the Golden Age of Comics. After the war the comics declined, only to experience a second, smaller boom in the early 1950s, during the Korean War. With peace, the field again contracted, but entered a third boom period in the mid-1960s, during the Viet Nam War.

This brief introduction is no place to analyze that record in depth, but if the three cycles of the hero comics and American wars are more than coincidence it certainly offers something to think about. Much as we all love heroic adventure comics, it would be a small price to pay if giving them up meant giving up war.

When he isn't involved with editing books like the present one, Don Thompson dons the spectacles and business suit of a reporter for the Cleveland *Press,* where he has covered assignments ranging from a crime-and-police beat to the financial page, to a suburban territory of somewhat eye-popping size. And when he finishes *that* job for the day, he comes home and writes short stories! (The first one he sold was "The New Science," to *Venture Science Fiction* magazine. And despite its title, it deals with witchcraft.)

In this chapter, Don treats a trio of superheroes—Captain America, Sub-Mariner, and Human Torch—whose own cycles have matched precisely that cycle of war and peace, boom and bust in the comics business. Perhaps his words will help you to figure out why.

CHAPTER 5

OK, AXIS, HERE WE COME!

by DON THOMPSON

★★★

The United States was at war with the Germans and Japanese from late in 1941 to mid-1945. Considering that we had so many comic book heroes on our side, one must grudgingly admire the Axis for their staying power.

Particularly when you consider that many superheroes were fighting thinly disguised Nazi and Japanese forces in the late thirties and continued to fight them into 1946, when the backlog of stories finally was used up, you have to be impressed with the Enemy's durability.

Some of the comic book heroes were too powerful to turn loose on mere human (or, if you prefer the wartime propaganda, subhuman) opponents. Superman, for one, steered clear of the war for the most part, with a lame excuse about how Our Boys didn't really need any help. The real reason, of course, was that Superman couldn't enter the war without ending it immediately—and, obviously, the war wasn't ending immediately.

The less-than-omnipotent superdoers could fight the Axis, however, and most did, both at home and abroad.

None threw themselves more fully into the fray than the heroes of the outfit known variously as Timely, Atlas and Marvel Comics. Their wartime heroes, particularly the Human Torch, the Sub-Mariner, and Captain America, fought the most elaborate plots, with no holds barred.

The casualties on both sides were tremendous—the complete obliteration of some European or South American country (or city) such as Holland (or Buenos Aires) was passed off by our heroes as a minor setback. Regiments of German and Japanese soldiers were wiped out at a blow, by floods and explosives.

It is hard to believe, in these days of racial tolerance and played-down violence—particularly in the comics—but it was once a common sight to behold the Human Torch burning the arm off a grotesquely deformed Japanese while a pretty girl gleefully cheered him on.

The Japanese all wore glasses and had buck teeth (or, often, fangs) and long claw-like fingernails. Their skins were usually yellow, often greenish-yellow. Reference to their racial inferiority was common—they were the Enemy, so it was all right to derogate them racially.

It was not always easy to recognize the heroes during those war years, except by noting who came up smiling at story's end. The heroes gloated so much over the maiming and killing of the Enemy that they seemed far more villainous than the villains. They were supposed to be better looking than the bad guys, but the art wasn't always good enough to make that clear.

Two of the three superstars of the Atlas-Timely-Marvel group were born in the same issue—*Marvel Mystery Comics* #1, November, 1939. That issue is today one of the half-dozen rarest comic books and commands fantastic prices in dealers' catalogs—$250 and up.

Frankly, it is not worth it. The art is bad and the stories are worse. The only items of real interest are the origin stories of the Human Torch and the Sub-Mariner, and both of those were reprinted in the mid-1960s in Marvel's modestly titled *Fantasy Masterpieces.*

The Human Torch was the cover feature and lead story and he looked different in each. The cover showed a blazing man who looked as though he was made of fire; the story showed a man who looked as though he was on fire. The cover version was never seen again.

The Human Torch was not human at all. He was an android, created in a huge test tube, complete with rubbery-looking tights. His tights were blue in the first story, red by the second. They remained red for as long as *The Human Torch* was published, though the design changed somewhat over the years.

The Torch was created by Dr. Horton, a relatively sane scientist, who sought only to create an artificial man. Because of some design flaw, his creation burst into flame on contact with the air. (The colorist didn't read the text very carefully—they seldom did, or do—because the flames were supposed to be blue and came out red. However, they looked better red, and stayed that way.)

The story opened with Horton calling a press conference to show off his creation, a well-built, square-jawed man with wavy blond hair. This magnificent man was frozen in an upright position, in a huge, air-tight glass cage. When Horton released air into the cage, the figure burst into flames and moved around. Draining the air left him flameless and immobile. The reporters were impressed: they urged Horton to destroy it.

(Nobody remarked on the creation's ability to survive in a total vacuum, an ability which must rank as at least equal to the power of self-conflagration.)

Horton refused to destroy his android, even after fellow scientists seconded the reporters' suggestion. All instruments proved inadequate to measure the heat generated by the blazing man (though the glass cage didn't melt), and Horton had no control over the creature.

Horton effected a compromise: instead of destroying the android, he had the glass container sealed in a steel tube and the tube imbedded in a huge block of cement, pending the time when he would find a way to control the flame-man.

Somehow, air seeped through concrete, steel and glass, and the tomb burst wide open one night, releasing the Human Torch. (He was named by newspapermen and never had any other name or secret identity.) Torch ran wild, igniting everything within several feet of himself.

At this point, with no previous training, he started talking. His first words, for posterity, were: "I'm burning alive!—Why must everything I touch, turn to flame?—" Not bad conversation for a first try, though he might benefit from some punctuation lessons.

Fire engines turned out to fight him, but water turned to steam on contact with the Torch, and their hose burned through when he stepped on it. Conscience-stricken at the damage he caused, Torch ran to an estate with a swimming pool (something owned only by the very, very rich in 1939), melted his way through the gate, plunged into the pool and extinguished himself.

The estate belonged to a gangster named Sardo, who promptly covered the pool with a huge sheet of glass he happened to have around, drained out the water and air, caught the Torch, and went into the fire insurance business. A warehouse owner refused to pay protection, so Sardo put the Torch in an airtight glass tank (he filled the pool with water and performed the transfer in a diving suit), took the whole thing to a warehouse and broke the glass with a rock. As he burst into uncontrollable flame and destroyed the warehouse, it dawned on the Torch that Sardo was a racketeer, using the android for nefarious ends.

Torch jumped to escape the warehouse and found that he could fly because "the combined blue and red flames made the Human Torch lighter than air." He burned down Sardo's house, accidentally killing Sardo by exploding a tank of sulfuric acid in the gangster's private laboratory. Torch found that nitrogen (called "nitro" by everyone in the story who mentioned it) could be used to turn off his flame. After some experimentation, he learned how to control his flame with his own will power.

After apologizing for the damage he had caused, he was released in custody of Dr. Horton, who blurted out his intentions of making a fortune with the Torch. Angered by the taint of commercialism in his creator, the Human Torch burned through the roof and set out on his own.

In later adventures, many of his powers changed or disappeared, and new ones were added. For a while, he was able to command fire by giving weird yells, but this ability was later restricted to flames of his own creation and then dropped entirely. He soon learned to throw fireballs (like snowballs, only hotter) with amazing accuracy, but this quickly got out of hand and became ridiculous when he started weaving webs of fire, surrounding villains with barrels of flame (complete with lids), and doing other outlandish tricks.

Sometimes, not always, a fire extinguisher would snuff his fire long enough to enable somebody to clout him on the head. Not only could he no longer stand up to fire hoses, but he could be put out by deep snow. He retained his ability to burn his way through steel and just about everything but asbestos, to melt bullets and knives aimed at him, and to fly.

He also acquired, in singularly prosaic fashion, a sidekick named Toro, a miniature version of himself. As was customary, Toro was an orphan and, which was nearly as common, worked for a circus when Torch found him. Toro, it seems, had never been burned as a child ("I used to pull baked potatoes outa the fire for the gang!") and was found unconscious in the flames of the train wreck which killed his parents, clutching a piece of molten steel.

So they called him Toro (apparently thinking it had something to do with fire; it is Spanish for "bull") and gave him a job as a fire-eater with the circus.

One day, as Torch was flying by, the kid burst into flames. Torch urged him to try to control it and Toro sent "a mental command speeding to his brain . . ." and became a miniature Human Torch. They teamed up and wiped out a strong man who was trying to take over the circus. This all took place in the first issue of *The Human Torch,* Fall, 1940.

Toro could be distinguished from Torch by costume—all the kid wore was bathing trunks—and by his flame. Toro's flame was clear, the Torch's flaming body had a lot of penscratches through it, which made him look somewhat dirty.

Neither had alter egos, but occasionally they would don street clothes or even formal wear over their costumes. Their clothing bill was staggering, because they frequently had to burst into flame without time to remove their outer garments. The police commissioner, for whom they worked, had a great many walls, floors, ceilings, and windows melted, as well. They were handy allies, but damnably expensive.

Frequently they burst into flame to the accompaniment of the cry: "Flame on!" These weren't magic words, as "Shazam" was, but more of a battle cry along the lines of "Up, up, and away!"

After a couple of stories in which the villains were burned to death, the Torch took an oath not to kill with his flame, which was why he spun ornate webs. Burning to death is *extremely* painful and it just wasn't possible to create villains who deserved it for every Torch story.

Then came World War II.

When the Japanese bombed Pearl Harbor and the Nazis began systematically murdering Jews, they abandoned all claims to sympathy. Torch was free to use his flame to the utmost and he did, resulting in some grisly stories and covers.

One typical cover showed the blazing buddies rescuing an attractive redhead from a Japanese soldier armed with a Samurai sword. Toro was melting his way through the ceiling and hitting an onlooking soldier in the throat with a fireball, and Torch had burned up through the floor and grabbed the would-be executioner by the arm, melting the flesh off down to the bone from shoulder to wrist.

The stories seldom had anything to do with the covers, but dealt with the plots of Nazi spies and Gestapo agents with names like the Rabbit and the Python. They were called that because they looked, respectively, like a rabbit and a python. The former had brown skin, long ears, buck teeth and an upcurving moustache; the latter had brown skin, striped with black. In spite of the brown skin, both were pure Aryan, or else they couldn't have been German villains.

Freaks were common in these stories, as in most superhero comics. There was the Parrot, who looked like a parrot; the End, who looked like death warmed over and allowed to congeal, and Dr. Smart, who looked and acted like a jerk no matter what his name, and the writer, said.

The Human Torch was the brainchild of Carl Burgos, who drew many of the early stories and signed even more. He appeared in one story, where Torch and Toro leaped from his drawing board to suggest lampooning the Germans (this was *before* the United States got into the war). In the story, Burgos got the okay from his boss and had his writers do a story. He then did some preliminary drawings and turned them over to a staff of hack artists to finish (commendable honesty to admit he didn't do the whole thing). The comics were dropped in Berlin, Hitler was almost laughed out of power, which irked him. He ordered the extermination of Burgos, and the Torch and Toro foiled it. During the whole of the story, Burgos went to absurd length to avoid showing his face, making it conspicuous by its absence. He did show Hitler, Goebbels, Goering, Churchill, and MacArthur, though.

Prince Namor, the Sub-Mariner, also bowed in with the first issue of *Marvel Mystery Comics*. He was the offspring of Princess Fen of Atlantis and an American naval officer, Commander McKenzie. McKenzie was in Antarctica, blasting away the great ice packs and churning things up in the undersea kingdom. The Princess, who looked human, was sent by her subjects, who looked like humanoid fish, to seduce the commander from his duty while they gathered an army. She fell in love with him and he with her, they married and so forth.

Then, on the day the army was massed beneath the ice, McKenzie's men began blasting away the ice to clear a path home. The shock waves wiped out the Atlantean army and Fen, angered, dived overboard and returned to her people where, after a suitable interval, Namor was born.

Princess Fen did not tell her son about surface people until after he, as a stripling, killed two, thinking they were robots because of their bulky diving suits. When he questioned her, she told him of his origin and explained that it was his duty to wipe out the surface people, a job he tackled with gusto.

In his early days, before and during the war, the Sub-Mariner was a brawny, broad-shouldered brute, with arms that tapered to small hands and a slim waist. His head, like his upper torso, was shaped like an inverted triangle. He looked like a musclebound Fred Astaire but had ears like *Star Trek's* Mr. Spock. He wore only black swimming trunks with a gold belt, though on occasion he would put on a cape of office (he was royalty, after all) or ordinary surfaceman's clothing. On his heels were tiny wings which enabled him to fly. He slimmed down in later stories and looked years younger.

All the early stories and many of the later ones were signed by Bill Everett, the artist-creator of the Sub-Mariner. If he really did draw them all, he certainly improved over the years. The early work was sloppy, hastily drawn, grossly exaggerated and anatomically ridiculous. The 1954 version was beautifully drawn, finely detailed, and anatomically pleasing to the eye.

It has long been reported that Mickey Spillane wrote many of the early Sub-Mariner stories, but Everett has denied this. Spillane, he said, wrote many two-page text pieces (the ones no one ever read, but the Post Office insisted on as a condition to granting second-class mailing privileges), but no comic book stories. Many of the two-pagers are clearly credited to Spillane.

The Sub-Mariner stories couldn't have contained any more brutality and violence if Spillane *had* written them, especially after sub-Mariner directed his efforts at the Japanese and Germans and the war permitted him to pull out all stops.

In one story (in *Sub-Mariner Comics #5*), he gleefully watched his lieutenant machinegun a Japanese landing party, blasted a destroyer with an incendiary bomb and danced for joy. However, the Japanese torpedoed Namor's boat and killed his crew, which made him mad. He righted an overturned Japanese torpedo boat, rode it head-on into a destroyer, jumped overboard before it hit, salvaged a depth charge, and used it to sink an aircraft-carrier, machinegunned some more landing parties, turned a flamethrower on them ("I'd give anything to have the Torch see me now! He thinks *he's* hot stuff!") captured a submarine, brutally beat its commander, then torpedoed another sub. He laughed when British machinegun bullets riddled the submarine commander.

There was even more, but you get the idea. There was no plot, just gore, as he sank another couple of destroyers, two more landing parties, and a brace of airplanes.

The dialogue was so bad it was embarrassing. Namor constantly made such exclamations as "Great Pickled Penguins!" "Suffering Shad!" "Holy Halibut!" "Flyin' Flounder!" "Cackling Catfish!" "Hopping Herring!" "Galloping Guppies!" "Slithering Eels!" and, the *pièce de résistance,* "Chuckling Clams!"

(Incidentally, the editors always insisted that Sub-Mariner's name was to be pronounced with a short "i," as in "The Ancient Mariner." Every kid I ever knew pronounced it "Sub-MahREEner," which is probably how you have been mentally pronouncing it as you read this chapter.)

Namor was very short tempered, very susceptible to flattery and more than normally stupid. He had a number of girlfriends who came and went. Most prominent was Betty Dean, the first surface woman to befriend him, and one of the few people who could control

him when he went on his frequent rampages. There was, briefly, a
Venusian girl named Jarna who, though very humanoid herself,
commanded an army of unhuman little men. And there was Princess
Rathia of Atlantis who urged him to conquer the world. Finally there
was a female counterpart named Namora.

Sub-Mariner and the Human Torch did not get along well together. Usually, comic book heroes were disgustingly buddy-buddy;
Torch and Namor were welcome exceptions.

Their rivalry started early and cropped up frequently before they
became grudging allies. It was fire versus water, a natural war,
helped along by Namor's desire to wipe out the human race and
Torch's determination to save it. They frequently fought to a draw,
even though Sub-Mariner was the villain, listed in the fifth issue of
The Human Torch as one of "The four horsemen of destruction,"
along with Hitler, Mussolini, and Death. This was the Fall 1941 issue written and released before the United States entered the war.

In the course of that battle in *Human Torch #5*, an army of British
soldiers drowned, Gibralter was captured by Namor, the Italian
army was wiped out, Africa was flooded, the polar ice cap was melted sending glaciers over Europe and North America, a tidal wave hit
New York City but was stopped by a stream of lava which turned it
to steam (not a great improvement), and President Franklin Delano
Roosevelt was shown reading a copy of *Marvel Mystery Comics.*

(Torch and Sub-Mariner were both given command of armies in
this story and the army invariably was wiped out. Yet all they had to
do was ask for more men and they got them, along with praise for
their leadership abilities and effusive expressions of gratitude and
unswerving loyalty from their new batch of followers.)

After the war, Namor drifted into a series of innocuous little adventures before he faded out in 1950. He was reintroduced rather
briefly in 1954 in an attempt to recapture lost glories his absence was
explained as a longer-than-usual "people are no damned good"
mood) but this reincarnation did not take. More on him and the
Torch (who was reincarnated in 1954 after having been buried in the
desert until an atomic bomb test revived him) later.

Marvel's other mainstay character was Captain America, who
burst forth in his own comic book with no preliminary appearances.
He was the creation of Joe Simon and Jack Kirby, creators of many
of the comic book superheroes of the forties. In many ways, he was
their best.

The first issue of *Captain America* introduced several long-term in-
gredients of the good captain's career—Captain America himself, his

boy associate, Bucky, and his favorite villain, the Red Skull. All in one 64-page issue, 45 pages of which were devoted to Cap himself.

The cover also introduced some permanent features: Captain America was smashing a Nazi nest and giving Hitler himself a crack on the jaw, while four Nazis fired at him, bullets bouncing off his shield.

(There was a lot more than that going on on that cover, since Timely's covers were among the most cluttered in the world. A Nazi with a microphone was watching a television screen on which a "U.S. Munitions Works" plant was being blown up by a Nazi spy; papers labeled "sabotage plans for U.S.A." lay on the floor; a large insert showed Bucky saluting the readers; there were six swastikas in evidence; bent and broken bars over a window indicated how Cap came in. This is crowded, all right, but it is far from the most crowded Timely cover ever printed. All of them had cluttered covers, often filled with fiendish machines, carefully labeled "Death Ray Camera" "Poison Gas Cannon." The cover of one issue of *Marvel Mystery* had seventeen labels explaining the action and I still couldn't figure out what was happening.)

With that television screen and Cap slugging Hitler, it may come as a surprise to learn that the first issue of *Captain America* was dated March, 1941. Seems there was a danger of invasions from within and the fifth column was busy sabotaging America. The army had been infiltrated with spies and President Roosevelt, after wistfully wishing the Human Torch were not just a comic book character, announced that FBI Chief J. Arthur Grover had a plan.

The plan involved injecting a "strange, seething liquid" into a scrawny 4-F named Steve Rogers. Rogers turned into a massive, muscular man. The doctor who injected him named him Captain America and said he was "the first of a corps of super-agents whose mental and physical ability will make them a terror to spies and saboteurs!"

However, one of the Army men watching the transformation was one of those Nazi infiltrators. He killed the doctor, destroyed the only vial of the serum, and proceeded to shoot everyone in sight (including FBI Chief Grover) before Rogers beat the whey out of him and knocked him into the laboratory equipment, which electrocuted him.

Now the only one of his kind, Cap donned a red-white-and-blue uniform based on the American flag and started smashing spies. However, now that he was healthy, Steve Rogers was drafted. In the Army, he met Bucky Barnes, boy "mascot of the regiment," who discovered him changing his duds. Captain America made the kid a red-yellow-and-blue costume and then Bucky joined him in his spy-smashing.

Captain America, patriotism personified, was a giant blond who covered the upper half of his head with a blue skull cap (by the second issue, it had become a tight-fitting hood attached to the torso of his costume). There were tiny wings just above the ears and a large white "A" on his forehead. In the first issue, he carried a triangular shield, with three large stars and red, white and blue stripes. By the second issue, it had become a circular shield with red and white concentric stripes, like a target. His costume was blue with white sleeves, red-and-white vertical stripes around his middle, red boots and red gloves.

Bucky wore red gloves, red leggings, blue boots, a loose blue jacket with a yellow collar, and blue shorts. He wore a black string eye mask and was called Bucky, whether he was in costume or not.

Cap carried no weapons except his shield, with which he bashed people. He could throw it with unbelievable accuracy, ricocheting it off several spies at once.

In the fourth story of that first issue, Cap battled the Red Skull, leader of a bunch of spies and murderer of several high-ranking Army officers. The villain wore a red skull hood and a loose-fitting maroon coverall with a white swastika on the chest. At the end of the story he was killed and unmasked as George Maxon, head of Maxon Aircraft Inc.

Two issues later, however, the Red Skull was back in action and was never unmasked again, nor was any mention made of his death. He became Cap's number one villain, fighting him time and again all through the war, until Cap finally killed him when World War II ended.

However, after the war, *Captain America* comics metamorphosed briefly into *Captain America's Weird Tales,* a horror comic, and Cap went to Hell to fight the Red Skull again.

In between battles with the forces of evil, he was Private Steve Rogers. Whenever trouble broke out he'd desert his post, duck into a convenient foxhole, and emerge as Captain America, leaping valorously and long-leggedly into the thick of the fray and emerging victorious. After each battle, however, Private Rogers and Mascot Barnes generally wound up peeling potatoes for deserting under fire. Rather inglorious, but the Articles of War permit shooting the offender for that crime, so they really got off pretty easily.

After the war, Cap became a schoolteacher, with glasses, and Bucky became one of his students. He fought petty crooks in very short, very unimaginative stories and faded away. In 1954, he was revived along with Torch and Sub-Mariner.

The blurb read: "Yes, the greatest champion of democracy is back with his pal Bucky . . . back to fight the worst menace the freedom-loving peoples of the world have ever faced! Together, they battled fascists and Nazis, but now they're needed again to fight 'The Betrayers'! They fought and battled all through World War II, these valiant and courageous patriots! But, with the coming of peace, there was still no rest for them! Communism was spreading its ugly, grasping tentacles all over the world!"

Maybe the readers were sore at them for sitting out the Korean War, but, in any case, the revival was short-lived.

Captain America, Sub-Mariner, the Human Torch, a flying super-heroine named Miss America (no relation to the Captain), a super-fast man called Whizzer, Bucky, and Toro teamed up as the All Winners Squad in two issues of *All Winners Comics.* The stories were poor, hastily done imitations of the Justice Society of America stories in DC's *All-Star Comics.* Two appearances were more than enough.

Much more successful were *The Young Allies,* a kid gang headed by Bucky and Toro. The rest of the gang included the usual kid gang lineup: Tubby, the fat slob; Knuckles, the pugnacious kid from Brooklyn; Jefferson Worthington Sandervilt, boy inventor who vociferated exclusively in polysyllabic pronouncements of imposing grandeur and resplendent vocabulary—and Whitewash Jones, the inevitable minstrel-show caricature of a Negro, superstitious and watermelon-loving, with pendulous lips, bulging eyes, a zoot suit, and natural rhythm.

Their first adventure had them battling the Red Skull; being patted on the head by Hitler ("My! My! Vot nice Cherman boys!"), who didn't notice Bucky's costume, Toro's swimming trunks, or Whitewash's non-Aryan coloring; being imprisoned in a concentration camp; breaking out; flying to Russia, where they were nearly sent to Siberia; flying to China; returning to America, and being rescued by Captain America and the Human Torch. Whew!!

(During the course of the story, Bucky disguised himself as the Red Skull by painting an ordinary human skull red and putting it over his head. God knows how.)

The Timely-Atlas-Marvel publications spawned a number of subsidiary costume heroes. There was the Patriot, who was distinguished primarily for the silly-looking long-legged eagle emblazoned on his chest. There was the Destroyer, who wore gray-and-red tights with a skull on the chest and had a gray face and gray teeth when in costume. There was Electro, a red-yellow-and-green robot that looked like a Technicolor fire hydrant; Ka-Zar, a second-rate Tarzan; the Vision, who appeared in mist or smoke to fight evil; the Angel, a non-powered guy who started out as a direct steal from Leslie Charteris' The Saint. The first Angel story, in the first issue of *Marvel,* was a plagiarism of *The Saint in New York.*

The Angel was the creation of Paul Gustafson, apparently the only person who ever signed the artwork. Exactly why he wore a costume is anybody's guess—probably exhibitionism—because he had no secret identity. Even while in ordinary clothes, he was called only "the Angel," but he always put on his costume when trouble arose. He wore blue tights with leather bands at his wrists, and a pair of large yellow wings decorated his chest. He wore a red cape, had yellow hair and a thin black moustache. At the end of each story, when justice was triumphant, the shadow of the Angel fell across the scene. He had no special powers, except the casting of that shadow on the most inaccessible places.

The most ridiculous Timely-Atlas creations were The Fin, who wore tights, boots and goggles—and a two-foot shark's fin jutting from his head, which may have made it difficult going through doorways, but established copyright—and the Blonde Phantom, a curvy blonde, who wore an elaborate, slit-skirted, low-necked red evening gown plus a mask when fighting crime. Besides the inefficiency of such a costume when engaged in hand-to-hand combat, it must have taken her hours to get dressed, by which time any emergency is either over or beyond control.

The whole line of superheroes faded out around 1954, when the Comics Code Authority showed up to clean up the comics and put an end to juvenile delinquency forever. It was just as well; they had all become anemic. The Atlas-Marvel-or-whatever line became devoted to war stories, bad westerns and dull, non-frightening (remember the Code) fantasy stories involving monsters named Tim Boo Ba and Fin Fang Foom and Groon and Gorr.

Until 1961, when it became apparent that there was a new audience for the costumed superhero, National-Superman-DC had revived Flash, Green Lantern, and Hawkman in new guises and were making money with them.

Stan Lee (writer-editor) and Jack Kirby (artist, the same Kirby who created so many superheroes with Joe Simon) looked up from their ridiculous fantasy comics and stupid westerns and decided to bring forth some superheroes. Lee had been writing comic books since the early forties, when he was seventeen. Kirby had been creating and drawing comic books since he was a teenager. Both had worked on every kind of comic book from funny animal to western, from romance to weird horror, from superhero to *Classics Illustrated.*

They wanted to do something different, so they crated the Fantastic Four, a group of non-costumed superheroes who did not get along very well at all together, who had psychological hang-ups and financial difficulties.

The four were scientist Reed Richards, whose brown hair was white at the temples; muscleman and pilot Ben Grimm, who had a surly disposition; Sue Storm, Reed's girlfriend; and Johnny Storm, a hotheaded teenager, Sue's brother.

These four were the unlikely crew of a spaceship built by Richards. They flew out into space and were hit with strong radiations. When they returned to earth, they found that they had turned into strange, nonhuman creatures. Reed Richards could stretch his body into weird shapes and extend himself over long distances (*à la* Quality Comics' long-defunct Plastic Man); Ben Grimm turned chunky and orange, with beetling brows, beady eyes, and an overall skin texture which resembled flowerpot fragments pasted over a bulky body—in short, he looked like the unimaginative monsters Lee and Kirby had been creating for the previous several years; Sue found she could turn invisible, and Johnny found he could burst into flame and fly.

They gave themselves names: Reed modestly called himself Mr. Fantastic; Ben aptly dubbed himself the Thing; Sue, of course, became Invisible Girl, and Johnny—why, Johnny was the Human Torch!

The beginning was inauspicious but the seeds of glory were there. The four bickered a lot and Johnny quit the group at the end of the third issue of *The Fantastic Four.* In the fourth issue, he wandered into a flophouse and read an old Marvel comic about Sub-Mariner. And who do you suppose that seedy old bearded amnesiac in the next bed turned out to be after Johnny burned his whiskers off? Prince Namor the First, the Sub-Mariner! Naturally.

Subby got his memory back when his whiskers went and he resumed his battle against the human race in general and the Fantastic Four in particular. For a while, there was a rivalry with Reed Richards over the affections of Sue, but Reed wound up marrying the girl and Sub-Mariner was given his own strip, later his own book, and an Atlantean girlfriend called Lady Dorma.

Lee and Kirby also created a superhero called Thor. He started out as a lame doctor who could turn into the Thunder God, with shoulder-length blond hair, a red cape, an elaborate blue-black costume, and a big sledgehammer which enabled him to fly (he had a

wrist-thong on it, see, and he'd put his hand through that, then throw the hammer and be pulled along behind it). Later, he turned out to be the real Thor, son of Odin, and had many multi-installment adventures in Asgard. He started out in *Journey Into Mystery,* one of those drab fantasy books, and eventually took over the whole thing, changing its title to *The Mighty Thor.*

Thor joined with Ant-Man (who could make himself ant-sized and control the ants mentally), the Hulk (a skinny scientist who was exposed to a nuclear blast and became a huge, green, stupid, impossibly muscled hero-villain), and Iron Man (a wounded playboy inventor who built a chest-plate to keep his heart beating and added armor to it to become a flying superhero) as *The Avengers.* In their fourth issue (there must be a magic about fourth issues: it was *Fantastic Four #4* when Sub-Mariner returned), a man was found floating in a cake of ice.

He was thawed and, lo and behold, it was Captain America, young and strong as ever. Seems he had been frozen in the ice after he and Bucky unsuccessfully tried to stop a rocket bomb in the last days of World War II. Bucky was killed and Cap became something of a whining necrophiliac, moaning about his lost partner and keeping his spare costumes in the closet of his apartment for years. Finally, in late 1968, he was given a new partner (who wore Bucky's old costumes), Rick Jones. Jones was the kid Bruce Banner was rescuing when he caught the nuclear radiation that made him the Hulk.

There is a lot of crossover in the modern Marvel Comics Group. A war comic, *Sgt. Fury and His Howling Commandos,* featuring World War II war fantasies, had a guest appearance by Captain America and Bucky in one issue. Fury himself later became a super secret agent with a second book of his own, *Nick Fury, Agent of S.H.I.E.L.D.* At one time or another, all of Marvel's superheroes have met, usually to fight under the impression that the other was a villain.

The new Human Torch once fought the old, in the 1966 *Fantastic Four Special #4* (an annual "giant" comic which, for 25 cents, gave you the same 64 pages you used to get for a dime). However, the original Torch was beset with moans because he was a mere android, not a true human, and he was killed saving the Fantastic Four.

Marvel, masterminded by Lee and Kirby, had managed a feat unmatched by anyone in the comics business: they had successfully revived their superheroes, sometimes in new identities, and made them superior to the originals.

In addition, Marvel produced several new superheroes of outstanding quality, such as Spider-Man. Spidey was the creation of artist Steve Ditko, though Lee wrote the dialogue and continued the character (Marvel's biggest seller) long after Ditko left the firm. Spider-Man was puny Peter Parker, a high-school student, when he was bitten by a radioactive spider and given the proportionate strength and wall-climbing ability of a spider. He designed a fancy red-and-blue costume with webbing designs, invented a web-spraying device and set out—*not* to fight crime, but to make a fortune in television! He was a smash on a TV show, but was paid by check and couldn't cash it because he carried no identification as Spider-Man. He couldn't reveal who he really was because his enfeebled Uncle Ben and Aunt May with whom he lived wouldn't approve. Sore because he wasn't making money, Spider-Man refused to get involved and permitted a burglar to flee past him, pursued by police. Later, that same burglar killed Uncle Ben. Spider-Man caught him, vowed to devote himself to getting involved, and proceeded to fight crime.

Other Marvel characters of note included Dr. Strange (another Ditko creation), a sorcerer who devoted himself to fighting other sorcerers; Daredevil, a blind attorney who had radar senses which were better than eyesight and extreme agility which seemed to be better than superpowers (he bore no resemblance to the Daredevil of the forties, except the name); the Black Panther, the world's first Negro superhero (Marvel led the comics field in race relations in the sixties—they featured many Negro supporting characters and even Negro villains); the Silver Surfer, a silver-skinned alien who rode the skies on a surfboard, looking for all the world like Hollywood's Oscar come to life; and a green-and-white costumed spaceman named (choke) Captain Marvel.

Marvel's villains (which included the Red Skull, alive and well and permanently red-skulled) were out of the ordinary, too. Chief among them was Dr. Doom, half man and half robot and an even greater scientist than Mr. Fantastic, with whom he fought. Dr. Doom had an advantage most comic book villains lack—as ruler of the middle-European country of Latveria, he had diplomatic immunity. The Fantastic Four could fight him, but not jail him. He even got his own book.

The Marvel method of preparing a story was to hold story conferences in which a rough plot was outlined. The artist then drew the story; Lee or one of his other writers (Roy Thomas, Gary Friedrich, Archie Goodwin, and Arnold Drake) wrote the dialogue and captions, and another artist inked the whole thing. It sounds like a backward approach to the problem, but it worked.

At a time in the late 1960s when the superhero craze was fading, Marvel kept inventing new ones. Several companies climbed on the superhero bandwagon with too little, too late. American Comics Group introduced a couple of limpwristed supernatural superheroes—a ghost named Nemesis and a magician named Magicman—both of whom were costumed as if for ballet. ACG folded. Dell brought out some unimaginative, badly drawn superheroes based loosely on Dracula, Frankenstein and the Wolfman. The comics folded and Dell remained only peripherally in the comics business. Other companies entered and left the superhero lists.

DC, the giant of the field, introduced a horde of titles which lasted fewer than a half-dozen issues each—*Beware the Creeper,* a revived *Plastic Man,* a superhero parody called *The Inferior Five*—and killed off *Blackhawk,* a survivor from the early forties.

Through it all, Marvel kept expanding its line, adding *Captain Marvel,* giving the Silver Surfer his own book, putting Spider-Man into a 35-cent comic magazine, *The Spectacular Spider-Man* in addition to his regular book, *The Amazing Spider-Man,* and they showcased proposed new characters in *Marvel Super-Heroes.* They revived and revised Ka-Zar, that second-rate Tarzan, and the Vision, who was an android in this incarnation.

One reason for the success of the new Marvels, besides the generally high quality of the art and writing, was that Lee created a personality cult around himself. Where DC comics were edited by a generally faceless lot of men whose names were unknown to the general public, Lee *was* Marvel. Every story in every Marvel comic listed his name first among the credits, either as editor or as writer, and in letters usually larger than anyone else's.

It infuriated many fans and brought heavy-handed jibes from DC (a lackluster humor book from DC, *Angel and the Ape,* included a comic book editor named Stan Bragg), but it worked.

Barring a sudden burst of the balloon—it has happened before—the Human Torch, Sub-Mariner, and Captain America should be around for years to come, creating new glories for tomorrow's nostalgia and dimming the memory of the past with a brighter present.

INTRODUCTION TO

ONE ON ALL AND ALL ON ONE

When you were a kid, you probably belonged to a gang (or tried to). The gang may have been two or three kids who tried smoking or a dozen kids who made an enthusiastic but ill-advised attempt to build a clubhouse. The odds are that you were not the leader of the gang, due to the shortsightedness of your friends. In addition to the local gang, you may have belonged to national groups such as the Captain Marvel Club or the Tom Mix Straight Shooters. For the first time, you were a part of society.

Tom Fagan belonged to Little Orphan Annie's Junior Commandos and helped them collect scrap in World War II. He is one of the three leading Batman fans in the world (no, we aren't going to name the other two), remembers that the first comic book he read was *Detective Comics* No. 32, and has been chairman of the annual Batman/Halloween Parade in Rutland, Vermont, since 1960. He was chosen Batmanian chieftain in a national election of Caped Crusader fans. He even includes a stylized bat in his signature. After a varied career—candy merchant, artist on a TV cartoon safety feature, reporter, city editor—Tom assumed his true identity as promotion director of Charles E. Tuttle, a Rutland book publisher.

Tom relates the adventures of comic book gangs, who were more likely to get into a scrap than collect scrap.

CHAPTER 6

ONE ON ALL AND ALL ON ONE

by TOM FAGAN

★★

The Gang has been inherent in literature from earliest times. Beowulf and his warriors against Grendel. Robin Hood and his Merry Men, taking to the outlaw holds of Sherwood Forest, rallying against tyranny. Peter Pan and the Lost Boys fighting a losing battle against conformity and the shackles of adulthood.

Tom Sawyer and his gang—Huck Finn, Joe Harper, Ben Rogers, and Tommy Barnes—and their oath as related by Huck Finn: "It swore every boy to stick to the band, and never tell any of the secrets; and if anybody done anything to any boy in the band, whichever boy was ordered to kill that person and his family must do it, and he mustn't eat and he mustn't sleep till he had killed them. . . ."

Another gang declaration was made in *Detective Comics* #64, June 1942, by a likeable but tough youngster: "Brooklyn's me name, see? . . . An' dat's me mob, see? . . . We're out ta get Hitler and his mob cuz dere ain't room for both of us, see?"

That was the blood promise of the Boy Commandos.

They are the words of a fighting kid gang, one of many such gangs in comics. They grew out of children's friendship with a superhero, gangs that existed to fight crime, and gangs that existed just because the members liked one another and enjoyed participating in adventures, real or imaginary.

The gang may be social or it may be antisocial. It may range in purpose from the Boy Scouts of America to Hell's Angels. It may lurk under everyday business suit attire or wear its colors as a warning sign.

Or it may broadcast its name publicly in costume or gang jacket. The range is from Shriners and Masons to Night Legion, Amboy Dukes, Black Rebels, Enchanters, Deacons, or Students for Peace.

Whatever they call themselves is an identity. It could just as easily be Commando Cubs, Comrades Four, Young Allies, or Teen Titans. The fascination of the gang lies in the sense of belonging, the essence of being one against all, no matter the odds . . . for fun, for fighting, for frolic—forever—for such is time to the gang.

The tradition of the gang is duplicated in American history: the Jameses, the Youngers, the Capone Gang, Bonnie and Clyde, children of the Depression whose out-and-out conflict with the Establishment created a new myth which encompassed many of the hopes and fears that lay within the American mind of the late sixties.

People against society and society against people. What more could you ask? World War II gave the answer: People united in common cause. The setting was perfect for the gang to take its place in the comic book medium that blasted into being, as gangs of one side prepared to wage war against gangs of the other.

Within the space of a single, shattering Sunday—the day of the death-dealing Japanese flight over Pearl Harbor—America became a nationwide gang, swept up in a holocaust of hatred. War was declared on Japan and, almost immediately afterward, on Germany. America was part of a Cause.

While a fighting-mad United States strapped on the sword, a new note crept into the "funny books." Mirroring the temper of the era, comic books began triggering imaginary youthful heroes into action, while real-life counterparts were hurling Molotov cocktails at onrushing German tanks or stealing on missions through mine-laden rice paddies in the Far East.

Detective Comics, which had produced the first kid hero, Robin the Boy Wonder, offered what an excitement-craving war-conscious public wanted: The Boy Commandos, creation of Joe Simon and Jack Kirby.

The editors of *Detective* seemed to feel an explanation was in order. Written at the bottom of the first page was this legend:

"What is this strip doing in *Detective Comics,* you say? The supercriminals who hold an entire continent in shackles can tell you! From the cauldron of war has risen new agents of justice, striking swiftly . . . silently! . . . From across the Channel comes a new challenge! The Nazi brute cringes in fear . . . for the day of liberation is on its way . . . Nothing can stop it! *The Commandos are coming!*"

Ungrammatical, but stirring.

Four boys and a man. But what boys and what a man! Tough-talking Brooklyn, wearing the comic book symbol of masculine toughness and low breeding, a derby hat, introduced his companions, his "mob."

As the Allies represented many nations, so did Brooklyn's gang. There were Pierre Chavard and Jan Haasen and Alfy Twidgett and the group's acknowledged adult leader, Rip Carter. Their words echoed the comic book sentiment of the forties—patriotic glee at being on the right side.

"Bon Soir, my friends . . . We are off to raid the Boche in France! The Commandos will avenge many of my enslaved countrymen tonight or my name is not Pierre Chavard!" (Apparently it wasn't; in later issues he was known as Andre.)

"I am Jan Haasen. The Nazis destroyed my family as they did my beloved Holland! . . . And I will stay and fight with the Commandos until my country is again *free!*"

"Cheerio, an' thumbs up, folks! Alfy Twidgett's going ta myke h'it pretty 'ot fer the Jerries tonoit!"

"I'm Captain Rip Carter, folks, my job is leading an outfit of tough commandos and keeping an eye on those young wildcats, our company mascots. We're a few against many . . . but how those Nazis run when we get started!"

Although they were referred to as boys until their withdrawal from comics in 1949, the commandos looked like older men with glandular disturbances, not like kids.

The first *Boy Commandos* story dealt with a cynical, embittered Frenchman, Leon LaFarge, who was contemptuous of his fellow man and of the ideals that prompt men to fight. Rescued from a beating by the Boy Commandos, LaFarge thanked them by calling them brats and ordering them to leave him alone.

But, with the promise of money, LaFarge agreed to help the commandos on a mission. Seeing men dying about him, LaFarge, still cynical, took the place of a French underground leader who was to be executed. His bravery did not cost him his life, however, because the Commandos battled their way into and through the prison to save him. Brooklyn, Alfy, Jan and Andre (Pierre) joined against Carter's orders in the "horde of howling demons sweeping into the courtyard, spreading death and destruction in the bewildered Nazis' ranks."

Evidently reader response was great. The Boy Commandos' adventures continued in *Detective Comics* monthly through issue 150. They also had 36 issues of their own magazine from 1942 to 1949.

Jan and Alfy left the team after the war. Jan was not replaced, but a rather uninteresting cowboy kid named Tex succeeded Alfy when he dropped out.

Without a war setting, *Boy Commandos* had trouble holding the public's interest. Such villains as Crazy Quilt, a costumed criminal employing colored lights for weapons, failed to maintain the strip's popularity.

But while *Boy Commandos* was in its heyday, it had many imitators. One came from the Family (Harvey) Comics line. Their answer was "a quartette of fighting queens" known as the *Girl Commandos*.

Like their male counterparts, the *Girl Commandos* represented different nations: America, China, Russia, and Britain. Their stories were told in *Speed Comics* and in *All New Comics*. *Girl Commandos* was a continuation of *Pat Parker, War Nurse*.

Pat Parker, naturally, took the initiative as leader. The *Girl Commandos* tales featured such diversified settings as Russian border posts on the Manchurian frontier, Alpine locales with "Japanese barbarians," and North African supply bases serving as stepping-off points "for the important Balkan invasion."

Besides Miss Parker, the girls were Ellen, Tanya and Mei-Ling. When they came up against the enemy, they didn't fool around. In one story, Mei-Ling faced death at the hands of a gun-wielding assassin. Her three friends arrived in the nick and, by clubbing, socking, and beating him, they subdued the would-be murderer and his companion. The girls then casually threw both opponents off a cliff.

Such scenes of brutality were common in *Girl Commandos* tales. One picture, lettered "Retribution—swift, deadly!" showed a Japanese prince, Hittika, pinned by three arrows against the flag of the Rising Sun.

Of course, these arrows were meant, originally, for the Girl Commandos, but that was hardly justifiable reason for the chubby Ellen to chuckle, "Coo! Looka Hittika! Number one Jap Pin-Up Boy!" It was this kind of writing and artistry that was later to bring public disapproval full-force on comics in general.

The Nedor (also known as Better or Standard) group of comics had its own commandos group: The Commando Cubs, who made their debut in *Thrilling Comics,* July 1943.

Uncle Sam himself introduced the Cubs, describing them as being "From every type of home, sent to England to learn the effect of old-world culture on kids of different backgrounds . . . marooned there since the war began . . . and now . . . 1943 . . . Let's see what's cooking!"

The reader then learned how the Cubs, while watching a commando drill, were inspired to be fighters on their own. To accomplish this, they trained themselves and eventually obtained military-looking uniforms.

The Cubs were Ace Browning, a "typical American boy" with plenty of grit; Spud O'Shea, a typical Irish boy; Horace Cosgrove II, an intellectual with a fondness for big words; Whizzer Malarkey, a plump kid, but fast when it came to fighting; and Pokey Jones, a Negro drawn in the stereotyped fashion of the day.

The Cubs primarily battled Germans, but fought the Japanese in two battles, once in December 1945 and again in February 1946, their last story with a wartime setting. Since the war ended in August 1945, their cessation of hostilities must be considered overdue.

Through the remainder of their career, the Cubs wore khaki-colored outfits with a star emblem and were a crime-fighting contingent.

Early Commando Cubs tales were written by Richard E. Hughes, who moved over to edit the American Comics Group in 1947, and were then drawn by Bob Oksner. Later stories were done by a variety of artists and writers, resulting in loss of continuity.

Kid gangs in comics often sprang from kids' friendship with a particular superhero. This was the case with the Little Wise Guys, who associated with Daredevil. Daredevil wore a skin-tight, hair-to-sole rubber costume of red and blue. It was striped vertically, one side red, one blue. He wore a spiked belt and carried a boomerang.

When Charles Biro took over writing Daredevil stories, the character had already gained popularity without the use of a youth group, appearing in solo action in several issues of *Silver Streak Comics,* the one-shot *Daredevil Battles Hitler,* and several issues of *Daredevil Comics.* Biro introduced the Wise Guys in 1942 and they eventually took the book away from Daredevil, lasting into the fifties.

The first Wise Guys story opened in an orphan asylum, where an elderly couple was preparing to adopt a fat little boy named Meatball, who had no wish to be anyone's charge. Meatball slipped away and, by chance, met Scarecrow, a tall, doltish youth who had been swindled out of two horses given him to sell by his farmer guardian. Fearing the farmer's wrath, Scarecrow, too, was running away. He and Meatball joined company and sought shelter in a barn.

The barn was owned by the father of Jock C. H. Herendeen, a boy who was to play an important part in both their futures. Jock, at the moment, was in a nearby city witnessing the beating of a small tyke by a larger boy.

Intervening, Jock—despite wearing short pants and being wealthy (two strikes against any kid in the popular American view of those years)—clobbered the bully. The small boy was Pee Wee, who, in sheepdog gratitude, followed Jock home, where they discovered Scarecrow and Meatball hidden in the barn. A friendship was formed and all, including Jock, moved into the barn.

Later, as they were playing in a field, they were charged by an angry bull. A boomerang sliced through the air and felled the bull. Immediately, the Little Wise Guys (christened contemptuously by their rescuer) wanted to learn the use of the boomerang, and Daredevil complied. Another friendship was formed, along with a partnership destined eventually to ease Daredevil out of his own comic.

Two issues later, *Daredevil* #15, a comic book classic, was published. Daredevil appeared in only some half-dozen panels in that comic book rarity, the death of a major character.

Rumble! Deadly, menacing with the Wise Guys' football team pitted against the Steamrollers, a delinquent gang which preferred robbery and vandalism to athletics. Pee Wee was taken captive and Meatball, after knocking Scarecrow unconscious to keep him safe at home, started off alone to rescue Pee Wee.

Heavy snow was falling as Meatball neared Steamroller territory; the appearance of gang members caused him to hide in the icy waters of a dark river. Pee Wee was saved, but at the cost of Meatball's life— he had contracted double pneumonia. Death became a reality for the Little Wise Guys and, for the first time, for many comic book readers.

Curly, a member of the Steamrollers, felt himself responsible for Meatball's death and joined the Wise Guys to defeat his old gang. Curly (called that because he was bald, with just a Sluggo-type stubble on his pate) took Meatball's place as one of the Wise Guys, and the team membership remained unchanged through the course of the series.

The title of the book remained *Daredevil,* though it was occasionally subordinate to the names of Pee Wee and the Little Wise Guys on the cover. (Pee Wee, feeling his name to be undignified, later took the name Slugger.) Daredevil eventually left the strip; he was absent for a long time as the guest of a Middle Eastern potentate, then returned to quit crimefighting and join the Air Force. The kids didn't even miss him.

Charles Biro emerges as one of the truly great writers in comic book literature. He believed, and still does, not only in telling a good story but also in imparting a message or moral with each story. He

wrote without sermonizing; his characters acted and spoke for themselves to get across the point Biro wished to make.

The three books he wrote for—*Boy Comics* (with Crimebuster and his monkey Squeeks), *Daredevil,* and *Crime Does Not Pay*—at one point were the top three sellers in comics, at a time when there were over 500 comic book titles on the market.

Biro was versatile. As a favor, asked by a harried editor at Hillman Periodicals to create a really outstanding character, Biro gave him Airboy. It was quite a favor: Airboy was Hillman's star character from 1942 well into 1953.

Biro was one of the crusaders in the comic book field. Firmly believing that comics had something worthwhile to offer, Biro sought another term to describe them. He came up with "Illustories," a name which never caught on but which is certainly a more apt description of the work Biro was doing.

Today, Biro is with the National Broadcasting Company in New York City and has worked on the creation of sets for top television shows.

The Young Allies had two famous members: Bucky Barnes, youthful fighting companion of Captain America, and Toro, the kid counterpart of that scorching nemesis of gangsters, the Human Torch.

Even before *Young Allies* #1, Summer 1941, hit the newsstands, its members, except Toro, had appeared in Captain America stories. Unnamed individually except for Bucky, the Allies were then only minor characters known as the Sentinels of Liberty.

In the first issue of their own book, Toro joined the group, immediately competing for leadership with Bucky. It took six issues before the feud was resolved, with Bucky finally the accepted leader. Toro, however, never slackened his conviction that the Torch was a better crimefighter than Captain America.

Young Allies featured high-powered action from the start. Their first enemy was none other than the infamous Red Skull, whom even the Nazis considered evil, though he was on their side. Torch and Captain America took part in the first adventure and some of the later ones—which didn't hurt the strip. Neither did the fact that Stan Lee was the series' editorial and art director almost from the beginning, nor the fact that Otto Binder wrote their early stories.

The lesser-known Young Allies were Knuckles, a tough kid blessed with the gentle name of Percival O'Toole; Jeff Sandervilt; Henry "Tubby" Tinkle; and Whitewash Jones. Marring the strip was Whitewash—drawn as a caricature of the American Negro, replete with rolling eyes, zoot-suit clothing, and minstrel-show dialogue.

Young Allies ran 20 issues in their own magazine. They also appeared in such other Timely Publications as *Marvel Mystery, Sub-Mariner, Kid Komix, Amazing Comics, Mystic,* and *Complete Comics.* They really got around.

The existence of Bucky beyond the years of World War II (the last issue of *Young Allies* was dated October 1946) may prove confusing to historians of comic book lore. Because, when Marvel Comics revived Captain America in 1964, Bucky was gone. Marvel said he had been killed while diverting a buzz-bomb type missile back in the war days, which certainly shook the faith of those who recalled Bucky's adventures with the Allies, and with Captain America as late as 1954—long after the war had ended.

Noting that comics of the forties were mirroring the effect of the war years presents a one-sided picture, and it should be made clear that comics also reflected other cultural, sociological, and economic aspects of a decade mixed with the problems, pains, and happiness common to any time.

One such problem is juvenile delinquency, and a kid gang called the Newsboy Legion kept their guardian, the Guardian, busy keeping them on the straight-and-narrow.

Star Spangled Comics for April 1942 introduced the Newsboy Legion—Big Words, Tommy, Gabby, and Scrapper, typical comic book kid-gang members. They had the makings of first-class juvenile delinquents. All four were orphans living in an unsavory section of Central City (later called New York City) known as Suicide Slum. The area also happened to be the beat of rookie policeman Jim Harper.

Harper had his troubles with Suicide Slum hoodlums right from the start. He was attacked during off-duty hours and severely beaten. The beating was intended to keep him in line; it had the opposite effect.

"This is the last straw," Harper said. "A guy can take just so much!" Spying a costume shop, he slipped inside and took several garments, leaving money behind while the store's proprietor was busy elsewhere. In full array, Harper went forth, thinking. "I probably look like a comic magazine superhero, out to grab crime by the horns!"

His battle attire was a costume of blue and gold, complete with a shield shaped like a policeman's badge. As the Guardian, Harper could go places and employ means a licensed law enforcer could not have used under legal circumstances. He confronted his former assailants and delivered a brutal thrashing of his own.

One of the punched-up thugs managed to gasp, "Who are you?" and Harper replied, "Why, I'm sort of . . . a . . . er . . . Guardian, I guess! *Yes, a Guardian of Society!* Against your kind!" Newspapers the next day carried headline accounts of this new crusher of crime, and the Newsboy Legion (they called themselves this because they all sold papers) were aware a happening had taken place in Suicide Slum.

They encountered Harper when he arrested them for stealing tools to build a clubhouse. Harper, to keep them out of the reformatory, agreed to be their (that word again) guardian. He was given a "few months" to effect rehabilitation of the boys.

It wasn't easy. The Newsboy Legion didn't like cops. It took all that Harper (and the Guardian) could do to turn the kids into law-abiding citizens eager to combat crime rather than commit it.

Until the strip's end in 1947, the Guardian rescued the kids or the kids rescued him in each story. Everybody played a little game of pretending not to know the real identity of the Guardian, though the kids would have had to be cretins not to know it was Harper. But that was the story line established by the originators—again Joe Simon and Jack Kirby—and it was maintained. The tedium was lessened by the refreshing artwork of Joe Kubert, which graced some of the stories in 1945.

It seemed to be the vogue in the forties to have a superhero as the mentor of a comic book clique. *Speed Comics* took up the trend with one of their big-name stars, Captain Freedom.

Newspaper publisher Don Wright constantly forsook the office to don the scarlet, blue, yellow, and white-star-flecked colors of Captain Freedom to aid his friends, the Young Defenders: Joanie, Lefty, Slim, and Whitey. Whitey was eventually replaced by Beanie (another bald kid), but otherwise the lineup remained static.

On covers, the Young Defenders battled Japanese and Germans, not only in the company of Captain Freedom, but also alongside *Speed Comics'* other notables, Black Cat and Shock Gibson.

Speed's covers were more than just a come-on to buy. Inside each issue was a text feature called "The Story Behind the Cover." A quotation from one of these is an example of the lurid turn comics writing could (and often did) take:

> But Captain Freedom reached forward quickly and in the brief moment that meant life or death to the Black Cat he seized her black-satin-garmented form before she could drop into the hideous acid. One yellow rat secured his Tommy gun, but before he got to use it Lefty was on him like a flash. He twisted one of the Jap's arms backward into a hammerlock until he cracked the limb just below the elbow. Screaming, the Jap fell into a faint. Another Jap had run into a corridor to get his sub-machine gun, but

just as he made ready to give Captain Freedom a burst of Jap lead, Joanie
sent fifty bullets into his chest. Joanie and Beanie had spotted a fixed machine gun in a crevice up on the wall, and anticipating a Jap retaliation
thought it would be wise to cover the Americans' sally. It was wise! The
Jap was dead before he hit the ground. One Jap lunged at Shock's unpro-
tected back, but this effort also came to grief as Beanie let fly one of his
largest stones smack into the bone behind the Nip's ear. With a low moan
the fiend slumped over and then lay still. "The only death list made out is
going to be Japan's!" shouted Captain Freedom. "After 'em!" cried the
Black Cat, and the Americans roared out into the night on the trail of
"HIM." Read the next issue of SPEED COMICS and find out the true identity of "HIM."

Without editorial comment (except to mention that all punctuation is as it appeared in the comic), let us roar out of *Speed Comics*
and investigate the ranks of the costumed kid gangs.

By their colors you knew them, which was a blessing, because the
gangs were so similar in appearance and purpose that they started to
blur after a while, even for the most enthusiastic reader.

DC's *Sensation Comics* had Little Boy Blue and the Blue Boys,
who appeared in the first 81 issues of that comic and made guest appearances in *Flash Comics* and the one-shot *Big All-American Comics.*

Little Boy Blue was Tommy Rogers, son of a newly appointed
district attorney who was out to rid their small home town of gang-
mob rule. Tommy wanted to help but was told to leave the job to
adults. So, Tommy and his friends Tubby and Toughy donned costumes and small town gangsterdom knew new terror.

All three dressed in blue, of course, with Little Boy Blue's outfit
distinguished from the others by a red hood and a chiffon scarf flowing back from the top. To summon his Blue Boys, he used a curved
horn and the sound of the "clarion call of justice" often echoed
through the tiny town as he stood on a rooftop silhouetted against a
full moon. It captured the imagination of the youthful reader and
this, plus the fact that they were just boys with no super powers,
helped to make the strip long-lived.

Other gangs, differing little from each other, were the Four Com-
rades (*Startling Comics*), Young Robinhood and His Band (*Boy
Comics*), Boy Heroes (*All New Comics*), Junior Rangers (*Headline
Comics*), Tough Kid Squad (*Tough Kid Squad*—one issue only),
Little Dynamite and His Gang (*Boy Comics*), Boy Champions
(*Green Lama Comics*). . . .

But you get the idea. The members of these gangs were tough
kids, fat kids, dumb kids, smart kids who used big words, and Negro
stereotype kids. An article listing them all would amount to a full
catalogue.

But there were standouts, such as Joe Simon and Jack Kirby's *Boys Ranch,* a regrettably short-lived Harvey title featuring Dandy Dolan, youngish ex-Union soldier; Wabash, a farmerish lad; Angel, a long-haired blond about twelve who was deadly with guns; Wee Willie Weehawken, an old Gabby Hayes-type of comic relief character; and Clay Duncan, adult guardian of the group.

Fine plots and good comic-book writing made the series memorable. In one story, "Mother Delilah," a saloon girl named Delilah won Angel's affection (no easy thing: he was a very bitter, unhappy, and dangerous kid), cut his hair, disarmed him, and made him a laughing-stock.

When his hair regrew, Angel returned to the town (the marvelously named Four Massacres). Backed by Duncan and the others, Angel shot it out with Delilah's backers. Delilah, who had grown honestly fond of Angel, deliberately stopped a bullet meant for him.

As Angel held the dying Delilah, crying for one of the few times in his life, a poet-dreamer who frequented the bar said, softly, "The innocent weep for the wicked, who in dying for others, are innocent in turn . . . Love's ever new—as morning's dew—and hating is as old as time!"

On the lighter side, there was the unnamed boys' club of *Little Lulu,* published by Dell Comics and credited to Lulu's creator, Marge—Marjorie Henderson Buell—but actually the work of writer-artist John Stanley. Lulu's fat little friend, Tubby Tompkins, was a member of the leaderless gang, which also included Willy, Eddie, and Iggy. In the best kid-gang tradition, Iggy was bald.

This gang's adventures consisted primarily of trying to keep Lulu out of the club and avoiding combat with the tough West Side Boys. It was all in fun.

Mostly in fun was Walt Kelly's *Our Gang* which ran for seven years in *Our Gang Comics,* eventually giving way to Tom and Jerry. The series was based on the MGM short comedy series, but Kelly soon adapted it out of all resemblance.

For one thing, he altered the Negro stereotype kid, Buckwheat, saddled on him by the movie version, to make him almost indistinguishable from the rest of the kids except by color. Bucky, as he became known, was one of the very, very few non-stereotyped Negroes in the comic books of the forties.

Our Gang dealt mostly in comedy, but they occasionally fought Japanese, counterfeiters, and pirates, occasionally getting embroiled in multi-installment serials that took them far afield, even to head-hunter country in the Amazon jungles.

The Pie-Face Prince of Pretzelburg (otherwise known as Dimwitri) was one of the wondrous creations of George Carlson, whose contemporary fables ran for forty-two issues of *Jingle Jangle Comics*.

Ibis the Invincible was born in ancient Egypt, slept for 4,000 years, and awoke in 1940 to find himself reincarnated as a comic book hero.

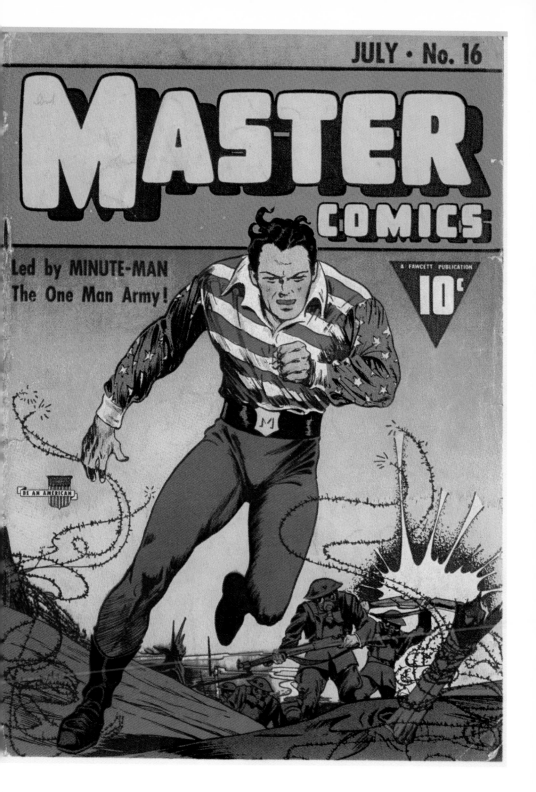

Minute-Man, secretly Private Jack Weston (he was later promoted to lieutenant), fought crime and
pies on the home front.

Spy Smasher was another one of those millionaire playboys who, during World War II, donned a costume to aid the war effort.

Batman was a frightening comic hero, often appearing in menacing silhouette. Copyright 1945 by Detective Comics, Inc., whose name was changed to National Periodical Publications, Inc., and reprinted by its permission.

This is the first meeting of the Justice Society of America. Evil-doers, beware! Copyright 1940 by All American Comics, Inc., and assigned to National Periodical Publications, Inc., and reprinted by its permission.

This is one of the half-dozen rarest comic books known, commanding $250 and more in dealers' catalogs. Its most interesting features are the origin stories of the Human Torch and the Sub-Mariner.

The Human Torch wasn't human. He was an android, created in a huge test-tube, complete with rubbery-looking tights. He and his sidekick, Toro, a miniature Human Torch, had the disconcerting habit of bursting into flame indoors.

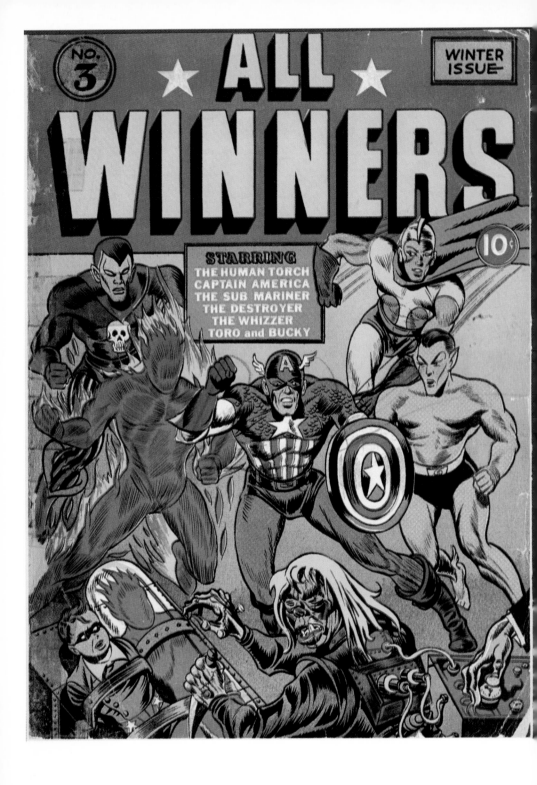

The All Winners Squad included Captain America and Bucky, the Human Torch and Toro, a flying super-heroine named Miss America (no relation to the Captain), and a super-fast man called Whizzer.

The Little Wise Guys, a kid gang associated with Daredevil, grew so popular they eventually eased Daredevil out of his own comic book. The kids didn't even miss him.

"We're a few against many … but how those Nazis run when we get started!" Copyright 1947 by National Comics Publications, Inc., whose name was changed to National Periodical Publications, Inc., and reprinted by its permission.

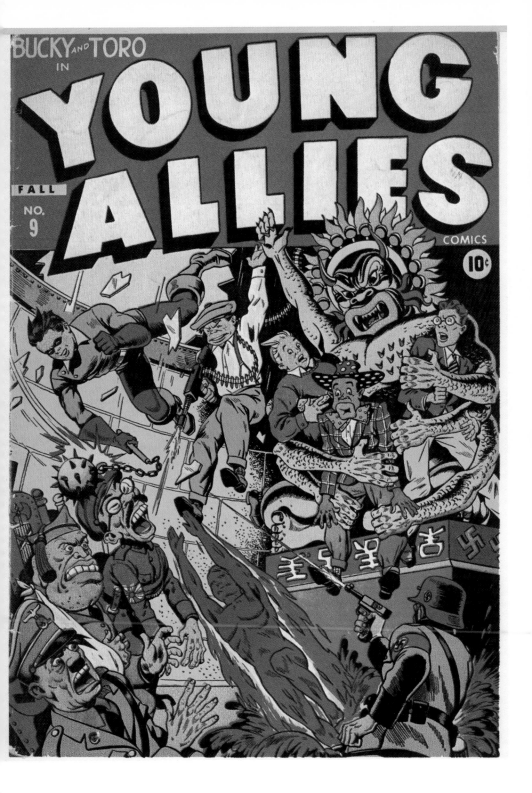

In addition to Bucky and Toro, the junior sidekicks of Captain America and the Human Torch, the Young Allies included Knuckles, Jeff Sandervilt, Henry "Tubby" Tinkle, and Whitewash Jones.

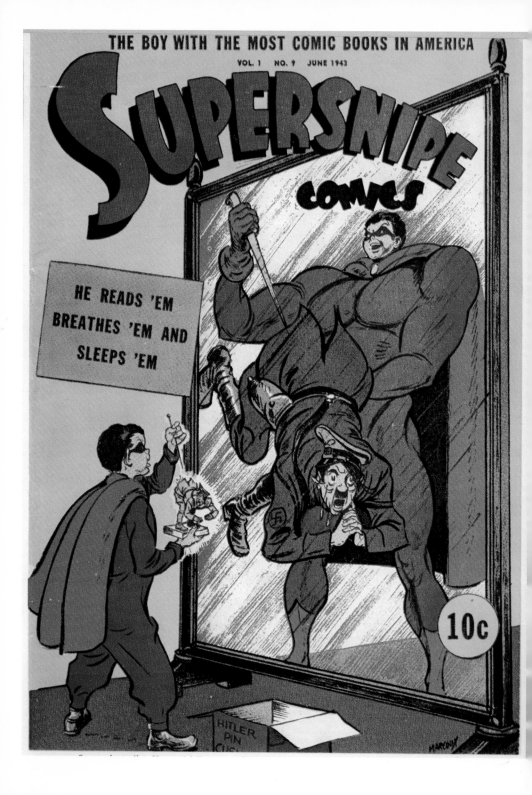

Supersnipe, alias Koppy McFad, was the boy with the most comic books in America. This charming parody of the whole super-hero idea wore red flannel underwear, his father's blue lodge cape and a domino mask.

Fine plots and good writing made this group stand out from the usual kid gang hi-jinks. The Boy's Ranch Team was made up of Dandy Dolan, Wabash, Angel, Wee Willie Weehawken, and Clay Duncan.

E. C. Segar's Popeye was part vulgarity, part compassion, a bit of raw aggression, a soupçon of protective gentleness, all spiced by violent waterfront humor and genuine "senskibiliky." "I yam what I yam, an' tha's all I yam!"

The strip continued until Kelly dropped it to syndicate his (deservedly) successful *Pogo,* which he had developed in *Animal Comics* since 1942, simultaneously with *Our Gang.*

Another lighter-side kid gang was composed of Herlock Dolmes, who fancied himself the world's greatest young sleuth and wore a long checkered coat and deerstalker cap; boy inventor Ulysses Q. Wacky; Trouble, a jinxed boy whose real name—which must have been part of the jinx—was Wilferd Berlad; and Roxy Adams, self-styled "girl guerilla."

Leader of the gang was Koppy McFad, alias Supersnipe, "the boy with the most comic books in America." (All those comics were published by Street and Smith—*Doc Savage, The Shadow,* etc.— who also published *Supersnipe.*)

Unlike Ed Wheelan's Comics McCormick, "the world's No. 1 comic book fan," who daydreamed adventures with parodies of popular comic heroes, Supersnipe actually fought crime, sometimes successfully.

He wore red flannel underwear, his father's blue lodge cape, and a domino mask. He remained a believable eight-year-old boy through all his adventures.

His only super-power was a one-time-only flying ability, achieved when Wacky made him a patched-rubber suit and filled it with helium. The Yapburg Fire Department tried to bring him down, a feat finally accomplished by Roxy with a well-aimed arrow.

Supersnipe stories were written by Edward I. Gruskin and drawn by George Marcoux. Gruskin, who wrote many while on combat duty with the army in Europe, told in the December 1947-January 1948 issue of *Supersnipe Comics* how the series was conceived.

"The original concept of Supersnipe was that of the late George Marcoux, the finest artist with whom it has been my good fortune to work. Supersnipe was 'born' spontaneously one day as George was watching a Labor Day parade in his hometown, Yonkers, N.Y. The floats and official cars, the marching men and women all passed by in dignified splendor. Then there was a break in the procession. The scream of a siren turned all eyes toward a ten-year-old boy, leaning low over the handle-bars of his speeding bicycle as he peddled up the boulevard, before the startled onlookers. A small cape flew from his shoulders, his front-wheel siren screamed his defiance of some invisible menace! A woman behind George clucked her tongue and muttered, 'Guttersnipe!' George's face lit up as he turned to her and said, 'You're wrong, Madam—that's SUPERsnipe!' "

Supersnipe and his pals mixed it up until 1949. Then came the April day when the New York *Times* carried the headline, STREET & SMITH GIVING UP PULPS. A smaller headline carried the message, "Oldest Publishers of Thriller Magazines also Scuttling Their Comic Books." The comics were *Buffalo Bill Picture Stories, Top Secrets, The Shadow, True Sports . . .* and *Supersnipe.*

The reasons they gave explained why many comic titles of all companies were folding. "A marked decline also has been noted in the sale of the comics, particularly since the end of the war. Reasons given for the decrease in sales of both 'pulps' and comics vary. The growing popularity of television is most frequently mentioned. Persons close to the field point out, too, that in the case of the pulps, readers have grown tired of the same 'format' and are turning to other types of fiction." The *Times* didn't say it, but the last statement applied equally well to comics.

Comic books muddled on, with some bright spots in the bland procession of cowboys, spacemen, and alien monsters, plus a few remaining superheroes who didn't wear their capes well.

The sixties brought back the mighty men and women in droves, but they didn't bring back the kid gangs. The few new kid cliques to appear seemed uninspired by comparison with the old. What happens when just anyone is admitted to a gang has been demonstrated by National's Legion of Super-Heroes, a feature of *Adventure Comics* since 1962.

The result is a population explosion on a superscale, with Superboy, Supergirl, Timber Wolf, Ultra Boy, Element Lad, Dream Girl, Matter-eater Lad, Colossal Boy, Shrinking Violet, Saturn Girl, Princess Projecta, Karate Kid, Lightning Lad, Brainiac 5, Bouncing Boy, Duo Damsel, Invisible Kid, Chemical King, Phantom Girl, Shadow Lass . . .

Not only that, but there is a Legion of Substitute Heroes, less kindly known as Legion Rejects. These include Polar Boy, Night Girl, Chlorophyll Kid, Fire Lad, Stone Boy and Color Kid. There are even stories about the Adult Legion and, to show how completely ridiculous something can become, a Legion of Super-Pets, featuring Comet, the Super-Horse; Krypto, the Super-Dog; Beppo, the Super-Monkey; Streaky, the Super-Cat; and Proty, a sort of Super-Amoeba.

National sicced another unbelievable kid team onto its reading public in 1964, the Teen Titans. This group—Robin, Kid Flash, Aqualad, and Wonder Girl—is a group of costumed teenyboppers who stay out after curfew to make sure ordinary teenagers sleep well.

   Marvel gave the teen scene the X-Men in 1963. Cyclops, Angel, Beast, Iceman, and Marvel Girl are supposedly teenage mutants, each with special powers. None of them look to be part of the under-twenty set; blame it on mutation.

   With the exception of National's Kid Guerillas of Unit 3, war orphans who fought in *Our Army at War,* none of the kid gangs of the sixties resembled the kid clubs of years gone by. An almost indefinable quality is missing. The kid groups of yesterday had a magic about them; not a magic evoked by present-day nostalgia, but one created in the midst of chaos. In a time when escape literature and youthful heroes were a needed respite from the frightening possibility of daily destruction, the comic books and their kid gangs answered the need.

INTRODUCTION TO

A SWELL BUNCH OF GUYS

OKAY, so you're a superhero. You spend a hard day saving the world from an assortment of mad scientists, crime syndicates, alien monsters, and so on, and then you come home to . . . what? A drab and lonely bachelor apartment? A splendid but equally lonely palace? Or, if you do surround yourself with a corps of fawning admirers, does their companionship not lack a certain something? Admit it, you'd give your best cape and tights to have some peers around you!

At least that's one school of thought, and its outgrowth has led to a number of the most popular and long-lived comic book features, as well as certain others which did not last so long. Groups like the Seven Soldiers of Victory, the Marvel Family, the All-Winners Squad, and others more obscure, have long since passed from the multicolored comics page. But the all-time favorite hero team, the Justice Society of America, not only outlasted its rivals of the Golden Age, but has made a comeback in recent years, albeit in slightly altered form.

Jim Harmon, born in 1933, suffered from poor health during most of his boyhood. As a result, his formal education was spotty, to say the least, but he made up for that by becoming a demon comic reader and radio listener (in the era of dramatic radio, that is). A freelance writer in recent years, he has sold over two dozen mystery and adventure novels under a variety of bylines. He has edited *Fantastic Monsters* magazine, and written several films including one with the unlikely title of *The Lemon Grove Kids Meet the Monsters*. His nonfiction book *The Great Radio Heroes* was, in his own words, "a modest best-seller" in its Doubleday hardbound edition, and was reprinted in paperback by Ace Books. A second volume on great radio comedians followed, and Jim promises still more to come.

In this chapter he chronicles the career of the Justice Society of America from its inception to its death and revival. A stirring tale!

CHAPTER 7

A SWELL BUNCH OF GUYS

by JIM HARMON

★★★

When comic books were new and still a dime a copy, few happenings on the colored page could cause as much talk and commotion at Lincoln Grade School in Mount Carmel, Illinois, as those occasions on which the hero of one book met the hero of another in a single story. Today, when comic book collecting, like most things, has been taken over by grownups from the kids, and has been organized and given a specialized jargon all its own, this summit meeting of secretive superhumans has been given a specific name. It is a "crossover."

We didn't know what to call it in the early forties, but our interest in it was as mighty as that of participants in the event. We were intrigued when Captain Marvel greeted his rival for fame and glory, Spy Smasher, like the good-natured Big Red Cheese the captain was. We were fascinated when the Sub-Mariner and the Human Torch met and instantly hated each other, just as water hates fire.

And we were absolutely enthralled when virtually all of the leading heroes of the Superman DC Publications line of comics met on the field of honor in *All Star Comics,* in a four-color tournament of invincible heroes, an Olympian festival of masked and hooded gods, a climactic Armageddon of the most sense-drenching comic book spectacular conceivable by man or boy.

This fascination with the crossover of one comic book hero into the world of another was an occasion equaled in fascination only by our interest in how each hero came to be, and his purpose in existing (other than to fill colorful pages and earn children's dimes). Again, the specialists have devised a term for these special events. They are "origin stories."

These costumed adventurers were *our* heroes, after all, and we naturally assumed that they had to have many of the same character-

istics, problems, and experiences that we all had. Like us, their readers, they had to find out where they came from and where they were
going. These biographical realities were required to make acceptable the biological fantasies of their existence.

Once convinced of the individual hero's existence there came a
need to place him in his society. We couldn't believe that Superman
was unique—after all, he had come from a whole planet full of supermen. And we couldn't believe that he would be content to associate forever and exclusively with people as mundane as reporter
Lois Lane and editor Perry White. Sometime, somewhere, even Superman must yearn for the companionship of his fellows, his comrades, his peers.

At times we kids fantasized such meetings between Superman
and Captain Marvel—his nearest compeer in the comics pages—all
unaware of things like copyrights and even antitrust laws that might
intervene. After all, every man—even Superman—needs a friend.
Even Superman had to feel himself part of society.

And in due course Superman's publishers provided him with an
appropriate society. It was the Justice Society of America.

The Justice Society was a "bunch of swell guys" in the words of the
Society's most enthusiastic member, Johnny Thunder. They were a
more remarkable group of friends than the Three Musketeers, of more
amazing powers, peculiarities, and inclinations. Their comradeship
was not, of course, so well defined as that of Dumas' adventurers, or
even as well documented as that of another trio in a coexisting medium, Jack, Doc, and Reggie of radio's *I Love a Mystery*.

But comic books, like radio, required us to use our imaginations
to fill in the details. What off-stage activities we created for our heroes to while away the weeks between the appearances of their published adventures! Did bright-clad adventurer meet bright-clad
adventurer somewhere in the menace-laden heavens, in incidents
unrecorded on those monthly pages?

Being bound by similar interests and occupations, how could the
masked and more-than-human crusaders who eventually became the
Justice Society of America not become also the closest of compatri-
ots? Their conspiracies, their goals, their passions, their world views
were all the same, and the same as ours, their admirers. They were
not only the best of friends to each other, but to us as well.

Our friends first got together in the winter, 1940, issue of *All Star
Comics*. Two other issues of the new quarterly had already appeared,
and had featured several of the same heroes—but only in individual
stories. *All Star* started life as a comics anthology featuring the most

popular of its publishers' features from other titles. This was not an uncommon practice at all, and both the DC line and several other houses repeatedly got added mileage from their successful features by starting titles of this sort.

But a dramatically new event took place in the third *All Star:* the heroes met face to face. The cover showed us the original eight members of the JSA seated placidly around a great circular table. Their costumes flashed vivid colors, predominantly scarlet and gold, picked out with a blur of green here, a patch of blue there. But the scene itself is too orderly, too businesslike to generate excitement. It looked almost like a grammar school class portrait.

But the editors must have liked it, for the picture is repeated on the first page of the magazine, as the splash drawing. Part of it is used later on as an internal ad. And it occurs still again, on the last page of the issue. There they sit, the mighty figures of the Atom, Sandman, the Spectre, the Flash, Hawkman, Dr. Fate, Green Lantern, and Hour-Man. They look for all the world like the entertainment committee of a junior high school masquerade party, posing for a portrait in their costumes the night of the dance.

Who has called these superhuman figures into conference? Who could exercise such influence over the grim figure of the Spectre, from whose black and umbrous eye sockets could spring fires to consume whole planets? What authority could command the appearance of Hawkman, who could soar as free as his namesake on huge, graceful wings of mysterious Ninth Metal? To whose will would the fabled power of Green Lantern bend? You never knew at the time, and it was just as well, for this first meeting of the Justice Society of America was called by a group of men in white collars and shirt sleeves gathered in a Lexington Avenue publisher's office in New York.

This new version of *All Star Comics* was conceived by the editorial staff of All-American Comics, Inc., a temporary spin-off of the Superman DC operation that was later reabsorbed into the parent firm. The staff included M. C. Gaines, managing editor and publisher; Sheldon Mayer, editor; and one of the pillars of the writing staff, Gardner F. Fox, a man whose writing credits would eventually include many historical and science-fiction novels as well as vast numbers of comics.

Fox wrote that first Justice Society story, and the next, and stayed on, in fact, for some three dozen of them. John Broome took over with the 37th JSA adventure (in *All Star* issue 39—remember those two pre-JSA editions) and continued to the end of the series. Sheldon Mayer remained as editor until issue 41, when he was replaced

ON EARTH-ONE, THE JUSTICE LEAGUE OF AMERICA HAS NEVER BEEN DEFEATED IN ITS CEASELESS WAR AGAINST CRIME AND INJUSTICE...

ON EARTH-TWO, THE JUSTICE SOCIETY OF AMERICA HAS TASTED ONLY VICTORY AS IT BATTLES AGAINST THE FORCES OF EVIL...

NOW MEET THE SUPER-POWERED BEINGS OF EARTH-THREE--TRIUMPHANT IN EVERY ONE OF THEIR MISSIONS...

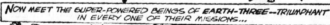

WHEN THE SUPER-BEINGS OF EARTH-THREE BRAZENLY ATTACK THE JUSTICE LEAGUE-- TO BE FOLLOWED UP BY AN ATTACK ON THE JUSTICE SOCIETY -- IT MARKS THE BEGINNING OF A SPECTACULAR INTER-DIMENSIONAL STRUGGLE THAT SHAKES THE VERY STRUCTURE OF THREE WORLDS!

CRISIS ON EARTH-THREE!

JUSTICE LEAGUE OF AMERICA, No. 29, August, 1964. Published monthly, with the exception of Jan., April, July and Oct. by NA-TIONAL PERIODICAL PUBLICATIONS, INC. 2nd and Dickey Streets, SPARTA, ILL. Editorial, Executive offices and Subscriptions, 575 LEX-INGTON AVE., NEW YORK 22, N.Y. Julius Schwartz, Editor. SECOND CLASS POSTAGE PAID AT SPARTA, ILL. under the act of March 5, 1879. Yearly subscription in the U.S., 95c including postage. For- $1.00 in American funds. Canada, $1.15 in American funds.

For advertising rates address Richard A. Feldon & Co., 205 East 42nd St., New York 17, N.Y. Copyright 1964 by National Periodical Publications, Inc. All rights reserved under International and Pan-American Copyright Conventions. Except for those who have authorized use of their names, the stories, characters and incidents mentioned in this periodical are entirely imaginary and fictitious, and no identification with actual persons, living or dead, is intended or should be inferred.   Printed in U.S.A.

by Whitney Ellsworth who worked with Broome until the very idea of a Justice Society seemed to lose its appeal to young readers (who were turning increasingly to crime and horror, westerns and funny animals and teenage comedy—anything except the fortunately, temporarily worn out costumed adventure heroes).

Associate editors who helped to plot these mind-staggering epics and to guide them through the publication mill seemed able to hold onto their positions (not to say their mental stability) for even shorter periods. Jerry Bails, one of the new breed of comics enthusiasts whose interests are cerebral as well as adrenal, has researched even this bit of history. He lists the *All Star* assistants as Ted Udall (1940-42 and 44-46), Dorothy Khubichek (1942-44), Robert Kanigher (1946-51) and Julius Schwartz (1944-51). Mark the name of Mr. Schwartz for future reference.

Only one man lasted through almost the whole glorious mess—art director Sol Harrison. This proves, no doubt, that Art can rise above human troubles, or even superhuman ones.

I'm afraid that such statistics as those I've just cited interest me now only slightly more than they did when I plunked my shiny dime down for a glossy copy of *All Star Comics.* As with the movies I saw, I was more interested in the stars in *All Star* than I was in the technical crew behind them. Oh, I was aware—we all were, back in Mount Carmel (and of course millions of kids were, wherever the comics reached)—that there was a writer behind those melodramatic SOCKs and WHAMs, that there was an artist behind those flowing capes and muscle-packed tights, even that there must be an editor overseeing the whole operation, and a production crew somewhere in the wings, and so on. But the *stars*—I endowed them with more wondrous life than even the strange powers of Dr. Fate or the magic ring of Green Lantern could bestow.

If I had little interest in the identity of the costume designers, I assuredly was fascinated by the uniforms worn by the All Stars themselves. A comic character virtually *is* his costume. His working clothes express his profession, his ideals, in brief, his character. Small wonder that modern collectors of comic book minutiae as well as the comics themselves will spend long hours discussing such earth-shaking matters as the changes in Hawkman's belt buckle. (He seems to have had at least two of them, one white, one yellow.)

Perhaps Hawkman wishes to be especially sure that he doesn't lose his trousers, since he already has to do without a shirt. His rippling muscles are accented only by criss-crossed yellow straps that hold on his great gray wings. His tight pants are green and he wears the superhero's frequent badge of insecurity, an additional pair of red shorts, over them. These and his red boots seem to come from the same outfitter that Superman uses. A golden hawk's head for a combination hat and mask completes Hawkman's ensemble. From this costume, we know that Hawkman can fly like a bird, swoop down like a hawk, and that he likes to show off his biceps, triceps, and pectorals.

The Spectre shares one particular characteristic with the "winged wonder" that might not be immediately discernible. While at first glance he seems to be wearing long underwear of a conservative white beneath a sickly green cape, cowl, gloves, boots, and slightly baggy trunks—a closer inspection, starting perhaps from those frighteningly dark eye sockets, reveals that the "ghostly guardian" is not wearing white tights at all. He is showing large portions of his dead white skin. Appropriate, since he is a walking (and flying) corpse. A Spectre indeed.

The occult powers of Dr. Fate are not revealed in so supernaturally eerie an appearance. He does appear formidable enough with bulging muscles revealed through blue tights, set off by a yellow-gold cape and shorts. An air of mystery is added by the matching golden helm that totally conceals his features, and a golden amulet completes the costume.

Green Lantern wears a red shirt with a device symbolizing his source of power as well as his name; the shirt is the standard skin-tight superhero model, although it had originally been rather baggy, and looked more like a bulky sweater. He also sports tight green trousers, red leggings, and a high-collared purple cape which, to-gether with a rather grim-looking eye mask, contrives to make him look sinister and mysterious. Yet it doesn't quite come off—a blond young man looking rather like Buster Crabbe can't look really sinister. Still, that is the "emerald crusader."

And speaking of the emerald crusader, the ghostly guardian, the winged wonder and all the rest—accustom yourself to these epithets and to many more like them. Comic book script writers and editors were seldom content with a simple *name* for their protagonists; almost from the start they were giving them nicknames as well. Thus the Phantom was known as "the ghost who walks." Superman was "the man of steel." Batman and Robin were "the dynamic duo." And so on, endlessly.

Back at the Justice Society, the black cowl of Hour-Man was also presumably intended to impart an ominous quality to his gaze. It looks rather like the green cowl of the Spectre, enough to make them look like brothers, or at least as if they were drawn by the same artist. (They were.) Hour-Man had an almost neurotic compulsion to check the time; he even carried a small hour-glass with him all the time, dangling from a cord round his neck and bouncing against his ebony shirt.

He wasn't just nervous, though. His super powers were provided by a sort of early technology pep pill, and wore off after exactly sixty minutes. What would have happened if he'd suddenly gone non-super while, for instance, holding an ocean liner above his head, is horrible to contemplate.

The Flash and the Atom were well matched in name, appearance, and personality. The one was a modern Mercury complete with winged feet and winged helmet, although he wore a few more clothes than his classical counterpart: blue pants and a crimson shirt shot across with a jagged *flash* of lightning; the hero's namesake as well as his symbol. The other—the Atom—was a tough little guy and, I've always suspected, a bit *mean*, too. He wore leather wrist bands to protect his wrists because his muscles were so powerful, just like all tough, mean little guys. His short pants seemed to be made out of brown leather, his legs were bare, and his shirt was open to the navel. A blue cloak and hood completely concealed his face— he sure didn't want anybody to know who he was. And you can easily guess that he went around picking fights with lumbering tough truck drivers who didn't realize how tough he was, and whom he accused of being crooks.

Then there is the Sandman. His costume is . . . are you ready? . . . a bright green double-breasted business suit, lavender cape, orange gloves, a bright golden slouch hat, and a yellow-and-blue gas mask that serves the additional purpose of concealing his face. Now all superheroes have their weaknesses, or at least they ought to. Making them totally invincible and invulnerable makes reader identification difficult and tends to make the stories all end on page two, when the hero steps in and-pow! ends the menace.

I have long suspected that in Sandman's case his fatal weakness was color blindness. The gas mask made sense in the early days when he put his foes to sleep with a gas gun . . . hence, at least allegorically, his name. Hence, also, a slightly suspicious similarity to the Green Hornet of comic book and radio fame. Later, the Sandman traded his garish outfit for a more conventional set of superheroic tights, and his gas gun for a harpoon gun (borrowed, perhaps, from the Tarantula) that he used to facilitate swinging from building to building. By then he had abandoned the gas mask—he didn't need it anymore.

The only member of the Justice Society who never wore a special costume was the bumbling, blond Johnny Thunder. However, he did seem to buy his bilious green suits off the same plain pipe rack that provided the Sandman's garb.

These were the original members of the Justice Society of America, who gathered that day in 1940 at the Society's charter meeting. And four of them, older, wiser, and somewhat changed by the passing years, were to be around for the very last meeting more than a decade later.

So were we, a good many of the original readers—also a bit the worse for wear.

That very first meeting, the origin story of the JSA which fascinates so many devotees of that biggest mass "crossover" of them all, had little in common with later lodge nights except perhaps the blundering Johnny Thunder.

The very first panel of the story (after a reproduction of the cover scene of the costumed knights at their round table) reveals Johnny shaking his fist at a rack of comic magazines including *Adventure Comics, More Fun,* and *Flash.* "The Flash—Spectre—Hawkman!" Johnny grumbles. "All members of the Justice Society! Say, you'd think those guys would invite me. . . .", And suddenly, miraculously, Johnny is plunked down in the midst of the JSA meeting.

How come?

Johnny was a very unconventional hero. He wore only street clothes (this in common with the excellent Sparky Watts of *Big Shot Comics*), and he was *meant* to be funny (this also in common with Sparky). Johnny's "power" was command of a magical, intelligent thunderbolt which was portrayed as a kind of bright pink djinn with a jagged lightning-like tail instead of legs. The thunderbolt was summoned by the Badhnisian hex words *cei-u,* a fact of which Johnny was unaware. But every time Johnny pronounced the phonetic equivalent of *cei-u* ("Say you") in ordinary conversation—presto! the thunderbolt. He would hang around for one hour, then disappear again until Johnny accidentally said the magic phrase once more.

Once at the meeting, although he generally comes across as a bit of a lightweight with bad taste in clothing, Johnny does have one good idea. He proposes to the assembled crime fighters "Suppose you each tell the most exciting experience you ever had? That'll entertain everybody!"

The Atom replies "It's a good idea—but where is Superman, Batman and Robin? They'd have some good stories to tell!" Or even pointers on grammar.

"They would," the Flash agrees, "but since *we're* all here, some-body's got to look after things and protect people. . . ." As anybody who reads comic books must know, that somebody certainly wouldn't be the police.

Artist Everett E. Hibbard continued in his smooth but uninspired style out of this first introduction into an individual chapter featuring his regular character, the Flash, who saved a lost treasure at the bottom of the sea for a kindly old sailor.

The next element of the JSA story concerns not water but fire—*Men Who Could Live in Fire,* as Hawkman titles his own adventure. The artist as well as the hero changed here, and we saw the fabulous work of Sheldon Moldoff, whose figures were often inspired by Alex Raymond's *Flash Gordon* newspaper strip. Jules Feiffer suggests that one could almost prefer the Moldoff version to the original, because there is such a special feel and texture of opulence, a certain "comic book grandeur," in these pages.

Moldoff was a very uneven artist. His best work—on *Hawkman,* and on another DC feature, the *Black Pirate*—showed magnificent design and draftsmanship. His worst—one recalls an EC feature, *Moon Girl*—could range from the merely uninspired downward through the utterly inept. Some critics have been so unkind as to suggest that Moldoff's good work was all the product of his "swipe file," an almost universal device used by comic artists to keep up with particularly good work of their contemporaries—and that the bad work is Moldoff on his own. Perhaps. But let's be more charitable than that, and merely say, again, that he was uneven.

The story itself deals with Men of Fire brewing destruction in a bubbling volcano, and the way that Hawkman smites them down with a selection from his private collection of ancient weapons. "The Hammer of Thor! He was a blacksmith, so his hammer should do all right!" Wait a minute, wasn't it Vulcan who was a blacksmith? Oh well, Thor did have a hammer. And the best part of most Hawkman stories was not the plot but the art—watching the play of line and shadow and muscle as Hawkman leaps and flies and strikes and carries his half-clad girl friend, Shierra, to safety.

The safety of all the earth is at stake next, as the Spectre and his illustrator, Bernard Baily, take over. The ghostly guardian is given the task of ridding the planet of a gargoyle god, Oom, who is ever "thirsting to kill." The Spectre must take a "short cut through the 'L' dimension" by hitching a ride on a shooting star to finally reach the strange planet, ephemeral Yzgartyl, where he defeats the flame-breathing dragon who guards the Red Moon Stone of Yzgartyl.

Of course the Spectre could do this because he could do *anything*. That is, except totally die, or marry a girl. A persistent death wish and justified doubts as to his own virility once plagued the coldest and the mightiest of all comic book heroes. He was far more powerful than Superman, in fact as powerful as God, with whom the Spectre once discussed his problems (disembodied conversational balloons were tastefully employed). Instead of Death, the Spectre was rewarded with a return to mortal life, and his relationship with his girl friend grew considerably warmer, but he never married her, instead preferring to spend his evenings with the boys down at the Justice Society. His change of heart established only, no doubt, that he was (currently at least) human.

Following the ghostly guardian is an undistinguished story-telling session in which Hour-Man ("Tick Tock" Tyler) gets enough charge out of a Miraclo pill to defeat a whole mob of jewel thieves costumed exactly like himself. Baily drew this too.

Then there is a story told by the Sandman, and executed (I use the word advisedly) by Chad Grotsky, one of the most primitive workers of the *All Star* art staff. In this tale a mad scientist who turns rats, cats, and people into giants is sandbagged by Sandman's gas gun. (His victims went "Kaff! Kaff!" It was a perfect phonetic rendering of the sound made by the Green Hornet's gas gun victims on the radio.)

The Dr. Fate story rather echoes that of the Spectre, albeit somewhat faintly. The panels by Howard Sherman are securely nailed into place, but they seem wooden. Dr. Fate explains that ". . . I am not human . . . I never was a child . . . I had no youth—the Elder Gods created me just as I am now, and placed me here on earth to fight evil sorcery."

Dr. Fate is able to leave his lonely tower in the Salem foothills—the tower boasts neither window nor door—to save his girl friend, Inza, from "dead phantoms . . . risen from their graves by sorcery of the vilest kind." At last Dr. Fate defeats that master sorcerer with a blast of magic flame from his fingertip. "Lest you reincarnate at a later age when I be not here—I dissolve you *ad infinitum!*" I have always suspected that one tap from the Spectre's green-gloved hand could have jammed Dr. Fate's golden helmet down so far over his ears, he could never get it off if he worked *ad infinitum.*

Next there is a two-page text piece about Johnny Thunder (did anyone ever read those two-page text stories?) and a story in which the Atom beats up some big guys for stealing millions from "one of the gold caches of the U.S. government." The Atom is severely hampered by *his* girl, Mary James (incredibly ugly as drawn by the careless Ben

Flinton). She says to him, of his alter-ego Al Pratt, ". . . he's such a weak sister at times that he gets in my hair!" *She* should complain!

Finally there is a Green Lantern story drawn by Martin Nodell, who must have felt right at home with Ben Flinton and Chad Grotsky. Kibitzer Johnny Thunder says "He can streak through the air, walk through walls, is immune to metals, and has other supernatural gifts to use by means of his *will power* when he wears his potent ring, made of part of a mysterious Green Lantern."

The emerald crusader exposes a crooked police commissioner in a rather mundane crime-fighting story. Gifted with many of the same supernatural powers as Dr. Fate and the Spectre, Green Lantern gained much greater popularity. He was not as ominous, foreboding, or frightening as the other two. Unlike the inhuman pair of Spectre and Fate, he suggested to us that perhaps *we* could work the same stunts if *our* will power were only strong enough. Maybe even *without* a magic ring. For the non-athletic kid, Green Lantern championed the cause not only of mind over matter, but of mind over muscles.

As the magazine—and the JSA meeting—draw to a close, there are further interruptions by Johnny Thunder, and by the Red Tornado. A word here about the Red Tornado. The comics, much to their credit, have always been able to laugh at themselves. Ma Hunkle was a typical frowzy housewife and mother in Sheldon Mayer's humorous "Scribbly," featuring a little boy of that name. To impress her own small offspring, Ma would dress up in homemade hero garb of red underwear, shorts, cape, and a cooking-pot with cutout eyeholes for a helmet, and pass herself off as the Red Tornado. She was very funny, and Sheldon Mayer is one of the unsung heroes of the comics industry. It was most fitting that Ma was in on that first meeting of the JSA.

But now finally the Flash zips back from stepping out of the room to reveal that he had zipped all the way to Washington to "the FBI chief, and incidentally, he's one swell guy. He wants all of us members of the Justice Society to come down and see him—*all together!* I told him I thought next Tuesday night would be okay."

It certainly was with all the members. They concluded their meeting, looking forward to really working on one big case together, the next time out.

In fact, that first JSA "story" wasn't really anything great. Not in terms of its own quality of artwork or writing. And as far as its content is concerned, it wasn't really a combined adventure at all, but a set of single-hero stories rather flimsily strung together by the framing device of the JSA meeting.

But the beginning was there. The first combined adventure of a major group of superheroes. The portent was here, of great things to come. For the next 54 issues of *All Star Comics* the Justice Society would work "all together" on one monumental problem after another. Great issues would be at stake henceforth.

In the fourth issue of *All Star*—the second to feature the JSA—the heroes *left* their meeting room, held their meeting with the chief of the FBI and set out to strike against espionage agents, "for America and Democracy." A crime syndicate leader, "the mysterious Mr. X," tried to kill off each member, although of course he failed and came to a sad end himself. I guess any assemblage of heroes like the Justice Society or any of its many imitators—the Seven Soldiers of Victory, the All-Winners Squad, the Marvel Family and so on—just naturally attracts the wrath of the underworld, rather as a tall structure is likely to draw all the lightning for a fair distance around.

I'm certainly not going to try to trace the adventures of the Society through 50-odd issues of *All Star Comics*. Instead, let's devote ourselves to those issues that recorded significant—really significant—occurrences in the history of the JSA.

Issue 6 contained just such a turning point, part of it indicated by the title of the story, "The JSA Initiates Johnny Thunder." Now one of the curious things about a built-up myth world like that of a comic book series is the quasi-legal set of precedents, rules, and conventions that are built up. The JSA, for example, had a charter; and it, and perhaps the economics of comic book publishing, dictated the rules under which *All Star Comics* was governed.

Even though the Flash had been a leading feature in *Flash Comics* from its inception, he shared its pages with Hawkman and a number of lesser fry. Now, a quarterly called *All-Flash* was being inaugurated, to be devoted exclusively to the adventures of the fastest man alive. The editorial board found that this was sufficient exposure for the Flash, and a place in the pages of *All Star Comics* could be better exploited to showcase the attractions of some less popular hero. So the JSA charter conveniently stated that any hero with a comic book all his own could not hold active membership, but would be obliged to resign and claim only honorary membership. That this device was not an afterthought, but part of the JSA rules from their inception, is evidenced by the fact that Superman and Batman had held honorary memberships from the first JSA story onward.

With the departure of the Flash from active membership, Johnny Thunder felt that he was a logical successor. He had been present at the meetings of the Society from the first, in a rather undefined status, and now the members decided to accord him full membership—after a good, rousing initiation stunt! (How playful these grim avengers could be, including as they did the walking dead and the mystically unhuman!)

Johnny's colossal snipe-hunt was for a balmy self-styled killer who printed newspaper headlines about his insidious career on a basement press. Bizarre, of course, but the bizarre in villains has always been a feature of the heroic adventure tradition. This time, however, "Killer" proved to be a harmless nut—but Johnny nonetheless managed to get himself thrown off a dock bound hand and foot, towed on a line tied to the tail of an airplane, locked in the trunk of a car . . . all at the hands of a motley crew of *genuine* crooks he managed somehow to get himself involved with.

Even with the assistance of his magic Thunderbolt, Johnny required the help of each member of the Justice Society: Flash saved him from a watery grave; Green Lantern rescued him from his sky-surfing; Dr. Fate rescued him from his automotive prison; and so on—until each member of the Society had showed his stuff, Johnny had been rescued, and a few crooks had been rounded up, almost in passing.

All that was left to do was to round up the *real* (but by now thoroughly terrorized) "Killer" McPanzee. At last, bumbling onto Killer aboard a steamship, Johnny ordered his Thunderbolt to drop the entire ship and the attendant problem into the laps of the JSA, thereby accomplishing his mission and simultaneously achieving his membership in the style that had long distinguished the Thunder family.

In the next issue, another significant event took place. And again Johnny was a vital agent in its occurrence. Again, a member had achieved a comic book of his own and was retiring from active membership in the Society. This time it was Green Lantern, and as a parting gesture, the emerald gladiator suggested that the JSA raise "$1,000,000 for War Orphans." Each member set out to raise his share of the million, and Johnny alone proved unable to perform. However, to pull Johnny's chestnuts from the fire, the honorary members of the Society made brief appearances and helped him to get the needed dollars. Not only did the Flash return to the pages of *All Star Comics,* but Superman and Batman also turned up. The few panels in which they appeared represented the first of only two appearances they were ever to make in *All Star Comics.*

I could say a lot about Superman and Batman, a vast amount in fact. Comic books in the form of reprinted newspaper comics had been tried over and over for decades, using a variety of sizes and formats. Something recognizable as the modern comic book had existed since *Famous Funnies*—a reprint series—began in 1932; and several periodicals—*More Fun, Adventure, Detective*—had presented a variety of rather primitive original material.

But it was not until the appearance of Superman in 1938, and Batman a year later, that the modern comic book came into its own, achieved its permanent role and sense of identity.

Why, then, these two greatest of comic book heroes played so little part in *All Star Comics* is an intriguing question. There are two main answers.

First there was the promotional aspect of a character's appearing in *All Star Comics.* By the very name of the periodical, and even more by the device of the regular conclaves of heroes, membership in the Justice Society was regarded as a promotional bonus for the characters themselves. Those who couldn't make it even *with* a boost from *All Star* were soon consigned to the limbo of discontinued heroes: Hour-Man was an early example and others followed.

Conversely, those characters already so successful as not to *need* the added wallop of the JSA were expected to forego its benefits in favor of others. Thus, Superman and Batman from the start; and, shortly, Flash and then Green Lantern.

Second, we should remember that the organization which ultimately evolved into the modern National Periodical Publications was not always monolithic in structure. In the early 1940s it was really a sort of bifurcated beast, with one side, under the tutelage of M. C. Gaines known as All-American ("AA"), and the other, with a variety of people on top but often identified with Whitney Ellsworth, known as Superman-DC. The DC stood for Detective Comics; this was the outgrowth of the original, pre-costume hero, operation.

Now most of the JSA members were "AA" characters—Flash, Green Lantern, Atom, Hawkman. *All Star Comics* was itself an "AA" product; and while it was not unknown for a "DC" character to be used on the other side of the line, there was obviously little desire on the "AA" side to have the two greatest "DC" heroes play a major role in *All Star Comics.*

In issue 8, in a story rather literally titled "Two New Members Win Their Spurs," there was another personnel change. Green Lantern had for some time been the featured story in *All-American Comics,* but now a *Green Lantern* quarterly was added, and he was obliged to retire to honorary status in the JSA. Simultaneously, Hour-Man, who was just not making it, conveniently applied for a leave of absence from the JSA; it was granted, and he never returned for even a minute, much less a super-powered hour.

The two new members were Starman and Dr. Mid-Nite. Starman was one of the many costumed heroes who was excellent in conception but rather disappointing in execution. Very cleanly and gracefully drawn by Jack Burnley, he wore a red suit blazoned with a golden star, the usual cape, and a Buck Rogers-like helmet. Known as the "astral avenger," he carried a Gravity Rod (actually it must have been an *anti-gravity* device) which permitted him to fly. Like so many others—Spectre and Dr. Fate come to mind at once—this attractively conceived character was largely frittered away chasing bank robbers and kidnapers when he would obviously have been more at home in more *outré* adventures.

The second new member, Dr. Mid-Nite, wore helmet and goggles and a black and red uniform beneath which lurked one Dr. McNider, a blind physician. The idea of a blind hero contains great potential—its use has ranged from the Bible to the modern detective character, Max Carrados—but in the comics, with their penchant for overdoing everything, Dr. Mid-Nite not only overcomes his handicap, but so thoroughly overcompensates that there is an advantage instead of an obstacle in it. Those goggles in Dr. Mid-Nite's costume permit him to see after all; in fact, they permit him to see in the dark.

(Permit me a small aside on the topic of how the comics repeat themselves. In the 1940s, the era of which we're speaking, there was a popular costume hero called Daredevil. He disappeared with hundreds of others in the cutbacks of the fifties, but just a few years ago the name was revived and applied to a new hero. Seeking a gimmick for the new Daredevil, his creator decided that *he* would be *blind,* and for a few stories the plight of a blind adventurer and the ingenuity he applied to overcoming his difficulties made the new Daredevil an outstanding feature.

(But very soon other, compensating senses began to appear. Before many issues had passed, Daredevil's "blindness" became only a convention of the strip—for all practical purposes, so thoroughly had he compensated, he was not blind, but in fact had greater sensitivity than a fully sighted person. So for Daredevil in the modern era, and so for Dr. Mid-Nite in the "Golden Age" of the comics.)

The next significant adventure of the JSA was the case of "The Bomb Defense Formula" in issue 10. This was by far the best JSA story to date, and proved to be one of the best ever. In it, the members of the Justice Society are sent into the future to obtain the secret of protecting America from enemy bombing attacks. Someday someone would devise an effective anti-bombing defense, and the JSA hoped to find it, in the future, and bring it back to those days of World War II. The time paradoxes of this move would have made an intriguing theme for a science fiction story (and in fact such paradoxes have been treated repeatedly with varying degrees of logical ingenuity) but in the simpler medium of the comic book they received scant consideration.

A Professor Everson, looking remarkably like Albert Einstein, sends the members of the Society on their way.

Hawkman arrives first in an Alex Raymond-ish land of tomorrow. Trouble erupts almost at once, as the futuristic cops don't believe that he is the legendary figure of the Twentieth Century. "Can't blame them," muses Hawkman, drawing a modest parallel, "Suppose Washington appeared suddenly before a policeman back in 1942. He'd be sent to a nuthouse . . . Wow! Hope they don't do that to me!"

But they do. Hawkman tries slugging it out, but futuremen have been bred to virtual supermen, and they effortlessly toss him into a barred cell better suited to a prison of the past than to a mental hospital of the future. (Genetics has progressed but obviously not psychiatry.) Now Hawkman remembers "My belt of Ninth Metal resists gravity. . . ." Pulling against the bars, the belt of Ninth Metal (could "*n*th metal" have been what was originally intended?) bends them apart.

Making his escape, the winged crusader learns from the televisabrary the location of various parts of the defense formula, and goes after the first one himself. Hawkman knocks out a future cop who gets in his way by *kicking* him in the jaw, since "the muscles in my legs are about ten times more powerful than my arms," and brings the information back through time to the rest of the members.

Hawkman's futuristic adventure should have given the flavor of the book by now. In comparable fashion, Sandman goes down into the mines of the future for his section of the formula; Starman into a city built atop giant trees; Dr. Fate to a new Atlantis built beneath the ocean; Dr. Mid-Nite performs an operation in utter darkness at a lush resort in the Sahara to establish his identity and gain access to his portion of the formula; and Atom goes to Sky City, home of giants who put him into a bird cage before he can manage to fly away with his share of the secret.

Finally, and in character with the usual treatment of the comic relief figure of the group, Johnny Thunder encounters trouble opposite to that of the rest of the Justice Society. The Defenders, a futuristic police force Johnny encounters, recognize him immediately as the legendary hero of the past and believe that he can do *anything*—

even capture Black Butch, the most monstrous criminal alive. Johnny can't, but his Thunderbolt can, and they get back with their segment of the formula.

The formula now complete, all members of the Society conveniently return to the identical moment in 1942, and America is saved from air raid.

In the next (eleventh) issue of *All Star* another new member is introduced, one with special status. The JSA got its first female member. Wonder Woman had been introduced in a separate story that appeared back in *All Star Comics* number 8, but that had, at the time, no particular relevance to the Justice Society. This was Wonder Woman's original story, drawn by Harry G. Peter, an artist with an awkward but highly distinctive style, and written by "Charles Moulton," actually William Moulton Marsden, a celebrated psychiatrist and prime innovator of the polygraph "lie detector."

Wonder Woman's origin and subsequent appearances in *All Star, Sensation Comics,* and the later *Wonder Woman* comics, revealed many curious aspects. She was originally Princess Diana of Amazon Island, exclusive home of a race of Amazons who had not seen a man for generations. When aviator Steve Trevor was forced down on the island, Diana "fell in love with a man," and was therefore forced to return to the outer world. Assuming the identity of Diana Prince, she became first a nurse, then a secretary, to army officers. Her friends in the new world were the Holliday Girls, college lassies dedicated to a gay life, it would seem.

Many comics, and particularly the costumed hero books, have been criticized for containing alleged perversions, thinly disguised pornography especially of a homosexual nature, which would presumably lead innocent children down twisted paths of unhealthy activities. Ninety-nine per cent of these charges are a load of hogwash. If they reveal anything twisted, it is the minds of the critics who see such content where none exists.

But when it came to Wonder Woman—the original Wonder Woman, I mean, not the drastically different version currently published—it would be hard to deny the charge.

Wonder Woman and her friends were constantly being whipped, trapped, chained, and tortured with lovingly delineated leather harnesses, bonds, and restraint devices. Of course Wonder Woman eventually triumphed in each encounter, and in each encounter men were portrayed as either hulking hairy beasts, twisted, scheming dwarfs, or totally ineffectual weaklings. In the end Wonder Woman would carry her helpless boy friend, Steve, to safety like a toy, then dump him to exchange hugs and kisses of delight with the readily available Holliday Girls.

It was a very sick scene. Since then Wonder Woman has undergone one sea change after another, being converted, in turn, into a kind of soap opera heroine, a straight adventuress, a member of a whole family of Wonder females including her mother, herself, and "herself" at several earlier ages; and, most recently, a mod-dressing, karate-chopping swinger clearly patterned on Diana Rigg, the former Emma Peel of the television series, *The Avengers.*

The Justice Society and Wonder Woman first encountered one another when the Society formed itself into the "Justice Battalion" to fight the Nazis and Japanese militarists in World War II. Each member joined a different branch of the armed services and fought the common enemy. Hawkman's girlfriend Shierra (remember her?) was sharing a room with nurse Diana Prince (Wonder Woman); Hawkman came to visit Shierra, met Diana, and in due course . . . No, she didn't steal away his affections: she became the Secretary of the Justice Society of America, a post which she first assumed "temporarily," but which she held until the last days of the Society.

Another outstanding adventure was "Shanghaied into Space" in issue 13. Its structure resembled that of "The Bomb Defense Formula" with space travel substituted for time travel. In the story's introduction, expertly drawn by Jack Burnley, the members of the Justice Society were overcome by a gas attack and rocketed to distant planets by Nazi scientists.

Each is sent to a different world, overcomes some menace to the local well-being, and returns to earth with a valuable tool for use in the war against the Axis. Only Dr. Fate escapes—he was "delayed on an important case," a device used innumerable times to excuse the absence of characters from combined-adventure tales. But, as if to substitute for him, Wonder Woman *was* caught, and sent to Venus where she received a kiss from a fairy queen engaged in a war against huge, brutal males. By the end of the episode the men were chained and kneeling in happy submission on silken cushions. Meanwhile, the fairy kiss enabled Wonder Woman to read the queen's mind—I'm not sure just how this power was of value in fighting Hitler, but Wonder Woman really dug it.

In issue 15, the JSA first encountered Brain Wave, the most prominent single villain they ever fought. In that story, Brain Wave created images by mental power to get revenge on the people who had caused the misfortunes of his life. In subsequent battles with the JSA he shrank all the members to a height of six inches, tried to drive them mad with weird dreams, and joined with a group of other villains—the Wizard, Vandal Savage, Per Degaton, and the Gambler—to form The Injustice Gang of the World. (Scholar's note: *cf.* Mr. Mind's Monster Society of Evil.)

Brain Wave was perhaps the ideal villain to oppose the Justice Society. He was little and ugly, and his only weapon was his brain. Naturally, he hated all those big handsome muscular hunks who had lots of friends, the enviable companionship of one another, and of course hordes of admiring girls. Brain Wave was independently wealthy, too, so it is no wonder that the JSA was never able to defeat him for keeps. Can such virtues as friendship and athletic ability and sex appeal ever really, permanently, triumph over money and brains?

The JSA continued for years in what comics publishers call "novel-length" stories. That is, each issue of *All Star Comics*—usually some 48 pages plus covers—was devoted to a single, long story, with "chapters" given over to each hero, rather than separate stories as in the usual "variety" comic like *Action.* They traveled again in time, propagandizing against the Nazis and juvenile delinquency and in favor of helping the handicapped. Quite a few issues involved time travel or inter-dimensional travel, chasing a murder weapon backward through history, or battling an invasion from Fairyland.

All Star Comics number 38 provided still another turning point. It was the last written by Gardner Fox, and the first to depart from the format of featuring an introduction and conclusion in which all the members were included, with intervening chapters featuring the individual heroes. The combined adventure had thus evolved to an additional level of integration. The first JSA story, remember, had featured wholly separate stories merely framed by the Society's meeting. The next 34 featured the heroes in their interrelated adventures. And now, at last, the members might appear together on any page, and any one of them or a group of two or three might go off on a mission.

Progress. Or . . . maybe not. For, without the spotlight falling on each member in turn, revealing his own particular powers and style of operation (not to forget the style of the particular artist associated with that hero), there sometimes seemed to be too many costumed clowns getting in each other's way, tripping over one another as they struggled to solve a problem that could easily have been solved by any *one* of the superpowered beings.

In this 38th *All Star,* the greatest villains of humanity's annals—Nero, Captain Kidd, Goliath, Cesare Borgia, Genghis Khan, and Attila the Hun—apparently succeeded in killing off the entire male membership of the JSA. (For that issue—the membership continued

to shift with the passing years, and a complete roster of every muscle-bound crime-fighter who ever appeared in *All Star Comics*
would be a truly staggering roll-call.)

But member Johnny Thunder had sent his girl friend, the Black
Canary, to summon secretary Wonder Woman and obtain help. Who
could help the dead?

The Amazon could, with the help of her friend, the reformed evil
scientist, Paula, now a sort of resident science-wizard on Paradise Island. The bodies were collected and subjected to Paula's miraculous
purple healing ray (it had once revived Wonder Woman from the
dead). The Society revived and went back into action to wipe up the
villains—imposters at that, as it turned out.

The death of the JSA was more symbolic than their resurrection.
It was the death of the Society under the old *All Star* format, and the
individual members were passing into limbo, even in their solo appearances in their own periodicals and in the variety comics like
Flash and *All-American*. Johnny Thunder only hung around for one
more issue, even in *All Star*. With the sole exception of Wonder
Woman, all the other members of the JSA—which is to say, the survivors of the old "AA" half of the National house—went out of business except for the crowded meetings of the JSA. And then, with the
57th *All Star Comics,* they disappeared, seemingly forever.

I was too old, and too young, really to grieve on that fatal day in
1951 when *All Star Western* number 58 was published. Yet it
seemed to me as if several old friends whom I'd known since grade
school had all moved out of town at once. Despite all the handwrit-
ing on the wall there had been no formal announcement of the dis-
solution of the Justice Society of America, and it was somewhat of
a shock when, somehow, in the few weeks between issue 57 and issue 58, the once-dazzling *All Star Comics* with its unrivalled lineup
of heroes and its incomparable Justice Society of America was converted into a book of cowboys and Indians.

And I was nearly 30, the mantle of mortality already hanging
heavy on me, before I again had a sustained thought about the Justice
Society of America.

In the 1950s National had started a (noncostumed) heroic adventure comic called *The Brave and the Bold,* featuring stories of
knights in armor, Viking warriors and so on. The magazine was less
than a runaway success, but rather than abandon the title altogether,
the publishers chose to convert it to a special "tryout" magazine
which would be a showcase of ideas for new comics. (This had
worked well in another periodical of the type, called, logically,

Showcase. Some of the *Brave and Bold* and *Showcase* features have been astonishing dogs—*Strange Sport Stories* comes to mind—but others have worked out so well that they were removed from the showcase pages and given periodicals of their own.

In *Brave and Bold* for March, 1959, a feature called *Justice League of America* was tried out. It was the third such revival from the old days of the "Golden Age" to be instituted by the one-time associate editor of *All Star,* Julius Schwartz. The others were the Flash and Green Lantern, not so much directly revived as recreated in refurbished and "improved" models, with new alter-egos, uniforms, etc. Now the JSA was similarly called up from the dust, transmogrified into the JLA. Carry-over memberships from the old organization were awarded to Flash, Green Lantern, Superman, Batman, and Wonder Woman (not merely as secretary). There was no nonsense about honorary memberships this time—the JLA needed all the consumer appeal it could get. Two additional members were Aquaman, a long-time feature who had never been a member of any such group, and J'onn J'onzz ("manhunter from Mars"), a sort of green-skinned alien Superman who had popped up in the interim years. (He has since popped back down.)

The first menace of the Justice League's new career was Starro, a villainous monster-sized starfish from space. This proved to be a typical foe for the new JLA. Others heroes were added to the roster as time went on. The revived-revised versions of Hawkman and Atom won their places in the organization anew. Green Arrow was added, circumspectly avoiding mention of his former association with the Seven Soldiers of Victory, a JSA surrogate that had run briefly in *Leading Comics* over on the DC side of the National house, back in the forties. New heroes like Metamorpho and Adam Strange made guest appearances in the JLA's magazine.

In *Justice League of America* number 21 (August, 1963), a monumental event occurred. In the separate adventures of the new Flash it had already been established that both the old and new versions of the fastest man alive "really" existed—on separate earths in parallel universes, another working-over of the old "worlds of if" science-fiction device. Now, crossing the dimensional barrier into the universe of Earth-Two, the members of the "new" Justice League share an annual, two-issue adventure with the members of the "old" Justice Society.

With that many superheroes, and with the modern comic book containing only half the pages of its ancestor, it *takes* a serial to get everybody in. Even a revived-revised version of the beloved old Red

Tornado turned up one summer, complete with Krazy Kat-like confusion as to his/her/its sex!

Perhaps I've changed. Perhaps I've grown older and lost the innocent accepting quality of a child. Or perhaps the changing times are to blame. But even though these new stories were written by Gardner Fox and edited by Julius Schwartz, the Justice Society in its guest appearances with the JLA just does not match its old magnificence of the days and the pages of *All Star Comics*.

But I remember the days when Dr. Fate frankly admitted his inhumanity, confident in the staunch friendship of his fellows in the Justice Society of America—the days when I firmly believed that there *was* a Society that promised Justice in America.

INTRODUCTION TO

THE FOUR-PANELLED, SOCK-BANG-POWIE SATURDAY AFTERNOON SCREEN

If you were a typical kid 20 to 30 or 40 years ago, your fantasy life would have had several major pillars. It was really too late for dime novels, but there might still have been a cache of them left around by an older brother or uncle or even Dad, and you could dig them up. There were certainly pulp magazines galore with titles that ranged from *Ace Mystery* and *Air Wonder Stories* to *Wu Fang* and *Zeppelin Stories.*

You surely loved the comics or you wouldn't be reading this book, and there were those dearly beloved and long-lost radio shows full of organ music and ingenious sound effects. But what about Saturday afternoon at the Bijou, or whatever *your* favorite movie palace called itself? (Sometimes it seems that they chose names in inverse proportion to their own cramped dimensions and shabby decor.)

The delicious ritual of standing in a line of urchins, coins clutched in your fist, buying your ticket, passing an usher clad as royally as an imperial grand admiral, and entering the hushed and seemingly incense-laden sanctum, there to see the latest chapter of your favorite hero's adventures portrayed in sparkling black-and-white by Dick Foran, Buster Crabbe, Ralph Byrd, Tom Tyler. . . .

Chris Steinbrunner was the urchin just ahead of you in that Saturday afternoon queue, and when he grew up he went into radio writing, doing scripts for the old science fiction shows, for *Dr. Christian* and for *Sherlock Holmes.* When dramatic radio died, Chris went into television, and is now manager of film services for WOR-TV in New York. He devotes his limited spare time to research into old (and new) film and radio.

But now, the decades run backwards. Once more you are a dirty-faced kid in sneakers and jeans, coins in your fist, and it's Saturday afternoon. . . .

CHAPTER 8

THE FOUR-PANELLED, SOCK-BANG-POWIE SATURDAY AFTERNOON SCREEN

by CHRIS STEINBRUNNER

★★★

Although memory may make a poor judge, it was *Radio Patrol* that best expressed the marriage between the radio serials and the comics. Each chapter opened with a youngster alone in his room, his eager face buried in what appeared to be a comic book. Over his shoulder we read it ourselves; four panels of action, synopsizing what has gone on in previous chapters. The last illustration dissolves into the real thing, and we're off and running, and another Saturday afternoon explodes into sock-bang-powie life.

Ah, those Saturday afternoons, those breathless sessions in darkened children's sections, wrapped up tight in the serial unfolding on the screen. It was in many ways as thrilling as poring over the color comics on Sunday morning, or the bright times when you traded for a comic book you hadn't owned before, or snatched one from the candystore racks.

Indeed, there were more than just emotional similarities between serials and the comics—many of the greatest comics heroes (and villains!) made the transition from the four-color panels or newspaper mattes to the screen. We followed them happily, and rather uncritically, even though the swingovers were in many cases somewhat surprising.

Serials had cross-pollinated tie-ins with the print media almost from their beginning as a movie form in 1916. Many of the early

Pearl White chapter-plays were simultaneously novelized, episode by episode, in the daily papers, which pushed up both newspaper circulation and movie attendance.

In the twenties, when serials were nearly as important as the main feature, and were openly enjoyed by grownups as well as children, the mystery and action themes of the serials were sometimes drawn from the works of such famous writers as Edgar Wallace and Earl Derr Biggers, and especially from Edgar Rice Burroughs' Tarzan stories. The adventure comics and strips which were later to lend the chapter-plays so much inspiration and cross-plugging had not as yet been born.

At the start of the thirties, sound came to the serials, and even though this gave the art a valuable new dimension (the heroine's scream! mystery-voice villains! ear-blasting, unending gunfire!), serials fell into decline. Taken by the new *double*-feature policy, grownups didn't want to see the chapters at all. The serials moved to Saturday afternoon and the one audience still loyal to them. On this level they enjoyed, by the mid-thirties, a renaissance soon to trigger a Golden Age. But the Hollywood studios manufacturing the chapter-plays, looking to widen their audience, hit on the idea of securing character rights to a very similar sister art: the four-panel, episodic, cliffhanging newspaper comic strip, another of the growing phenomena of the 1930s.

Universal, most venerable of the serial-churners, was the studio, and *Tailspin Tommy* the strip of their choice.

The "miracle" of flight, Lindbergh's solo odyssey across the Atlantic, and all the daredevil pioneer soaring of the first airmen had made those pilots the same sort of romantic, heroic figures in the public eye as astronauts are today—and, in fact, wildly more so. Hal Forrest's *Tailspin Tommy* was one of the earliest comic strips to exploit this public image, and because it dealt with the metamorphosis of *boy* into ace aviator, it was a likely first choice for the metamorphosis of strip into serial.

Universal packed as much as it could into the thirteen chapters, starting Tommy's adventures at a point before he has ever touched the controls of a plane. We find him as a mechanic in a rural Southwestern community appropriately called Littleville, dreaming of motors that fly and the comradeship of great pilots. A chance air crash and Fate bring Tommy to Three Point Airport; the boy immediately joins the milieu of the airfield and stays. Rather than concentrating on unfolding one specific adventure epic or the fight against one specific major villain (which is the way most serials are structured), *Tailspin Tommy* based itself rather closely on the first year of its comic source, and told a good many smaller stories across its 13 episodes . . . including how Tommy learned to fly; his tangling with air bandits, and even, briefly, a mad scientist; how he flew his injured pal Skeeter across the treacherous Rockies in a wild lightning storm; his entering and winning the National Air Races; and finally, because of some earthquake rescue work he has managed to squeeze in, his becoming a national hero and going to Hollywood to make a film!

And, not content with fading out as a mere movie hero, Tailspin crashes into the final chapter rescuing his gray-haired old mom from a railway disaster, and being hailed by old hometown Littleville in public ceremony as "one of the most spectacular figures in American aviation today." And that certainly packed a good deal into a single serial! It was a great success, which not only paved the way for a sequel in 1935—*Tailspin Tommy and the Great Air Mystery,* with a much more cohesive plot that took Tom to the bandit-infested jungles of a South American country called "Nazil"—but it was a success for the genre. Universal was now committed to raiding the comics for future serial properties. The studio decided its next venture would be in the direction of the science-fiction comic strip.

Science fiction of sorts had already made its appearance in serials. Gleaming futuristic cities often seemed to be secreted underground or undersea. In *The Lost City* Kane Richmond battled a scientific madman (played with alcoholic intensity by William "Stage" Boyd, not the William Boyd of *Hopalong Cassidy* fame) who threatened to ruin the world with the "ectromagnetic traditions" of his secret magnetic city under an African mountain. In *The Phantom Empire* good ol' Gene Autry gallops down to fantastic Murania, also under a mountain, but this great discovery pales before Gene's need to get back to his ranch daily to host a country-music radio show. (His contract was coming due.) Ray "Crash" Corrigan joined an Annapolis submarine team in a descent to the *Undersea Kingdom* of Atlantis, whose ruler, the usurper Unga Khan, vowed: "I will either become supreme ruler of the upper world, or destroy it!"

Universal, which previously had not turned out a science-fiction serial, turned for its inspiration to a Sunday-pages comic strip which, since its start two year before in 1934, had captured the public imagination with its different look and first-rate drawing style. It was Alex Raymond's *Flash Gordon.*

Universal could hardly have chosen better. Raymond with his skill and innovations had pushed the art of the comic strip up to a new plateau, and his inter-planetary odyssey was full of wonder. The studio used it all, faithfully re-creating the first year's adventures straight from the smash opening: college athlete "Flash" Gordon and airline passenger Dale Arden share a parachute descending from a plane crippled in a tremendous, cataclysmic storm which is tearing Earth apart, a storm caused by the wandering planet Mongo. Flash and Dale land near the secret lab of eccentric scientist Dr. Zarkov, who is convinced that on Mongo there is an evil intelligence deliberately plotting to wipe out civilization here, and who has been building a rocket ship to take him to the sinister planet. Flash convinces Zarkov that he and Dale must come along too—and the three of them take off in a sputtering, smoke-belching rocket for a serial adventure to end all serial adventures—far and away the best serial ever made.

Buster Crabbe, an Olympic swimmer turned actor, who had previously tried his swing as Tarzan, was a magnificent nostril-flaring Flash; Jean Rogers, just a teenager at the time but a sexy one, was a believably menaced Dale; and Charles Middleton as the superbly evil Ming, "Emperor of the Universe," dedicated to destroying Earth and bedding Dale, gave a portrait which was deathless. And very close to the strip, as well. Universal spent a big $350,000 to give the serial the same lush locales.

Fantastic futuristic cities, great fleets of rocket ships, barren monster-infested wastelands, palaces suspended in the sky on vast anti-gravity beams generated in great furnaces, lion men, winged warriors, horned apes, fire-breathing reptiles in caves, lands under the sea—wonders piled on wonders. "The hero of the heavens and all of his enemies ALIVE, and all their amazing adventures REAL! . . ." *Flash Gordon* was a smash success, and in some locales was billed ahead of the features it accompanied. It was the one serial reviewed by *Time.* And favorably!

Flash Gordon saved Earth from Ming—and saved Dale as well—in three separate serials. At the climax of the first, the Oriental-looking, long-caped Emperor has swished into a flaming crematorium, conceding victory to our hero. A short two years later, in 1938, in *Flash Gordon's Trip to Mars,* Ming is back, casually informing a minion that he is impervious to fire; he has changed his base of operations to the Red Planet and is happily bombarding us with a deadly Nitron lamp that causes earthquakes and cyclones. It takes a fast fifteen chapters on Mars for Flash, dashing across light bridges and befriending clay people, to put the Lamp out.

Ming isn't switched off that easily, though. One more year and we find him back in charge of Mongo, sending a spacefleet of plague-rockets to spread Purple Death on Earth. Flash blasts off for Mongo again, handily messes with an army of walking robot bombs called Annihilatons, wins the loyalty of a degenerate race of Rock Men, and wipes out Ming with one of his own superbombs. Says Zarkov: "Ming conquered the universe, and you have just conquered Ming. Therefore, Flash Gordon, you have conquered the universe!" Which is how the final serial in the series, *Flash Gordon Conquers the Universe,* got its name.

In between, Buster Crabbe also managed to star as Buck Rogers (1939), hero of the other most memorable science-fantasy newspaper strip. It was not as faithful an adaptation, but the Phil Nowlan and Dick Calkins vision of the strife-torn 25th century was by 1939 ten years old. Buck's jump across five centuries—to discover an America in ruins, with its remnants ruled by gangster methods—is retold somewhat differently: in the serial he is aboard a dirigible which crashes in the Arctic, releasing the suspended-animation-causing Nirvano gas. But the serial is more or less true to the spirit of the strip, with most of the familiar figures and locales: Buddy, Wilma, Dr. Huer, mobsterish Killer Kane, quick trips to the Hidden City, and incredibly quick trips to the Planet Saturn.

Space opera, of course; farfetched and juvenile. But they had a certain poetry. Flash Gordon and his interplanetary comic-strip odyssey brought the Saturday afternoon serials as close to true art as they were likely to come—and, because of him, they came pretty damn close. They had grace and zest; they sounded a high, pure, full-throated call to epic adventure. And because the public responded to this call, Universal went full speed ahead to acquire new comic-strip properties for their serial gristmill.

What better choices to make than the two other strips begun by the talented and busy young Alex Raymond? *Jungle Jim* was a fully clothed Establishment Tarzan, and *Secret Agent X-9,* a collaboration with two-fisted mystery writer Dashiell Hammett, became a serial filled not only with shadowy gangland activity but also missing crown jewels, and such unlikely mittel-Europeans as Shara Graustark and Baron Michael Karsten. War clouds were already hanging low over Europe, and at home the Depression and organized crime had all but toppled many of our most cherished institutions; by 1937 serials—and the comic strips—were sensitive barometers of the national disorder.

Displaying great expertise in translating the violent cops-and-robbers world of the strips to the screen was the director Universal hired to expand its serial department and specifically to handle *Jun-*

gle Jim and *X-9,* plus the serial version of Captain Eddie Ricken-backer's aviation newspaper strip, *Ace Drummond*—the great Ford Beebe, who had masterminded much of the earlier Mascot Pictures' brief golden age. Beebe, who is still alive and in happy retirement, reminisced recently (in an interview with Edward Reicher) that he would have liked to have *Jungle Jim,* his favorite of all his produc-tions, made in color. But this would have been too costly an innova-tion for Universal. Beebe was to innovate in other ways.

Ace Drummond, a grownup, slicked-down Tailspin Tommy, moved from Littleville to Outer Mongolia, even had his own song, which he broke into lustily once each chapter (it was a lyric worthy of an air ace—"Contact! Spin 'em around! Put her nose into the wind! Head for the sun!"). Often he was cut short by trouble—be-cause in those secret temples high in the Himalayas, over the whirr of ancient prayer wheels that were somehow also radios, hooded monks listened to those ominous words: "Ace Drummond must die! The Dragon commands!"

Tim Tyler's Luck, from the Lyman Young African adventure strip, followed 16-year-old Tim and the fanciful Ivory Patrol across the veldt in search of the boy's father, an expert in gorilla language who has disappeared. Opposing them is the villain, Spider Webb, in his marvelous steel-hulled "Jungle cruiser." Tim is a modern Andro-cles, making friends with every jungle creature from elephant to panther; the only friend he does *not* have in the serial is his pal, Spud, from whom he was inseparable in the newspaper continuity.

Radio Patrol brought crime right back where it belonged—to the steel mills, junkyards, and "Egyptian Villages" of the 1937 big city, with hypnotized killers making off with a formula for flexible steel, and with the two uniformed policeman heroes, Pat O'Hara and Sam, buzzing about in that modern crime-fighting wonder, the radio-equipped patrol car. The entire newspaper strip by Sullivan and Schmidt was based on that one police innovation—the radio patrol car—but, even so, it lasted a decade and inspired a good serial. (Not having the inspiration to invent a TV-wristwatch or space coupe, the strip is dead today.)

In *Red Barry,* another cop, again played by Buster Crabbe, chases crime down to Chinatown, where assorted sinister Chinese and some Caucasian types are after two million dollars in Russian bonds . . . closely based on the King Features syndicate strip. All of these seri-als were directed for Universal by Ford Beebe, and all of them fea-tured openings designed to point up their comic-strip origins: four line-drawing panels, much like the panels one would find in a newspaper, giving outlines of the previous chapters and dissolving into the live-action present. *Flash Gordon's Trip to Mars,* also co-directed by Beebe, went this gambit one better: the huge comic panels are being watched by Ming's men on an immense futuristic TV screen!

But Universal was not to remain the only studio to use comic heroes for their serials. Republic, a new studio founded in the mid-thirties and devoted to action themes, was already making a name for itself in the serial corner. Republic paid special attention to fights and stunting, and their detailed, accurate miniatures, on which they never seemed to stint, permitted orgies of destruction on public buildings, dams, power plants, and endless fleets of planes and trucks. For its fifth serial, Republic acquired the rights to the most smashing, potent newspaper strip of the day, Chester Gould's hard-hitting *Dick Tracy,* whose harsh lines and no-holds-barred war on crime had made it since 1931 the perfect police strip.

Republic's 1937 adaptation of *Dick Tracy* omitted many of the familiar faces of the strip—Tess Trueheart and Pat Patton were out, as indeed was everybody except the young kid, Junior—and had Tracy as a crimebusting FBI man rather than a police-headquarters plainclothes dick. The most familiar face of all—Tracy's own, with its eagle nose and razor-sharp hatchet jaw—was patently impossible to duplicate, but Republic came close with Ralph Byrd, a good, athletic actor who, if he did not quite jut that famed square chin—seemed to make up for it with Tracy's own determined aggressiveness and dedicated civic consciousness. He was the perfect Dick Tracy, and played him through four bang-bang serials. In the first, a scientific mastermind known only as The Lame One kidnaps Dick's brother Gordon, perverts his mind for evil with a brain operation—and, in the same smash opening chapter, mind you, builds a vibration machine to shake down a just-completed bridge. In 1938, *Dick Tracy Returns,* battling Charles Middleton, our old friend Ming, who is the two-gun dad of a brood of four racketeer sons. In 1939, *Dick Tracy's G-Men* go after terrorist Nicholas Zarnoff—"gnawing like a rat at the foundations of our democracy!" (And would you believe Jennifer Jones as heroine?)

In 1941, it was *Dick Tracy Versus Crime Incorporated*—specifically, an invisible foe called the Ghost, so up-tight about New York (his mobster brother has been executed) that he's busily polishing off the City Council and, at the end of Chapter One, has set off an explosion in the Atlantic which causes a huge tidal wave to rush at the metropolis. Naturally Tracy finds a way to stop the wave—which is a bit much to ask even of a one-man police battalion. But

Ralph Byrd carries it off beautifully, and when he pats the FBI on the back with a statement like "no criminal can outwit an organization which goes on forever, whose members never rest"—why, we believe him.

Republic also did a very memorable job with *The Lone Ranger* (1938), who started his career as a radio program hero but later became a comic strip hero as well. (Republic altered the legend so that no one knew the identity of the mysterious masked man until the finale. He was one of a diminishing group of Texas Rangers who were being killed off chapter by chapter!)

The Adventures of Red Ryder, in 1940, was an exciting Western serial drawn from Fred Harmon's newspaper strip, with Don Barry as Red—whose father is killed when the villain needs his ranchland as a right-of-way for the Santa Fe railroad. Naturally the serial also featured Red's Indian pal, Little Beaver, and the Duchess. (Red also became the hero of several features.)

Zane Grey's character, *King of the Royal Mounted,* a familiar adventure strip of the thirties, became a chapter-play in 1940, and one of the first serials to war with Germany—but not by name. The Canadians are mining Compound X to use as a treatment for polio—but the nasty Huns need it as a bomb detonator! King stops all this . . . in typical Republic action fashion.

Republic was not the only contender in the serial field—Columbia Studios also decided to gear their action department for serial production. A late starter, Columbia could never quite match the smoothness and slickness of Republic and Universal—but not for want of trying. And Columbia was especially keen on reworking comic-strip properties. Its seventh serial was *Mandrake the Magician* (1939), from the famed character created by Lee Falk. Brash and hyperthyroid Warren Hull was not as slicked-down and not very often as caped as Mandrake, the comic hero, and he could not gesture hypnotically with nearly as much aplomb. But he was very good (he was also good in two other serials as the pulp-novel hero, the Spider), and maintained a high pitch of excitement in tracking down the villainous Wasp—though his suit was crumpled and he hardly ever wore a tux. His close friendship with the African giant, Lothar, was a first in bringing racial integration to adventure films.

Chinatown was a frequent setting of Columbia's adaptation of *The Shadow,* which of course was a pulp series and radio show, but by the serial's debut, 1940, it was also a newspaper strip and a comic book. Victor Jory was the perfect cloaked Shadow/Lamont Cranston/Lin Chang, and when the evil Black Tiger rasped, "*Flint, you've failed again!*," it was perfectly chilling.

That year Columbia did a pedestrian version of *Terry and the Pirates* which captured none of the color of Milton Caniff's great work of art but used nearly all of its people: a teenage Terry, Pat Ryan, Normandie, the Dragon Lady, Connie (wearing painful-looking pasted-on ears) and Big Stoop. The China interior setting seemed close enough to the Caniff source, but all the realism and the heart were gone. Columbia made up for it though, in 1942, when it cast stuntman Dave O'Brien as Captain Midnight—an afternoon radio serial which also became a comic book. It had planes and explosions and a good villain—Ivan Shark—and encouraged Columbia to further their comic-character adaptations. That turned out to be a mixed blessing.

By the early forties Republic and Columbia were very actively mining the comics. Strangely enough, Universal—the studio which had really *discovered* comics for the serials—was beginning to back away. In 1942, it released a good version of Frank Martinek's sea-going strip, *Don Winslow of the Navy,* which had Don Terry as Intelligence Officer Winslow battling the spymaster Scorpion in Pacific island ports-of-call in the days just before Pearl Harbor. It was a beautiful job, and earned a sequel in 1943, *Don Winslow of the Coast Guard,* with both Don and the Scorpion shifting operations to foggy, wartime Seattle.

That same year Universal did a smashing version of Zack Mosley's aviation strip, *The Adventures of Smilin' Jack,* with Jack still finding time to smile while lined up against all the Axis powers. It was a great serial, but Universal's last look at the Sunday comics. By the mid-forties Universal had given up serials altogether.

In the meantime, Republic began looking for likely serial material not only among comic strips but also among those Sunday color-page spinoffs which had by the forties become an American phenomenon: the comic book. For some time the studio had attempted to acquire the rights to Superman, but there had been a last-minute dispute with National-DC and the deal had fallen through. It was very short-sighted on National's part, for Republic then turned to what it felt was an acceptable substitute hero, Fawcett Comics' *Captain Marvel,* and fashioned what many still think is the perfect serial. Shazam!

The Captain Marvel of the comics was "born" in an abandoned subway tunnel. Republic changed and embellished this origin somewhat: To a remote section of Siam, zealously guarded by unconquered tribes, comes the unwelcome Malcolm Scientific Expedition seeking knowledge of the ancient Scorpion Dynasty. In the expedition is teenage radio operator Billy Batson (Frank Coghlan Jr.), whose moral code is so straight he could easily become an idealistic pain in the neck: he declines to join them in breaking into a forbidden tomb.

Instead, splitting down another corridor, he runs into an ancient wizard who, because the curse of the Scorpion is about to be unleashed on the world, passes on to Billy the mantle of Captain Marvel. All Billy must do is call out the portmanteau invocation to Solomon, Hercules, Achilles, Zeus, Atlas, and Mercury—and amid an explosion and billow of smoke he becomes the red suited Captain Marvel (dark, brooding Western star Tom Tyler in his best role).

Meanwhile, the expedition has discovered a scorpion statue with five lenses in its moveable claws—five lenses which, when lined up, can turn base metals into gold! The lenses are divided among the five scientists in the group for safekeeping—but one scientist, driven by greed, becomes the black-cloaked modern Scorpion and attempts to eliminate the rest of the expedition.

The action shifts back to America, where Captain Marvel must deal with gangsters in the Scorpion's pay, and the scientists, despite his vigilance, are killed one by one. Finally the climax brings us back to the temple in Siam, where Billy and his friends must fight off an attacking desert tribe also working for the villain, and a reactivated volcano has trapped the new expedition inside the tomb. Ultimately, though, the Scorpion is unmasked and Billy learns he has transformed into Captain Marvel for the last time, his "work having been done."

Not only was this serial superbly plotted and constructed, but the great flying sequences designed by Republic's special-effects geniuses, Howard and Theodore Lydecker, made it especially memorable. Captain Marvel's flights through the air, his zooming up the sheer sides of office buildings, or shooting along a highway after a speeding truck or parallel to the rim of a dam, were so realistic that their trickery defied detection. (Actually, the Lydeckers used a full size dummy in flying position, arms pointed forward, pulled fast along an invisible wire across hundreds of feet, generally after a shot of Marvel himself leaping high into the air . . . from a concealed trampoline.) Mixed together, the fast-moving action and stunting, the fantastic flying effects, and the good basic story, made *The Adventures of Captain Marvel* a very successful serial, the joy of Republic's Golden Age.

The studio's next serial, *Jungle Girl,* reversed a trend: it *became* a comic book. The serial was very loosely based on an Edgar Rice Burroughs novel of the same name. The title character was a girl named Nyoka, who didn't even exist in the book. But the serial was sufficiently popular for Fawcett Publications to secure rights to the character of Nyoka and begin running a Nyoka serial in the pages of *Master Comics.* This in turn was so popular that Fawcett started an additional comic book devoted entirely to the adventures of Nyoka!

In 1942 Republic bought rights to a great wartime comic book, *Spy Smasher,* and fashioned another of its serial masterpieces, heralded in the comics themselves with pictures of Captain Marvel shaking Spy Smasher's hand, "welcoming him to the screen."

The serial opened with a blasting horn rendition of the first notes of Beethoven's Fifth ("V for Victory") Symphony; the serial moves from occupied France, where Alan Armstrong, the goggled counter-intelligence agent known as Spy Smasher, has just escaped a German firing squad, to America, where Alan reveals himself to his twin brother Jack, and together they fight fifth columnists who are infiltrating the home front.

Twin Jack was a departure from the comics, but essentially the serial was amazingly close to its source. Kane Richmond was superb in a difficult double role, and looked the part of Spy Smasher exactly. The action was breathless and ceaseless, and the death of Jack in one of the later chapters was both surprising and poignant.

In 1943, Republic made its final raid on the comics. *Captain America,* as created by Simon and Kirby, was a 97-pound weakling made superstrong by a wartime scientific experiment. Donning a red-white-and-blue costume complete with curved shield and assisted by a young sidekick named Bucky, our comic book hero goes out to fight Nazis, Japs, spies, and homegrown gangsters. The *Captain America* of the Republic serial was completely different from the comic. Both his curved shield and his sidekick Bucky are gone. The Captain's other identity is now "fighting" district attorney Grant Gardner (rather than Army private Steve Rogers, as in the comics), and instead of avenging himself against the wartime foes of the nation, the serial's Captain is content merely to go after the Scarab (fastidiously played by the marvelous Lionel Atwill), an archeologist who is using a poison known as the Purple Death to eliminate some fellow scientists.

There is no attempt to explain Captain America's origin and Grant Gardner's stopping to change into costume seemed at times only to impede the action. It was hardly necessary, at any rate, for by the last chapter everyone, even the Scarab, knew exactly who Captain America really was. The real mystery was left unexplained: why should a crusading district attorney, the one person in our society fully capable of running the machinery of justice, step well outside the Law for jungle combat with evil forces? It just didn't make sense.

Not that *Captain America* wasn't a fast-moving, adventuresome serial. It was . . . but it was also the last serial Republic was to draw from the comics. The studio was to continue to make serials of diminishing quality for some ten years. But it would never again invest the comic pages with its own aliveness and magic. In a way, it was the beginning of the end for Republic, and for the serials as well.

However, in the days of Republic's greatest success, Columbia Pictures also decided to travel the comic-book route to big box-office receipts. Their adaptation of Bob Kane's great National Comic, *Batman,* in 1943, was nowhere near Republic's standards, and had a particularly shabby look about the sets and props (the Batmobile, for instance, was a sorry, nondescript convertible). However, the serial still managed to retain some of the verve and charm of its source.

Lewis Wilson, who had a sort of Boston accent, made an aristocratic Bruce Wayne. And J. Carroll Naish, as the fiendish Japanese espionage agent, Dr. Daka, with headquarters inside an amusement park dark ride, an alligator pit next to his office for disposal of unwanted visitors, and with an army of zombies at his command, was tremendous. *Batman* was box-office, and Columbia raided the comic book stands for more titles.

Lee Falk's jungle strip *The Phantom* was next, and Tom Tyler (who had played Captain Marvel) made a visually perfect Ghost-Who-Walks. The serial was obviously made on a skimpy budget, and Lee Falk to this day remembers it with pain.

Undaunted, Columbia next tried its hand at Dale Messick's lace-frilled newspaper strip *Brenda Starr, Reporter*—a slightly above average crime yarn enlivened somewhat by Kane Richmond as the cop in love with Brenda—and three years later decided to bring to the screen the most famous comic-book reporter of all: Clark Kent.

This was not the first time Superman had come to the screen. Several years earlier, under the sponsorship of Max Fleischer, he had appeared in a series—not a serial—of animated color cartoons from Paramount. These cartoons were an interesting experiment in using the format of the short animated film for serious adventure stories instead of the usual funny animal romps.

The Superman cartoons hewed closely to the comic book appearances of the characters, and borrowed the voices from the radio series (most prominent being Bud Collyer in the dual role of Clark Kent and Superman). Even today these cartoons hold up well in terms of dramatic impact and imagination, but after the one series of

Superman cartoons, the animated shorts went back to comedy, and the adventure stories went back to "live."

Actually, in the three years before Superman (1948) Columbia fashioned serials out of several radio heroes—*Hop Harrigan, Jack Armstrong, Chick Carter, The Sea Hound*—and such comic book characters as *The Vigilante,* a modern Western with Ralph Byrd joining Ace Drummond as a singing serial hero, and Clarence Grey's science-fiction strip *Brick Bradford,* with Kane Richmond as Brick traveling by Time Top both to the moon and to pirate waters in the 18th century. By the time Columbia was ready to try Superman, Sam Katzman was in charge of the studio's serials—a man well known for the fact that his films never lost money, nor that they were very big in the budget or the quality departments.

Superman, with Kirk Alyn in the title role, was somewhat disappointing. Although it had elements of action, and some fine villainy in Carol Foreman's Spider Lady, it sorely needed Republic's production care. Instead of even attempting to copy Republic's ingenuity for the flying scenes, Columbia had Superman leap up, up and away via a crudely obvious line-drawing cartoon. Despite its obvious deficiencies, though, the serial earned a great deal of money, especially in foreign sales, and Katzman happily signed up any comic character on which he could lay his hands.

Tex Granger, from antiseptic *Calling All Boys* magazine, was to solve the riddle of Mystery Mesa. *Congo Bill* was to stumble onto a white virgin ruling a jungle tribe—the virgin in question was the formidable Cleo Moore, all bust and sarong. What was *she* doing in a kid's serial? *Bruce Gentry* hopped into his plane to give chase to flying-disk saucers—more crude animation here—only to learn that they were being sent by a mystery man out west.

Sam Katzman next attempted a sequel to his first success, *Batman and Robin* (1949), which appeared even less costly than the first version. This time Batman was played by Robert Lowery, and his car was even more dingy. Every set—Wayne Manor, the Bat-cave, police headquarters—seemed to be another cramped corner of the Columbia lot, with almost no room to turn around.

But despite the laughable moments, which were many, the serial had a certain manic charm, especially in its traditional villain, the black-hooded Wizard, who stopped all electric motors everywhere with a device on his secret submarine, who barked insane orders to his men and wild challenges to Batman, and at the finish revealed his true identity as somebody's twin brother—the most ridiculous conclusion a serial ever had. But it still made money.

Unstoppable, Katzman then put Kirk Alyn back in trunks for *Atom Man Versus Superman.* Atom Man was the alias for the man of steel's arch-enemy, Luthor (played with bald pate by Lyle Talbot). Lots of kryptonite ignited in this one, and a flying saucer which Luthor operated gave Katzman another opportunity to trot out the same old line drawings. The final chapter title—*Superman Saves the Universe*—is a sentimental reminder of Flash Gordon, but nothing else is. Very crude and simple, it still made money. But it was the last time Superman was to fly in a movie serial—television was on the horizon.

Still looking for likely tie-ins, in 1951 Katzman made a serial version of the hit TV adventure series (and comic book), *Captain Video.* The Captain was a sort of pocket Flash Gordon, for he and his Video Ranger fought villains not only here on Earth but on the Planet Atoma, ruled by a Ming-derived meanie named Vultura. It was not an excessively intelligent serial, but it moved with terrific speed, as if haste could cover its defects—and often it did. Despite its lean budget, *Captain Video* had certain of its scenes on Atoma tinted, and many of the chapter climaxes in monochrome—for whatever draw a touch of color could have against the encroachments of black-and-white television. It was already too late, though.

The following year Katzman tried two more comics. Buster Crabbe made his final serial appearance—nearly two decades after Flash—still looking very fit as Thunda in *King of the Congo,* a pleasant and even sexy African adventure from the Thunda comic book. (Itself an obvious copy—there were many—of Tarzan.)

The serial version of Reed Crandall's *Blackhawk* reduced that international team of fighting air aces to only four members, but it was so loaded with healthy action, pleasing fights, and interesting locales—including a quick trip to Mexico in the later chapters—that it hardly deserved to be the last comic-spawned serial. But it was.

It was hardly Katzman's fault. He had tried to keep the serials going as long as he could, but he realized that television would soon absorb the talent, the financing, and even the audiences of the serial art for its endless low budget programming. So the Saturday afternoon sock-bang-powie screen dimmed a little, and those of us who in our youth fed on and drew strength from the serials grew up and were replaced by—no one.

But like seeds taking root even on enemy soil, serials themselves became an early television staple, infecting a whole new generation. And from the first, TV had adopted and adapted comic heroes, from Dick Tracy to Buck Rogers to Blondie to the 104 endlessly rerun episodes of the TV Superman show which both immortalized and destroyed George Reeves. (Reeves committed suicide as a result of becoming so typecast as Superman that he was unable to obtain any other roles.)

Expensive, if not altogether accurate, live-action color series have been made out of *Batman, Tarzan,* and *Green Hornet,* and there have been some amazingly faithful Saturday morning animated cartoons: *Superman, Batman, Superboy, Aquaman,* and, in one series, the whole multi-heroic *Justice League* of *America.* And, from another publisher's stable of costumed adventurers, the *Fantastic Four, Spider-Man, Iron Man, Captain America, Sub-Mariner,* and the *Hulk.* Plus TV originals, obviously inspired by the comic book heroes, Birdman, Shazzan (note the spelling), Space Ghost, Jonny Quest, and Super-President (believe that one if you've never seen it!). Several of these—and others—have traveled the adaptation route backwards to become the basis of comic books.

Pop art and the camp craze have brought outside attention to the comics, some of it unwelcome, and, as a result there have been commercial films of *Batman* and *Barbarella*—the latter as close to Flash Gordon as the sixties can come. Have you ever considered Jane Fonda as a female Buster Crabbe?

In the Beatles' marvelous animated feature, *Yellow Submarine,* there are brief—almost subliminal—guest appearances by a slew of comic characters, including the Phantom, Mandrake, and Flash Gordon. The superhero on the screen may have fallen on lean times, but he dies hard and is not yet to be counted out.

The current revival of interest in serials, though, cannot duplicate the Saturday afternoons of our youth—the purity of our passion as Flash fought, Marvel flew, or Murania crumpled under the disintegrator ray. Our world crumpled, too—swept away. It could have been a good world, full of simple brave men doing good deeds, full of great inventions and miraculous devices, full of zip and dash and things looking dark but coming right at the end. It would have been a good world, except the serials ended and we grew up, and look what kind of world it is now.

INTRODUCTION TO

CAPTAIN BILLY'S WHIZ GANG!

IT was, and is, the goal of many comic-book readers to be cartoonists or writers. Naturally, most don't make it. Roy Thomas, once a Missouri schoolteacher, broke into the comic-book-writing field with a script for Charlton Comics' short-lived *Son of Vulcan*. Encouraged by this, he accepted an even more short-lived (less than two weeks) job with National (DC) Comics, where he wrote a never-published *Jimmy Olsen* story. Leaving that position, he went to Marvel, served an apprenticeship by writing *Millie the Model* stories, and went on to become associate editor. He now writes *Dr. Strange, The Avengers, Sub-Mariner* and similar books. He has even written adventures of *Captain Marvel,* a recent pretender to the rank and name of the fabled Big Red Cheese.

When Roy was a comics fan instead of a comics professional, he had a particular fondness for the (real) Captain Marvel and his fellow Fawcett heroes.

The Cheese's associates included magicians, costumed non-superheroes, dozens of cowboys, floppy animals, some sailors and fliers, and many super doers. Not all were interesting, but many were.

(Roy reveals in this article an anachronism in Meredith Willson's *The Music Man.* The musical is set in turn-of-the-century Iowa, but refers to a publication called *Captain Billy's Whiz-Bang,* which wasn't conceived until years later, as we shall see.)

CHAPTER 9

CAPTAIN BILLY'S WHIZ GANG!

by ROY THOMAS

★★

A long, long time ago, during what is sometimes still called, affectionately if not accurately, the Great War, a large publishing company was born. The troops who witnessed this blessed event were doubtless unaware of it at the time—all they saw was a mimeographed joke-and-cartoon paper put out by their captain, Wilford H. Fawcett, and entitled somewhat flamboyantly, *Captain Billy's Whiz-Bang.*

But, as the song says, it was the start of something big.

After the war Fawcett returned to the "Whiz-Bang Farm" in remote Robbinsdale, Minnesota, but somehow managed to continue his paper as a professional magazine (an occasional copy still turns up in the used-magazine shops): digest-sized, saddle-stitched, not too different in appearance from the *Army Laffs*-type magazines published to this very day. Since war does not teach us anything, Fawcett even kept the title *Captain Billy's Whiz-Bang,* a title which passed, in a small way, into the very fabric of our culture. If you doubt this, listen carefully to the lyrics of the song, "Trouble," from Meredith Willson's musical, *The Music Man.*

Captain Billy's Whiz-Bang was the first venture of what was later to become Fawcett Publications, publishers of movie magazines, women's service magazines, "men's sweat" magazines, pulps such as *Triple-X,* the original *True Confessions*—and *comic books!*

It seems that even 20 years of peacetime publishing did not diminish the erstwhile soldier's veneration for his humble beginnings. Upon entering the comic-book field in 1940, at a time when the mushrooming success of Superman was making the fantastically endowed costumed hero the ideal of American youth, Fawcett's first major underwear-character was *Captain Marvel,* alias *Billy* Batson, the first of the innumerable comic-book captains to appear. And it's not merely coincidence that at almost the same time he also started a magazine called *Slam-Bang Comics.* Then, having run out of titles reminiscent of his career in the military, Fawcett came up with, almost simultaneously, a third comic-book called *Master Comics*—or did he?

Slam-Bang Comics, with a bunch of nondescript characters headed by a hero named Diamond Jack, soon perished, but the others were successes from the beginning, especially *Whiz* with Captain Marvel. At least National Comics thought so, for they immediately launched that lawsuit against Fawcett which was eventually settled out of court with Fawcett's agreement to cease publication of comics featuring the members of the Marvel Family (something it was doubtless ready to do by 1953 anyhow)—but that story appears elsewhere in this book.

During this period of slightly more than a dozen years, Fawcett was the number two publisher of comics, right behind National in most ways, and ahead in others. Of course, next to the Big Red Cheese and the other members of the Marvel Family the rest of the Fawcett characters sink into relative insignificance, but a few of them were rather good, and the others could at least hold their own with some of National's lesser features. And so, ignoring for the most part the Marvels, let's take a look at some of the superdoers who composed the second string of Captain Billy's Whiz-Gang.

All of the features under discussion fall into the general category of super or costume heroes, but for purposes of identification, three distinct if occasionally overlapping groups can be differentiated.

First of these would be the crime fighters. Virtually *all* of the *National* superdoers would fit under this classification. The second is war heroes, the costume heroes whose popularity and activities rested largely, if not solely, on their wartime doings. The third and relatively minor group is the magicians, who are distinguished mostly by method, rather than purpose, from the other groups.

Most popular of the crime fighters not involved with the war was Bulletman, who first appeared in *Nickel Comics* #1, dated May 17, 1940 (only a few months after the February 1940 debut of the Cheese himself). The first issue of this primarily experimental comic featured Bulletman, "scientific marvel of the age, whose super-powerful brain and perfectly-trained body enable him to overcome all physical obstacles in waging his tireless battles against the forces of evil," a description which could have fit any number of "underwear boys" in the early forties.

His origin, done rather primitively both artistically and story-wise (for example, the captions were printed at the bottom of the panel about half the time, and rarely belonged there logically) was pretty typical, too. Pat Barr, "fearless police sergeant," was ruthlessly gunned down by mobsters, leaving his young son Jim an orphan. The boy, waiting impatiently for the day when he could don a law-man's uniform, studied criminology and ballistics furiously, to the exclusion of more normal boyhood activities. He even worked for a long time on a "crime cure" intended to cleanse the human body of all germs and thereby, in some mystic way, rehabilitate even sworn criminals. ("Crime is a disease.")

However, when Jim went to take the police academy entrance examination, he found that his years in the college laboratory had taken their toll. The first panel on page two showed him jauntily entering the police department door; in the second he came out, dejectedly mumbling: "I've failed. Too short . . . too skinny . . . bad marksmanship . . . This would have broken Dad's heart if he'd lived."

However, Jim's laboratory training stood him in good stead, for he was soon working as a civilian police laboratory criminologist, living up to his childhood nickname of "Bullet Barr" with his work in ballistics.

Meanwhile, of course, he had not abandoned his great desire to perfect a "crime cure," and, thinking that at last he had developed one, he tried it on himself to test its effects.

Predictably, he woke up the next morning with splitting pajamas due to remarkably accelerated growth and bulging muscles. He tossed his bed around and knocked a hole in the wall to celebrate. Then, lest his new stature attract undue notice, he went out and bought a new wardrobe of oversized clothing and went to work.

Nobody noticed that he had shot up several inches and gained many beefy pounds in weight overnight. And naturally, that very morning, a gangster was cornered at his impregnable hideout. A newspaper headline blaring "Do We Need a New Robin Hood?" set Barr's mental processes to work and in no time at all, with his newly accelerated brain power, he designed a bullet-shaped Gravity Regulator Helmet which enabled him to fly. At the same time he "salvages a costume that will strike fear to evil-doers," so the book says— it looks pretty harmless to me, unless crooks are afraid of pin-headed crimefighters in yellow-and-red tights—and zoomed off.

In no time at all Bulletman had captured the cornered killer, plus other assorted hoodlums, and had achieved great fame. One newspa-

Bulletman DISPLAYS A HANDFUL OF TEETH!

TEETH!

YES, BUT FALSE TEETH-- EACH WITH A SMUGGLED JEWEL INSIDE! THAT WAS THEIR METHOD!

BULLETMAN AND BULLETGIRL LEAVE, THEIR JOB DONE!

DID I HEAR A RUMOR ABOUT A VACATION?

NEVER TAKE RUMORS SERIOUSLY!

SURE IS A VACATION, WITH BULLETMAN AND BULLETGIRL AROUND, EH, KIDS?

--ER-- YES!

UH HUH!

But THERE IS NEVER A VACATION FOR BULLETMAN AND BULLETGIRL, AS THEY AID THE FORCES OF LAW AND ORDER EACH MONTH IN MASTER COMICS!

COMING UP! FOUR NEW SMASHING ADVENTURES OF **BULLETMAN & BULLETGIRL!**

1- THE MAN WHO WAS DRESSED TO KILL!
2- THE MURDER PROPHET!
3- DOCTOR RIDDLE!
4- THE FAT FIEND!

ALL IN **BULLETMAN No.5 10¢** ON SALE *MARCH 11*, AT YOUR NEWSSTAND! **DON'T MISS IT!**

per even offered a $1,000 reward for a photo of Bulletman, which Jim sent with instructions to send the money to the police pension fund.

The newspaper did not print the picture, however, so Bulletman decided to investigate. What did he find? "Don't miss the next great issue of *Nickel Comics*," but I did miss it, and if anyone has *Nickel Comics* #2 and will tell me what Bulletman found, I shall be very grateful. For kids in 1940, however, it wasn't much of a wait, because the short-lived book came out every other Friday. Even bi-weekly, it had the greatest frequency of publication that any newsstand-distributed comic ever had, tied later for a short time by the hugely popular *Captain Marvel Adventures.*

The all-time frequency champion was *The Spirit,* a slim *weekly* comic featuring Will Eisner's wonderful crime fighter Denny Colt and several lesser characters, and introducing the early work of such talents as Jules Feiffer and Harvey Kurtzman. But *The Spirit* was a special case: it was produced and distributed as a supplement to such Sunday newspapers as the old Philadelphia *Record.* Under the circumstances *The Spirit* was very much a special case, not fairly comparable with more conventional comic books, and when The Spirit did appear in regular comic book series, as he did several times, those periodicals were issued on much more conservative schedules.

Actually, after a somewhat mediocre beginning, Bulletman turned out to be a good feature, especially after the art was taken over by Mac Raboy. Bulletman's costume, which originally consisted of a yellow neckerchief, a tight red shirt slit to the belt to show off his bulging chest, and yellow riding pants plus boots was modified: the gravity helmet was improved so that it attracted the bullets which would otherwise have struck the mighty but not impregnable Jim; it also enabled him to fly. And, as happened so often in those days (and these), he picked up a partner in his Crusade Against Crime. This was his long-time girlfriend, Susan Kent, daughter of the police chief. She became Bulletgirl soon after the feature began, and continued in the series until its demise. She gave the strip, I always thought, a strong resemblance to the old Hawkman feature in *Flash Comics.* Much later Bulletman and Bulletgirl were joined by a little boy in a costume-party Bulletman suit, whom they humored in a few adventures, and even, for a time, by Bulletdog, complete with Gravity Collar. But these were minor developments.

When the apparently impractical *Nickel Comics* ceased, Bulletman survived by moving into *Master Comics,* where he soon proved popular enough to earn (as did an astonishingly large number of those early Fawcett heroes) his own comic. The first issue of *Bullet-*

man appeared in 1941, only a year after the first swig of the supposed crime cure. With its logo printed in silvery metallic ink, a beautiful Raboy cover and excellent interior artwork, that first issue is now a rarely seen, mouthwatering collector's item.

In 1941, its 68 pages cost exactly one thin dime, and you could have as many copies as you could lug home from the newsstand, as long as your dimes held out. Sob!

Like most superheroes of the day, Bulletman fought a large array of unusual criminals. In *Bulletman* #1, for example, the crimebuster battled a costumed crook named the Black Spider, a monkey-faced villain known as Dr. Mood, and a nameless but terrifying giant who was over 20 feet high. Also, in one later story foreshadowing the Injustice Society stories in *All-Star Comics,* he and Bulletgirl fought three of their old enemies who had combined into a "Revenge Syndicate." They were the Weeper, who always cried before killing his victims; the Black Rat, a superstrong guy who in costume looked just like a rodent; and the Murder Prophet, who foretold evil and then made his prophecies come true. These three, before pulling a crime, would always throw dice to see which of them would be the leader for that evening's evildoing. The Flying Detectives brought them to an untimely end in a flaming building. Small loss.

Bulletman's switch to *Master Comics* came at an opportune time for that magazine. Like *Nickel,* it had started off in an experimental format. Priced at 15¢, *Master* was billed as the "World's Biggest Comics Book" and, in one sense at least, it definitely was! Though its 52 pages made it somewhat smaller than the usual 68, the *size* of the pages was roughly the same as that of today's *Life* magazine. Back in those halcyon pre-World War II days not only Fawcett but Fiction House as well could put out tabloid-size comic books. But whereas the primeval jumbo-size *Jumbo Comics* had only one-color printing, *Master* was all in color for a dime-and-a-nickel . . . and it was soon cut to only a dime.

Begun as a monthly, *Master* featured for a short time a thoroughgoing Superman imitator called Master Man, who was consistently if immodestly billed as "the world's greatest hero."

Originally a skinny kid, as young "Bullet" Barr had been, he was given some magic capsules by a "wise old doctor" and grew up into the strongest man on earth. He wore a sort of page-boy costume, with blue shirt and bright red pants, and built himself a lofty castle of solid rock on the highest mountain peak in the world. From there he could see all the evil in the world and "race to destroy it instantly."

Therein lies an interesting point about these Fawcett heroes—very few of them could fly. Bulletman could, of course, but that was by means of a mechanical device. But Master Man (in imitation of the earliest days of Superman and Captain Marvel), like the rest of Fawcett's non-Marvels, could not. Master Man could *run* like the devil, though, and in the first seven-page story he outran raging winds, a speeding automobile, and a falling bomb. In virtually every way he was like D.C.'s Superman, so National sued *him,* too; for once, perhaps, with more justification than commercial greed, and Fawcett dropped him at once. I doubt that he had anything near the potential of Captain Marvel, anyway.

At about this time, *Master* became a regular-sized comic and, after featuring a hero named Minute Man for awhile (to whom we shall come in due course), began to cover-feature the recently created Captain Marvel, Jr., with unsurpassed drawing by Raboy. So Bulletman had to wait for his own comic to receive that particular type of glory. *Bulletman Comics* lasted well into the middle forties, much longer than most of Fawcett's non-Marvel magazines about a single character.

Mr. Scarlet, of the soon-to-come *Wow Comics,* was as much an imitation of the early Batman as Master Man was of Superman. An attorney in his secret identity (when he worked, which seemed rarely), this mustached crime-fighter wore a red, red suit, though in later days some silver trimming was added. He had no superpowers, and, like the early Batman, also used a gun when the occasion demanded. Of course he picked up a kid partner, Pinky, in *Wow* #4.

During his early days, Mr. Scarlet was featured often, with several tales in each issue of *Wow,* coming about as close to having his own comic as a costume hero can without actually achieving this goal. The arrival of Mary Marvel as a regular feature drove him off the cover, however, and finally limited him to one story per issue.

Two costume heroes worth mentioning briefly under the admittedly imprecise heading of crime fighters are the Devil's Dagger and the Hunchback. The former was another Batman type, but wore a black tux, top hat, and half-mask, red cloak, and, utilizing a lethal dagger as well as a not-infrequent pistol, was featured in the first few issues of the giant *Master.*

More interesting, though not much longer-lived, was the Hunchback, who in actuality was a rather handsome young man who donned a grotesque disguise to frighten criminals, whom he evidently assumed to be quite superstitious. The Hunchback wore a set of green tights, devoid of ornament, and he either donned a fright-wig or arranged his otherwise immaculate hair into the semblance of one, and carried a gnarled T-shaped crutch. With the crutch, he battered criminals, vaulted walls, and, on at least one occasion, deflected a knife hurled at himself so that it was imbedded—fatally—in the throat of a criminal.

In one story the Hunchback traced a criminal conspiracy, leaving corpses scattered in his wake, to the police commissioner himself. To dispose of the master criminal he seized him by the throat and, with detailed pictorial representation, throttled the life out of him. A brutal, fascinating mutation of the costume hero.

One character who could undoubtedly be mentioned under either this or the war heroes category is the quite popular Captain Midnight. Originating in a Dell comic entitled *The Funnies* in the late thirties, he was a World War I aviator, a *real* captain, code-named Midnight for a special mission. After the war he came out of retirement, not as a real costume hero, but just as an adventurous aviator.

Soon the hero of a popular and long-lasting radio series as well as a movie serial, he was picked up by Fawcett in 1942 and revitalized into a costume hero wearing a modified aviator's suit in red, a purple-blue helmet with goggles that doubled as a mask, and the symbol of a winged clock face on his manly chest. Still accompanied by his Secret Squadron, and still basically an aviator, Cap cut quite a formidable figure, whether dealing with criminals, or, as he often did during the days of World War II, spies.

Fawcett revised his origin in the first issue of *Captain Midnight* (he started off immediately with his own comic book): in his alter ego as Captain Albright, famed inventor, he had decided to retire from the rigors of crime fighting, helping for his fellow man as a scientist instead. However, with the rise of the Axis menace, he decided to become once again Captain Midnight, using his inventive powers against the enemies of the nation. The first issue even featured a cover depicting Captain Marvel himself welcoming Captain Midnight into the fold. (Captain Marvel often graced the first covers of fellow Fawcett characters, as official greeter.)

In the actual comeback story, Albright was kidnapped because of his new invention that the Nazis wanted to get their hands on. But, left alone in a locked room, he changed into Captain Midnight, climbed into the next room in typical daring manner, and mopped up the enemy agents.

One of the most fantastic and appealing things about the comic book Captain Midnight was the web-like projections between his arms and his sides, or presumably, the arms and sides of his costume. Called gliderchutes, these enabled him to parachute at will from planes or buildings without fear of injury. I always wondered what happened to them when Cap wasn't using them. They just seemed to disappear—now you see 'em, now you don't. However, the thought of being able to glide around like a flying squirrel always fascinated me.

After the war, Captain Midnight lasted longer than most of the Fawcett heroes having a basis in the war. This was probably due to the continuing popularity of his radio show. With the war over, the comic book followed two different paths. Midnight had always fought criminals, and he continued to do so in half the stories. In place of the half formerly devoted to war, there was now a science-fiction trend, with fantastic inventions, invaders from outer space, and all the rest of the Buck Rogers atmosphere.

Even with the death of the comic, Captain Midnight has not been forgotten. A rarity in the comics industry, Captain Midnight was owned, not by a publisher, but by the Wander Company, the manufacturers of Ovaltine. Ovaltine had sponsored the long-lived Captain Midnight radio series, and Ovaltine now sponsored a new television series of Captain Midnight adventures. (If you haven't seen it under its own name, reruns are still occasionally telecast, under the name "Jet Jackson" in deference to Ovaltine's proprietary interest in the name Captain Midnight.)

From the transitional figure of Captain Midnight it is only a short step (from red to green, to be exact) to another popular Fawcett hero, Spy Smasher. These two heroes were similar in a great many ways.

When he started out as a supporting hero in the first *Whiz,* Spy Smasher wore an almost standard aviator's suit of brown, decorated with a red diamond on the chest (a symbol never explained in all the years it was used), and a brown helmet-with-goggles, the goggles again serving as a mask. As a gimmick in the early issues, Spy Smasher's face was usually hidden, or colored black, so that his features—if you can call them that, considering the poor quality of the artwork in the early tales—were unseen. The reader was challenged at the end of some stories to guess the secret identity of Spy Smasher. However, unlike the later Sparkman who used the same gimmick with *three* possible secret identities, Spy Smasher had only *one*— that of Alan Armstrong, one of the apparently unending supply of millionaire playboys who during World War II aided the war effort as costume heroes.

Within a few issues, Spy Smasher's basic costume was changed from brown to green (no explanation in the story), and it was obvious to all concerned—if indeed it had ever been a secret—that Alan Armstrong was the mystery man. Obvious to all, that is, except the ever-present fiancée and potential father-in-law, and the other characters in the strip. In 1941, *before* the costume change, Spy Smasher gained his own magazine, which he kept for a few issues. A new and much better, although unfortunately anonymous, artist was brought in and the stories rose above the pitiful (even for comic books) level of the 1940 *Whiz* stories.

Spy Smasher remained in *Whiz* until the end of the war, at which time, under the mistaken assumption that there were no more spies to be smashed, he abandoned his costume for a trench coat and became a private detective called Crime Smasher. That didn't last long enough for anybody to count the issues, but the sad downfall of Alan Armstrong illustrated a point particularly noticeable about Fawcett's war heroes (and those of other publishers, as well).

Almost without exception, these characters died off within a short time after the end of World War II. Even the mighty Captain America of the Timely group switched to a weird story comic for a short time and then disappeared altogether. It was as though the holocaust of the 1940s produced the need for these heroes, and so they multiplied, but, with the end of hostilities, they had no worlds left to defend. Fighting crooks alone did not generate as much excitement, and so the heroes who were military in nature began to die off.

Probably the most colorful of Fawcett's various warlords was Minute Man who, when danger called, wrapped an American flag around himself—at least, that's how his rather baggy costume always looked to me—and was fit as a fiddle and ready for war. Even more than Spy Smasher—who at least had a gyrosub (You've never heard of a gyrosub? It was a combination tank/submarine/vtol aircraft. Now you know.) for flying to other continents in a hurry—Minute Man was a hero who fought spies and enemy agents on the home front. Though ostensibly a private in the U.S. Army (he went to officer's candidate school and made Lieutenant later on), he always found the opportunity during any emergency to duck behind the nearest kiosk and change into a slimmed-down version of Captain America. For a short time during his adventures in *Master Comics,* he fought crime and spies without a mask, somehow preserving his secret identity. But, soon after he got his own short-lived comic, he donned a small half-mask.

Unlike that of some of the other strips, the artwork on this series was fairly good—or, if not that, at least somewhat *dramatic.* Most of the stories of Minute Man in *Master* were done by Phil Bard, whose work was mildly reminiscent of that done by Simon and Kirby about the same time. There were some eye-arresting villains, too, including some vampires and an unexplained phenomenon called the Skeleton, a ten-foot Nazi monster, who was one of the creepiest villains ever encountered in a comic book.

In connection with Minute Man, a few words should be said about a great difference between National and Fawcett in the way they handled their stables of super doers. Unlike the National group, Fawcett featured a large number of crossover stories in which two or three of its heroes would get together for an adventure of special interest. For example, a Nazi-hypnotized Spy Smasher battled for months with Captain Marvel in the early *Whiz* issues; Bulletgirl appeared in a story in *Mary Marvel* #8; Spy Smasher and Captain Midnight teamed up at least once in *America's Greatest Comics,* Fawcett's fat 15¢ answer to DC's *World's Finest Comics.* One of the best of the crossover stories occurred in *Master Comics* #41.

As the tale opened, the members of the Crime Crusaders Club—Captain Marvel, Jr., Minute Man, Bulletman, and Bulletgirl—all regulars in *Master*—were having a meeting when Junior discovered that Minute Man was lost in thought, looking unhappy and perplexed. Upon questioning, he revealed that he was in the midst of a bond sale campaign and that "everyone in the country has contributed with the exception of *one* class"—the criminal class. So Minute Man, seizing upon an accidental suggestion of Captain Marvel, Jr., decided upon a treasure hunt of sorts to raise the money he felt the hoodlums should pay to the war effort.

Soon afterward, pamphlets were distributed by the other Crusaders, saying that Minute Man was selling chances on himself: "Buy a Bond and Get a Shot at Minute Man!" Gathering in an abandoned amusement park, as stipulated, the criminals handed over their guns to Bulletman and Bulletgirl, having been previously promised full immunity from arrest till midnight. To raise additional funds, the Flying Detectives sold back the crooks' guns for $100 apiece, with bullets proportionately priced.

The result was a rather interesting chase, with one crook attempting to cheat by using a hand grenade he had smuggled past Bulletman. However, it was caught in mid-air and exploded harmlessly by Junior. Attempting to flee the area in a racer, Minute Man himself crashed into a road barricade set up beforehand by the wily criminals, and was knocked unconscious. As they lined up to shoot the unmoving figure, however, a mysterious cloaked and monocled Nazi with a thick accent showed up and declared that he intended to take Minute Man to Berlin with him. While he pointed a loaded pistol at the crooks, Minute Man escaped in an airplane, only to be shot down by the hoodlums, who stole their own aircraft from a nearby base and gave pursuit.

Parachuting into some construction works, Minute Man figured he could escape before the crooks touched ground, but became hung up and helpless. The cloaked Nazi approached and leveled a gun at him—and then turned out to be his old friend, Bulletman, in disguise.

As the flying crime buster helped the entangled Minute Man get free, the latter inquired as to their exact whereabouts. "Why, we're on the outskirts of Weston, Pennsylvania," replied Bulletman.

"Swell, I made it!" cried the exalted ultra-patriot as he bolted away. "I'm going to spring my trap!"

"I don't understand," queried a puzzled Bulletman. "It's not midnight yet. Aren't you going to keep your word?" (Comic book characters are very moral.)

"Only an hour left till midnight!" came drifting the cries of the crooks, who were still in hot pursuit. Suddenly, out of nowhere, Minute Man came rushing at them. Naturally, mere tommy-guns could not stand against his mighty fists, and the hoods were all neatly confined in the jaws of a friendly steam shovel. "Yer a liar!" they cried as one man to a disappointed-looking hero who explained that, to the contrary, he had merely led them eastward into a different time zone. It *was* midnight in Weston, Pennsylvania.

Chalk up $100,000 for the war bond drive, courtesy of Minute Man. And as a touch of irony, the readers knew that Minute Man's secret identity was Private Jack—Weston!

Minute Man presents something of a paradoxical figure among these heroes. Evidently popular enough to have deserved his own comic for a short time as well as a featured spot and a number of cover-shots in *Master Comics,* he perished before the end of the war. Outlasting him by some years were a couple of relatively minor war types from *Wow Comics,* Phantom Eagle and Commando Yank. The latter was a gray-and-blue clad eager beaver of the Spy Smasher type, except that most of his fighting was done abroad. His secret identity was Chase Yale, war correspondent (and, after the war ended and until his demise, a "roving telecaster").

Quite similar in some ways was a character even closer to the Captain Midnight type, Phantom Eagle. In his regular identity of "young Mickey Malone," the baby-faced soldier whom his sergeant constantly referred to as "too young to fly," he spent most of his time wiping the wings of the airplanes on the English base where he was stationed. However, in his spare time, he had built his own secret fighter plane—a not inconsiderable feat—and had started a career fighting Nazis on his own.

Along the way he also picked up the "Boy Commandos" of the air, a group of youngsters from various Nazi-occupied countries who *all* had their own private warplanes and who, under the command of Mickey, went forth to battle the Nazis under the aegis of the Phoenix Squadron, so named in the confident expectation that their homelands would someday rise from the ashes of German occupation.

The Phoenix Squadron used to disappear at the end of each story, when their continued presence might prove embarrassing for Mickey. And, incidentally, none of these enlisted costume heroes ever got arrested for going AWOL. Steve (Captain America) Rogers and his pal Bucky used to get guardhouse duty galore, but Jack Weston, Mickey Malone . . . never!

At any rate, in his orange grease-monkey suit with an eagle on the front, the Phantom Eagle flew his own raids into Nazi territory, and whenever he flew over, Mickey Malone's Sergeant Flogg was very stern and disapproving. "It ain't good for morale to have one guy bargin' off by himself that way," Flogg grumbled, "but he sure gives them Nazis a headache." Not too articulate, but accurate. After the raid, naturally, Flogg usually questioned Malone as to his recent whereabouts and always received the pat answer, "Just catching up on some sleep, Sarge. Anything exciting happen this afternoon?"

After the war the Phantom Eagle more or less abandoned his Mickey Malone identity and, under the auspices of a private international airline, became a sort of "guardian of the airways," as the subtitle of his strip now read. He also kept up a sporadic hunt for a legendary Golden Chalice on which was engraved the Formula for Peace. He still looked all of fifteen, too—I'm surprised no one ever asked to see his pilot's license. He lasted (as did Commando Yank) until about 1947 by converting to civilian activities, but there was a noticeable lack of vitality in both these features after the war ended and the editorial stock of war stories (cleverly published as "secret war archives") was used up.

Curiously, one of Fawcett's most interesting War Hero types was not even invented until 1944. In May of that year, in *Captain Marvel Adventures* #35, a young army private named Pep Pepper demonstrated his ability to read minds. During an exhibition boxing match in which the Big Red Cheese was unable to lay a superpowerful hand on his dogface opponent, he turned briskly around and slugged Major Stuff, his commanding officer, announcing that his superior officer was actually a Nazi spy. When the real major showed up, Pepper's wild tale was credited. And so when he announced that he also had "radar vision" which allowed him to see long distances, Captain Marvel was ready to believe his statement that a super-missile had just been launched toward them by the Germans, and Captain Marvel was able to fly and intercept the missile.

Such a talent was naturally invaluable to the Allies, and Pepper was soon discharged from the army and flown by Captain Marvel to a secret meeting place where he was ushered into a dark room containing the leaders of the Allied nations. Roosevelt, who was present with Stalin, Churchill, and Chiang Kai-shek, explained that the darkness was necessary so that Pepper could not read their minds and appointed Pepper the vanguard member of an international police force which was to maintain peace after the war ended. Until then he was to work unofficially under the code name of "Radar."

Immediately thereafter, the Radar series began in *Master Comics,* more or less replacing the by-then defunct Minute Man. Ordinarily wearing a green plaid trench coat and false mustache, Pep Pepper had only to take off the lip spinach, reverse his coat to white-side-out and, presto, he was Radar, the International Policeman. Now that, by gosh, is a secret identity if I ever saw one, unmatched until the recent Mystery of the Jaguar's Missing Mustache. (The Jaguar, a short-lived Archie Comics hero, had a mustache which appeared and disappeared with a flip of the identity-coin.)

Captain Marvel appeared in Radar's first story in *Master* to give the new hero a briefing (and to assure the new feature a first reading), but Radar soon proved that he needed no help, and for the next couple of years he was on his own.

When Fawcett started a short-lived comic-book idea entitled *Comics Novel* in 1947, the first (and unfortunately only) issue starred Radar in a well-written, feature-length battle with a sinister-looking villain named Anarcho, Dictator of Death. A full-fledged *Radar* comic never emerged, however. A recent *John Force, Magic Agent* comic put out by the now-defunct American Comics Group was a conscious or unconscious copy of Radar, but it evidently went to an early and deserved grave.

Significant among the several magicians whom Fawcett carried over the years—and proportionately there were a fair number of them—was Ibis the Invincible, who appeared in the first *Whiz* and all issues thereafter and who, like so many others, had his own comic for a short time in the early forties.

For the origin of this unusual hero, we were taken to the year 2000 BC, and to Egypt, where the new ruler, known affectionately as the Black Pharaoh, wanted as his bride a luscious princess named Taia, who, however, was "under the protection of Osiris, the god of justice." To combat this state of affairs, the Pharaoh summoned a master of black magic to conjure up Set, Egyptian god of darkness, who gave the Pharaoh control over a number of demons. This crew was then used to turn Egypt—which had formerly been a "land of free men," we were informed with more fervor than historical accuracy—into a state of slaves.

The good Prince Ibis objected, led a revolt, and was imprisoned for his pains, but escaped when he was given the mystical Ibistick, a sort of magic wand with an ibis represented on it. The demons and the Black Pharaoh were defeated, but in the battle the lovely Taia, who was also beloved of Ibis, was fatally wounded by an arrow—or so it seemed at the time.

Grief-stricken, Ibis ordered the Ibistick to kill him also, only to find that the wand could never be used to harm himself. As it turned out, this prevented a tragedy of coincidence, for Taia had only been put to sleep for a mere 4,000 years by the potion on the arrow. So faithful Ibis used his super-sparkler to do the same to himself, so that he and the princess awakened at the same time—1940—though in different lands, because of some meddling archaeologists.

After this beginning, which has overtones of *Romeo and Juliet,* the Mummy movies, and Hawkman, Ibis turned out to be a pretty good and durable character. Attired during the early years in a black suit and red turban, he later added a purple cloak (which he lost still later, as the strip neared its end).

He survived longer than most Fawcett heroes, possibly because of the increased interest in horror comics around 1953. In fact, he survived the Fawcett line altogether, being sold along with a few others to Charlton Publications, who featured Ibis for a time in a comic book called *Danger and Adventure.* Though ogres, witches, *et al.* (that *et al.* also includes further encounters with Charon and various other demons) appeared throughout the career of Ibis, these tales became noticeably more gory and monster-filled in later days.

One Ibis story concerned a demoniac character who was the personification of the fear of darkness that mankind has felt in all ages and who resembled a skeleton in priestly robes with a cowl over its head. The story began with Fear killing a frightened caveman in the dim past and ended in a grisly fight between this creature of man's own imaginings and Ibis the Invincible. When the Egyptian prince managed to utilize his Ibistick to destroy the horror, he observed that "Now mankind need never live in fear of darkness again." I recall that I felt, at age eight, a complete sympathy and identification that I have never felt with *any* other character in *any* form of literature. Such stories were the exception, of course, but they did exist.

The other magicians were, by and large, an uninspiring lot when compared to Ibis. Warlock the Wizard in *Nickel Comics,* however, held some interest. Accompanied by a raven named Hugin which perched on his shoulder, Warlock went about practicing his white magic, as comic-book wizards were wont to do. He possessed his own magic wand, called the Golden Hand, which resembled a fist-shaped popsicle, and which, growing to gigantic size when Warlock spoke the magic word "Abraxas," would carry out the wizard's command by grabbing beautiful girls away from evil ogres and the like. He died with *Nickel.*

Others were a monocled magician named El Carim (spell it backwards) in the bedsheet *Master Comics* and Balbo, the Boy Magician. There was also Atom Blake, Boy Wizard, but he was primarily a precocious inventor so he doesn't count.

As time went on, the preponderance of costume heroes in comics of the Fawcett line, as in other lines, diminished, but there were a number of good characters who don't fit in these categories. Nyoka the Jungle Girl, straight from the Saturday matinee, was one of the most famous ones; Lance O'Casey was a fair-to-middling high-seas adventurer for a long time in *Whiz;* the Companions Three were not bad as general adventure-type adventurers; and Captain Venture was a fairly promising semi-costume hero who somehow aborted after the earliest issues of *Wow.* Fawcett's western heroes make a complete—and large—category themselves. The best and longest-running title was Golden Arrow, the Robin Hood of the West, for many years in *Whiz Comics,* and for a while in *Golden Arrow Comics.*

One excellent adventure strip was *Doctor Voodoo,* a time-travel high-adventure series beautifully drawn by Raboy in *Whiz,* using the no-balloons style developed by Hal Foster and Alex Raymond for Prince Valiant and Flash Gordon.

Perhaps it is significant, however, that as ghost stories, teenagers, and war tales filled the pages of Fawcett comics prior to the 1953 decision to drop all comics along with the Marvel Family group, the last adventure hero to be introduced by Fawcett was Captain Video, an offspring of television, the medium many blame for the decline of the comic book business.

In 1953 the last of Captain Billy's Whiz Gang died. They had not been totally without influence, however, nor will they soon be forgotten. There had been movie serials based on Captain Marvel, Spy Smasher, and Captain Midnight; the last-named still had a full life on TV ahead of him. The Big Red Cheese in particular had enjoyed an immense popularity which had manifested itself in tee-shirts and wrist-watches (*I* had one and it worked beautifully—I wish I still had it!) and other paraphernalia. And Fawcett is now publishing *Dennis the Menace*. It ain't much, but at least it's a Fawcett comic and . . . someday . . . who knows?

INTRODUCTION TO

THE SECOND BANANA SUPERHEROES

Contrary to popular belief, comic book heroes did not always win. The publishing landscape is littered with losers, past and present and, undoubtedly, future. A scanning of today's comic book racks (if you can find any) will show you several titles doomed to a briefer lifespan than that of *The Beautiful Phyllis Diller Show*. Without mentioning the thought processes that lead publishers to think there is a market for superheroes with mongoose blood, Ron Goulart recounts a few of the farthest-out failures of comic books' Golden Age.

Ron Goulart, who won an award for writing a commercial in which a man got hit in the face with a pie, has been writing science fiction and humor since the early fifties. He has four books out so far (and an Ace Book on the pulp magazines forthcoming) and has had about a hundred stories and articles published. He has appeared in most of the science fiction magazines and in *Show, Saturday Review, 1000 Jokes* and *Playboy*.

Once an addict, Ron now says he can take comic books or leave them alone. Considering some of the ones he encountered, it is not surprising that he took the cure.

CHAPTER 10

THE SECOND BANANA SUPERHEROES

by RON GOULART

★★

Although I'm as nostalgic about comic books as the next member of the over-25 generation, I also happen to suffer from total recall. When some trivia quiz asks who wore a red-and-blue costume and leaped over tall buildings I'm as likely to answer the Wizard, the Angel, or War Eagle as I am to blurt out Superman. While others are worrying about what the letters in Shazam stand for I'm muttering Johnny Quick's magic formula—3X2 (9YZ) 4A—under my breath. And so while some celebrate the big name super heroes I find myself more concerned with the obscure, the second fiddle, the third string, the short-lived, and the out and out flop mystery men of the past.

Heroes with names like Hyperman, the Blazing Skull, and the Black Owl who were products of the moods of the 1930s, Depression, and approaching war. Heroes who were invented by cartoonists and writers who remembered Prohibition, had seen movies like *Scarface, Lost Horizon,* and *The Mark Of Zorro,* listened to the Lone Ranger and the Green Hornet on radio and read the pulp magazine adventures of the Shadow, Doc Savage, and the Phantom Detective. The patchwork superheroes fought everything from gangsters to crooked politicians, even worried about kid problems like cruel teachers, and were fighting World War II a good year before it started officially for America.

If you read Frazer, Lord Raglan, or Margaret Murray you can probably find some good anthropological, even psychological reasons why our early superheroes acted and dressed as they did. But the overriding reason was the financial success of Superman. To get in on it, a publisher had to make sure of instant product identification. In the years just before the War a superhero needed a bright costume, a dual identity, and a wild talent.

One of the most important things to us then was "who he is and how he came to be." The origin. Brand new origins are not easy to think up and once the superhero deluge hit there was a certain amount of repetition. "Some men are born great, some acquire greatness and some have greatness thrust upon them."

That's about how it broke down with mystery men, too. Superman came from superparents on a remote planet, Batman studied for years to develop his mind and body, Billy Batson had only to wander into that abandoned subway. The most appealing idea to a kid was the short-cut origin, with magic powers thrust upon you. Doing pushups and studying chemistry were too much like school.

Many of the men who became superheroes by accident had the kind of accident that would permanently fell the usual guy. Take the Blue Bolt, for instance. One day in the summer of 1940, Fred Parrish, Harvard football star, is practicing punting when he is struck by lightning. He barely gets over that when he takes off in his private plane and crashes in a lost valley. There the "great Dr. Bertoff" shoots him full of radium, dresses him up in a blue costume and crash helmet, and christens him the Blue Bolt. For awhile the Bolt stays in the lost world, shooting his lightning gun and battling a tinted Dragon Lady named the Green Sorceress. As war approached he returned topside. The first artist on the Blue Bolt was Joe Simon, soon joined by Jack Kirby. After the Simon-Kirby team quit, the feature was taken over by the very good George Mandel.

That first issue of *Blue Bolt Comics,* where the Bolt was born, was filled with accidents, but Sub-Zero Man had an even more difficult time. His super-atom ship, while carrying him from his home planet, Venus, to Earth, gets frozen by an asteroid. Crash landing near Salt Lake City, Utah, he finds he's turned to ice. Fortunately he was able to shoot himself in the head with his atom pistol and thaw out temporarily from time to time. Suspect at first, he was gradually accepted by America. And Sub-Zero, getting his powers of freezing under control, became a crime fighter. When it came time to pick a boy companion he chose an Eskimo.

Explosions were always good for turning one into a superman. When the Germans bombed the Belgrade lab of scientist Basil Brusiloff, the subsequent blast turned him into Blackout. Brusiloff wasn't even distressed at finding himself covered from head to foot with black fur. Another exploding scientist was Vapo-Man, one of Centaur Publications' many short-lived characters. When Nazi agents caused his lab to go up, it turned young Bradford Cole into a superhero, Vapo-Man, whose chief ability is the dubious one of being able to turn into steam. This was one of the many ill-fated heroes drawn by Sam Gilman. (Gilman has since became an actor and was seen briefly on the quickly cancelled TV series, *Shane.*) Roy Lincoln was working in his father's lab when crooks broke in. To save the secret explosive he swallowed it and this turned him into the Human Bomb. All the explosive power of 27-QRX settled in Lincoln's hands. For a costume he wore a white asbestos suit and in later *Police Comics* episodes the Human Bomb acquired a girlfriend, but they never held hands.

At the Eastern Color Printing Co., editor Steve Douglas was thinking up enough terrible accidents to unsettle any insurance agent. First, Bob Blake accidentally got a remarkable solution spilled all over him. This caused "him to disintegrate and become a pool of water on the laboratory floor." Blake finally turned back into flesh and blood and got things enough under control to turn to water at will. Wearing a goggled airplane helmet and a bulletproof cellophane suit he fought crime and foreign agents as Hydroman.

This 1940 *Heroic Comics* character was drawn by Bill Everett, who has done more waterlogged heroes than anybody. Hydroman never became much of a success, although the idea of entering a room by way of the plumbing had appeal.

Another *Heroic Comics* hero was Pat Dempsy. He worked in a foundry, one of the few superheroes with a working-class background, where a vat of molten metal dropped on him. Instead of dying he turned into Man O'Metal. He never had a costume and always went around barechested in work pants.

My favorite misfortune was the one that overtook Bruce Bravelle in Timely's *Red Raven Comics.* Working in a lab, Bruce got hit by lightning in the midst of an experiment. Alter this, he discovered opposing currents in his body. By crossing his wrists he could spin round and round, which he considered an asset. He then donned a blue-and-red costume to right the world's wrongs as the Human Top. This early Dick Briefer strip lasted only one issue.

A misfortune nearly as good hit Bob Frank in Timely's 1941 *USA Comics.* Dying of fever "deep in the jungles of Africa," Frank is given a transfusion of mongoose blood by his scientist father. "Returning to New York, Bob Frank chooses a distinctive costume to clothe himself in" and becomes the superfast Whizzer. His distinctive costume was actually Blue Bolt's, colored yellow, but you couldn't expect a man with mongoose blood in his veins to be any good at fashion design.

The costumed hero who worked hard to become one was not as frequent. Besides Batman, the heroes who studied for their trade included the Shield, the Firefly, the Target, and Dick Cole. In *Pep Comics,* Shield writer Harry Shorten made a virtue of the fact that Joe Higgins had paid his dues. "No importation from another planet, nor accidental freak of nature. He is the product of years of painstaking toil, the climax to brilliant scientific research."

Collaborating with Bob Wood, Shorten also created the Firefly. Harvey Hudson studied biology and chemistry in college, devoted years to learning the secrets of insect strength. Finally, he trained himself to be as strong as an insect, and was finally ready to crusade against crime as the Firefly. It's a little disheartening to find Shorten, who was so dedicated to the idea of hard work and original research, making his living today by writing an imitation Hatlo panel.

Bob Wood's the Target spent four years in college studying metallurgy and becoming a four-letter man. After crooks killed his DA brother, who looked just like the then New York DA, Thomas E. Dewey, Niles Reed made himself a bulletproof suit out of a metallic cloth he invented and became the Target.

Dick Cole, Wonder Boy, didn't have much choice about training for the hero business. He was left as a baby on the doorstep of "kindly and well-known Professor Blair" and the professor himself made up his mind to test his child-rearing theories on the orphan. By the time Dick Cole was in his late teens he could do about anything the non-magic mystery men can. He entered Farr Military Academy and, since many of his classmates were scoundrels, homosexuals, and even a wonder boy gone wrong, he never ran out of problems to fight.

Drawn by Bob Davis for *Blue Bolt Comics,* Dick Cole was the only strip to successfully mix the Frank Merriwell/English schoolboy story format with the new comic book notions about heroes. Bob Davis, who also did the Chameleon in *Target Comics,* had a single-minded, easygoing style. It had a naive running, jumping, never standing still look and there'd be no place today in comic books for its uncluttered approach. Davis' career ended early in the forties.

A few heroes, besides studying and training, had to go through an initiation. Often the rite of passage took place in Tibet. Because of *Lost Horizon* and the Shadow, Tibet was pretty much the superhero capital of the world in the late thirties and early forties.

In the mountains of Tibet "the Council of Seven selected an orphan of superb physical structure, and each did his part to develop in the child all the qualities of one who would dominate the world of men." Before the Seven would allow Aman, grown by 1939 to a man of 25, to leave Tibet, he must pass a series of tests. These included having knives stuck into him, beating an elephant in a fight, and killing a snake with his teeth. One of the Seven had also given Aman the ability to turn into green mist at will. With all this going for him Aman, now known as the Amazing Man, returned to America.

The plots of the early Amazing Man stories, running in the Centaur Line magazine of the same name, all seemed to be clouded by green mist. One other member of the Council of Seven, the Great Question, was a villain and he was continually taunting Aman by means of telepathy. All this went on while Amazing Man battled gangsters, swamp raiders, and enemy agents.

In the beginning, Aman worked in a double-breasted blue suit, but he eventually switched to shorts with crossed suspenders. The first episodes were drawn by the versatile Bill Everett and later Sam Glanzman, calling himself Sam Decker, took over.

A complex initiation was undergone by Dan Lyons in *Mystic Comics.* For some reason the Blackfoot Indians were short on braves who could outrun a deer, beat a salmon upstream and hit a bull's eye with an arrow. When Lyons stumbled into the Blackfoot camp, he was allowed to take the tests. Exactly why the chiefs then gave the successful Lyons a black superhero costume and red cape and named him the Black Marvel was never made clear. They may have figured that after putting him through all the tests they had to give him something. The Black Marvel appeared only a few times, drawn first by George Mandel in his effective, slightly Caniff school, style. Mandel, now a novelist, also drew such second banana heroes as the Angel, the Patriot, and Doc Strange.

Whether because of the psychological hangups of the Golden Age artists and writers, or because of the overwhelming influence of Edgar Rice Burroughs, there were a great many waifs and orphans. Little boys were continually being left in remote spots, to be raised by some rather unlikely foster parents.

Little Richard Grey's explorer parents were wiped out by Yakki raiders on the bleak steppes of Outer Mongolia and the child was reared by condors. Environment won out over heredity and Dick learned to fly. He got filled in on the human side of things by Father Pierre, a helpful hermit. Back in civilization, he put on shorts and cape and became the Black Condor. The exceptional artwork on the early *Crack Comics* Condor stories is by Eisner sideman Lou Fine.

Meanwhile, David Merrywether's parents were doing scientific research in deepest India when jungle wildmen did them in. Little David was brought up by a tigress and acquired tiger power, plus a cat's traditional nine lives. After adopting a "suitable garb," in this case Tarzan's leopard skin and Batman's cowl, he became Catman. Catman first appeared in the short-lived *Crash Comics* and devoted himself, like most of the heroes of this publisher, to beating up subversives at home. When he got a magazine of his own Catman changed his costume and artist, going from Irwin Hasen to Charles Quinlan, and became even duller. The idea that he had nine lives was exploited for awhile, with Catman getting knocked off and coming back to life once a month. It must have finally occurred to someone that you could only use the device for about nine issues, and so the idea was dropped.

The approach of World War II, and the growing certainty that America would be involved, produced superpatriots and superpacifists. The superAmericans, violating all rules of flag handling, usually wrapped themselves up in Old Glory and used it for capes, pants, tights, and tunics. The problems they coped with were a mixture of legitimate 1940 worries and right-wing paranoia. Fifth column sabotage of defense plants and invasion by enemy troops were their most frequent preoccupations.

Everybody knows about Captain America but there were many others, among them Minute Man, Pat Patriot, the Spirit of '76 and Major Victory. This last was the creation of Charles Sultan and showed up briefly in some awful magazines put out by Harry "A" Chesler, Jr. Major Victory was blown up by enemy agents in the fall of 1941, and brought back to life by Father Patriot, a mixture of Uncle Sam and Santa Claus. The Major's main problems centered around the recurrent Nazi invaders who insisted on marching into Midwest towns in full uniform and taking over the radio station. Since we weren't officially at war, Sultan always drew the swastikas backwards. His style in general was a clumsy, overblown imitation of Lou Fine's.

A magazine called *Captain Fearless* was a hotbed of superpatriots, featuring not only the Captain himself but Miss Victory and Citizen Smith. Captain Fearless' name really was John Fearless and he came from a long line of military men. While walking through Boston Cemetery he encountered the ghost of the first John Fearless, a veteran of the Boston Tea Party and the War of Independence. Though young John was a military cadet, his ancestor did not want him to fight overseas, but rather to concentrate on "enemies harbored within our borders!" Old John vanished, but left a package behind. (Apparently, they gift wrap where he came from.) The package contained a Daniel Boone costume and a magic horn inscribed: "Blow only in great danger." The Captain donned the buckskin and went on to thwart foreign agents with names like Von Groon.

Miss Victory was in reality a Washington, D.C., secretary. She, too, fought subversion at home and, not having any super powers, had to depend on a second-hand convertible for transportation. Her opponents usually made it pretty easy for her and listed themselves in the Washington phone book under names like Mr. Axis.

Citizen Smith, being a professional common man, didn't wear a costume. He ran around in rumpled slacks and shirt. What powers he had also came from a ghost, this one being his father, the Unknown Soldier. Smith's first caper involved him with a foreign agitator named Herr Greeder. Greeder had taken over the union in an airplane plant and talked the workers into a strike. Citizen Smith decided no loyal worker would possibly strike unless pushed by outside troublemakers. He beat up Greeder and the workers forgot all about higher wages, shorter hours or whatever it was they were going to strike about. The artwork on Smith was by Irwin Hasen in his early bat-it-out manner.

The spread of the war in Europe also produced a small band of pacifist superheroes. They were usually off-planet aliens, synthetics or robots. In its first issue, *Target Comics* introduced the White Streak by Carl Burgos. The Streak was an android found in South America. "I'm Manowar," the Streak explains, "keeper of peace, breaker of war mongers, who fight for profit with men's life as pawns!" Before a year was out, though, he'd taken on human form and gone to work for the FBI.

The Centaur Group's resident pacifist was Man Of War. He started up in *Liberty Scout Comics,* a half year before Pearl Harbor, done by Nils and Paul Gustavson. Mars, the war god, gets the notion of erecting an image of himself to promote war on earth. Due to a slip-up he picks Dayton, Ohio, as the place to create the likeness. What he gets is a clean-cut Pat Boone type in red, white and blue with an eagle on his chest. "You forgot one thing," Man Of War tells his creator. "You created me in a peace-loving nation, not an aggressive one . . . And your own deadly blazing sword is in the hand of someone more powerful than yourself." It's hard to believe someone so in tune with our continuing national goals could flop. But Man Of War did. He appeared in his own magazine a couple of times and that was the end.

One more aggressively named pacifist was Bombshell, in *Boy Comics*. This time Mars was his father. Mars is mellower here. "War was never meant to be turned into reckless slaughter," he says, sending his teenage son to Earth to combat Nazis with a magic sword that can "destroy the machines of war but which can not take human life." By the time the debut issue of *Boy Comics* hit the stands we'd entered the war. The early artwork on Bombshell was by Mort Meskin, an excellent cartoonist, who opened up the page, used layouts like no one else's, and introduced a quietly exaggerated concept of drawing the figure in action.

Bob Davis' Blazing Skull in *Mystic Comics* had a go at stopping war. Alias Mark Todd, the Skull operates in Europe, fighting Nazis and, in one case, teaming up with Churchill. This was a gloomy sort of strip and Davis must have sensed he was up against impossible odds with an anti-war hero in 1941. Todd's costume had cross bones on its chest, he wore a skull mask, and, of course, in German *Tod* means death.

Since a hero needed a new villain each issue there soon got to be quite a gallery of bad guys. There was such an abundance of villains that some of them were able to star in strips of their own. The favorite villain of this century has been the sinister Oriental. DC went to the source and featured Fu Manchu in early issues of *Detective Comics* and then introduced a swipe in *Adventure,* Fang Gow. The opposition in each was pretty prosaic: Inspector Nayland Smith and fighting Irishman Barry O'Neil. It took the Hollywood-influenced minds of the New Friday comic group (later the Gleason-Biro-Wood outfit) to come up with the logical comic book form for Oriental villains.

They mixed the idea with some King Kong and got a supervillain several stories high, the ultimate in fiendish Asians—the Claw. Thinking him up exhausted his creators, and for several months there was no hero to match. Initially, the Claw, calling himself the Green Claw, popped up in "the remote mountain regions of Asia," surrounded by a cult of devil worshippers. He breathed flame, killed frequently, and was also a scientific wizard. The sight of that 50-foot-tall monster tinkering with a tiny microscope was always an inspiration to the science-minded child.

The first hero to buck the Claw was Major Carl Tarrant, a scientist adventurer. After Tarrant came Jerry Morris, an ambassador and a pretty capable man with the test tube himself. Finally Bart Hill, "rich playboy," decided to tackle the job. He dressed up in a simple half-red, half-blue costume, called himself Daredevil and from then on the Claw was second banana.

Most of the early confrontations between the Claw and Daredevil, the best of the also-ran mystery men, took place in *Silver Streak Comics* and the artist was the highly effective Jack Cole. Don Rico attempted to draw the feature next, using a style apparently inspired by the murals in remote South American post offices. When Biro-Gleason-Wood put Daredevil into his own magazine, Charles Biro drew the feature. Even after he gave it up he continued to do all the Daredevil heads. He provided each new artist with stats of Bart Hill and insisted they clip them out and paste them on.

The other early star of New Friday was the Silver Streak. I missed the episode where he got his red and gold suit, but I know he got some of his powers from a swami who built racing cars as a hobby. Every time the swami entered his best machine, also called the Silver Streak, in competitions . . . giant insects swooped down and killed his drivers. He finally had difficulty recruiting drivers and had to resort to hypnotizing a clean-cut young taxi driver into shape for the job. A giant fly killed the cab driver, too, but the swami brought him back to life and the young man took to driving around in the racing car, calling himself the Silver Streak and hunting for the giant insect maker, a Dr. Katan.

The debut episode was drawn by Joe Simon, solo. Shortly, Jack Cole took over and the Silver Streak became a costumed hero with the speed his name implied. With Cole, the strip became a well done, light adventure feature, somewhat in the Plastic Man vein. Bob Wood had a turn with the Streak, adding the inevitable boy comparison. Like Daredevil, the Silver Streak finally fell into the hands of Don Rico and he went from there into oblivion.

The Timely company was a good source of short-term heroes. Publisher Martin Goodman used the same techniques in his comic books that he'd learned in the pulps. If a title or character didn't sell, he would drop it for something else. The Goodman magazines *Daring* and *Mystic* changed casts completely from issue to issue.

Where once you found the Blue Blaze, Dr. Gade the Invisible Man, and the Dynamic Man you next met the Super Slave, the Black Widow, and the Terror. Or maybe Moonman, by the always-individual Fred Guardineer. *Daring Comics* dropped Zephyr Jones, Joe Simon's the Phantom Bullet, and Trojak the Tiger Man to introduce the Thunderer by Carl Burgos, the Fin (yet another of Bill Everett's aquatic heroes), and Blue Diamond by Ben Thompson. Thompson, now a gag cartoonist, was one of those ambidextrous artists who could borrow from both Milton Caniff and Alex Raymond.

The champion for erratic heroes was Lloyd Jacquet's Centaur line, which included *Amazing Man Comics, Stars And Stripes,* and *Keen Detective.* They were in a state of eternal auditioning, and even the characters they stuck with shifted magazines and artists in no predictable pattern. At one time or other Centaur featured the Masked Marvel, Air Man, the Eye, Fantoman, and the Fantom of the Fair. They had Speed Centaur, who was part horse, and Super Spy, who was without super powers at all. *Amazing Man Comics* remained relatively the same with Aman, Mighty Man, Minimidget, the Iron Skull, and the Shark. The Shark was a Sub-Mariner type and drawn by magazine illustrator Louis Glanzman under the pen name Lew Glanz.

Even when you were strongly predisposed toward all superheroes, you had to admit that sometimes a dud got into print. For me, and my neighborhood contemporaries, the man who towered above all the others as the prince of flops was Phantasmo.

Clothed in what looked like yellow cellophane, subtitled *the master of the world,* Phantasmo blundered around in Dell's *The Funnies.* I'm still not sure who Phantasmo really was. He sometimes lived inside the body of a Randolph Scott looking guy named Phil Anson. Whether he was Anson's astral projection or simply a guest was never too clear. Anyway, the Phantasmo part of the team learned "the mastery of mind and body" in, oddly enough, Tibet. Coming back to New York after 25 years he picked up a bellhop, Whizzer McGee, and they took up residence together. Whizzer never assisted Phantasmo directly and never got to know him well enough to call him anything but Mr. Anson. The stories, when comprehensible at all, were hallucinatory things about Phantasmo growing as big as buildings or small enough to swim through drain pipes.

Many of the heroes from the pulp magazines got into comic books, too. Street & Smith put the Shadow, Doc Savage, and Bill Barnes into strip form. After a few issues in his own magazine Doc Savage, then drawn by Jack Binder, was turned into more of a superhero by the finding of a powerful magic hood in, of all places, Tibet. This was always a dull-looking feature, except for the few times William A. Smith, now an illustrator and painter, drew it.

The best strip Street & Smith had in comic books was a new one, *Supersnipe.* It was a parody of the whole superhero idea, written by Ed Gruskin and drawn by newspaper strip veteran George Marcoux. Its boy hero, Koppy McFad, was billed as "the boy with the most comic books in America." He did all the things the superheroes did: Wore a red flannel costume, kept it and a cape under his clothes, jumped off roofs. For Supersnipe, unfortunately, the fantasy was not shared by anyone else in his world. Nobody went along with him and he was spanked for butting into people's affairs, laughed at for the lumpy appearance his hidden costume gave him. A realistic, sometimes funny exploration of what might really happen to a superhero, *Supersnipe* lasted only a few years. Considering the way it kidded us I wonder why we put up with it at all.

You had the impression back then you could never exhaust the supply of superheroes and masked men. There were always new ones. Mirror Man, Iron Vic, Boomerang, Captain Truth, the Black Cobra, Captain Combat, Yankee Boy, the Green Turtle, Professor Supermind & Son, the Voice, Lady Fairplay, Steelfist, Shock Gibson, Pyroman, the Magnet, Kangaroo Man, Airboy, The Great Zarro, Power Man, Wonder Boy, and the Blue Streak. Plus Atomic Man, Red Rogue, the Green Lama, Golden Lad, Atoman. Those increasing references to the atomic bomb meant the end of World War II, the start of the Cold War, and, as Wolper documentaries say, the end of an era.

There are superheroes around again and millions of kids love them again. But old codgers know nothing ever happens the same way twice. The wildly eclectic period between the end of the Depression and the start of the Second World War is almost three long decades behind. There weren't giants in those days maybe. But still quite a few compelling, exciting, sometimes ridiculous, facsimiles.

INTRODUCTION TO

COMIC OF THE ABSURD

Comic book readers of the past and present, and certainly today's collectors and sometime scholars, rate their "literature" in a hierarchy of values. Comics about super-powered adventurers are (and always were) at the top of the list. Non-powered costume heroes ran a close second, followed by cops-n-robbers, cowboys and the rest. Those periodicals that were clearly intended for "the little kids" drew nothing but the scorn of their eight, nine, or ten-year-old seniors.

Jingle Jangle Comics was never an outstanding success during the Golden Age, and is even more obscure in retrospect. It was a "little kids' comic"; it featured fairy tales and similar stories for the youngest members of the comics audience, those who, rather than reading the books had to have them read to them by their elders. It was, to all outward evidence, just one more commercial periodical introduced to meet a market and discontinued when that market ceased to sustain it.

And yet Harlan Ellison, a man whose first appearance in print was in a comic book (albeit on the letters page—"My parents join me in congratulating you . . .") maintains that one laborer in the vineyards of *Jingle Jangle,* the otherwise forgotten George Carlson, in fact possessed a genius, a vision of such proportion that a modern rehabilitation is the very least he deserves. All about Carlson's remarkable stories in this chapter.

About Harlan Ellison himself, that's another matter. He can perhaps be described as a human whirlwind, an unbelievable bundle of energy racing between Los Angeles, New York, London and Rio, leaving in his wake a trail of short stories, magazine articles, novels, screenplays, and astonished onlookers. Winner of awards as both screen writer and science fictionist, his two-volume science-fiction anthology from Doubleday (*Dangerous Visions* and *Again, Dangerous Visions*) has proved among the most controversial and simultaneously most successful multi-author books in the history of science fiction.

CHAPTER 11

COMIC OF THE ABSURD

by HARLAN ELLISON

★★★★★★★★★★★★★★★★★★★★★★★★★★★★★★★★★★★★★★★

When the aliens come from Tau Ceti in 2755 A.D. and begin scrabbling like dogs digging bones, in the rubble that is left of Civilization As We Know It, they will surely unearth the finest works of the geniuses of Art. They will discover Bosch, and Van Gogh, and Vermeer, and Monet, and Dali, and Wyeth, and Rembrandt, and Picasso. They will also discover George Carlson.

Beg your pardon? Who?

I said: George Carlson.

I sense your outrage. This unknown, in company with these undisputed greats. I hear your question. I see your beetled brow. You want to know, *who the hell is George Carlson?* And, *by what right do you presume to link him with the greatest masters of Art?*

Who is George Carlson? I'm glad you asked. It's about time someone did.

George Carlson is Samuel Beckett in a clever plastic disguise. He is Harold Pinter scrubbed clean of the adolescent fear and obscurity, decked out in popcorn balls and confetti. He is Ionesco with a giggle. He is Genet without hangups. He is Pirandello buttered with dream-dust and wearing water wings. He is Santa Claus and Peter Pan and the Great Pumpkin and the Genie in the Jug and what Walt Disney started out to be and never quite made.

George Carlson is . . .

Or, rather, he was. He's still alive; I have it on good authority, though I've been unable to track him down. (And in a way, am rather glad. I once received a letter from Edward Gorey, and considered going to meet him, but decided it was better to let gods live in their valhallas, and not muck them about with the realities of acquaintanceship. The same goes for George Carlson.) But Carlson is no longer an "is." He's a "was." He doesn't do *that* anymore.

Again, I hear you: what *that* is it he don't do no more?

Well, he don't chronicle the adventures of the youthful yodeler and the zig-zag zither; he don't tell what happened to the toothless scarecrow and the tamed wildflower; he don't reveal the startling tale of the fashionable fireman and the soft-boiled collar-button; he don't hip you to the extra-salty sailor and the flat-footed dragon; he don't regale you with the facts in the contretemps of the coffee-eyed hermit and the unprisoned princess; he don't . . . well, he just *doesn't,* not any more. And that, woeful folks, is terrible sad-making.

Because the man known as George Carlson, the incredible artist who—for forty-two issues of *Jingle Jangle Comics*—scripted and drew a series of unparalleled contemporary fables called "Jingle Jangle Tales," no longer draws. *Jingle Jangle Comics* is long-since gone. It died in December 1949. At Christmastime. During a season of joy and colored lights and children's laughter, George Carlson went away, taking with him one of those rare and marvelous gifts we had been joyously allowed to savor from March of 1943 till that emptiest of Christmases. He went away, and he took the "Jingle Jangle Tales," and most of all he took "The Pie-Face Prince of Pretzleburg."

It won't mean much to kids today—surfeited as they are with post-puberty sex-symbols like Jim Morrison of The Doors, historical myth-figures like Clyde Barrow and Bonnie Parker, or authentic heroes like Yuri Gagarin and Frank Borman—but back in 1943 when I was nine years old, Dimwitri (The Pie-Face Prince) was a very special person in my world.

Sitting here now, writing about Carlson and his mad brood of improbable characters (was there ever a more convulsive duo than the self-winding organ-gander and the overstuffed bull-fiddle?). I find it barely short of incredible that he happened as he did. For Carlson was easily thirty years ahead of his time. Without the rampant sex, he was in the mode of R. Crumb and Gorey and Tomi Ungerer and Ronald Searle and even Rowland Emmett. He was one of the first cartoonists of the absurd, and a) how he came to develop his style in a time when cuddly animals were the going thing, b) a publishing house like Famous Funnies that trafficked in cuddly animals employed him, and c) kids like myself who really couldn't have understood what he was about, dug him . . . are improbabilities too staggering to deal with.

His drawing was neither simple nor retarded as was the bulk of the line-work being done. His style was one of pre-*Mad* goodies secreted here and there in the panels; of jumbled and overlapping shapes that delightfully bedeviled the reader; of fats and thins that gamboled and bumbled everywhichway; of plot-lines surfeited with double-level puns and plays on words an Oscar Levant would have treasured. Carlson was a *rara avis.* One of a kind. His like had never been seen before, and since him it has all been the sincerest form of flattery.

I suppose pedants would find his little flummeries filled with examinations of Man and His Times, of the eternal struggle between Reality and Fantasy, of the Essential Absurdity of Existence. They're probably all there, replete with literary and allegorical allusions. But what a drag. Dissection of Carlson's work would merely leave lying about a great many rocketeering doodle-bugs and nonskid dickys, with no world-view or *weltweisheit* obtained.

Carlson, you see, was like cotton candy. Very sweet, very good for you, and totally unclassifiable. Tearing him apart would have served no end, and serves no end now. And like cotton candy, he was ephemeral, dissolving even as you tried to grasp him. His meanings were about as obvious as "Waiting For Godot," and to those who seek meanings (in either) a Kafkaesque exercise.

What he had (and what these cartoon fables have even now, in the crackling, brittle pages of comic books well over twenty years old) was magic. Come on, I'll show you.

We can begin with the incredible adventure of the Colly-Flowered Walrus and the Woggle-Eyed Carpenter, from *Jingle Jangle Comics* #39. June, 1949.

Once, long ago (Carlson begins), there lived a near-wealthy but colly-flowered walrus. His favorite three-tune radio, now of age, had come down with a razz-berry fever on the very day he was going to sell it to the king. So he took it to his dumbest friend, a busy woggle-eyed carpenter, saying, "Look, ole top! The king wants a snappy unwatered concert t'day. Fix th'goofus on this radio so it works, and bring it to him, and I'll pay you when I get that royal job as royal TRIPE INSPECTOR!"

(The panel shows the walrus, a rotund tusky chap with albino fur more like a sheep dog than a walrus, wearing a pink flowered vest, a green morning coat, huge floppy red shoes—certainly adequate for ballet—white gloves, and bearing a battered radio with three birthday candles stuck in it. It also shows the carpenter who, over a fire composed of a burning firecracker, is boring a hole with chisel and bit in an alarm clock resting awkwardly in a frying pan. I don't interpret these things, I just tell you how they look to me.)

In the next panel, the carpenter is dashing off bearing the radio, saying, "Wait! All it needs is a new grimmick! And I know where to get one . . . almost."

In the next panel, the walrus, whose crimson bowler has just blown off his head in consternation, is saying, "Oh—oh, I forgot! I left my triple-best sneezing powder inside that radio! An' if the king gets a whiff of *that*—oh, I must get it out before he finds it!" In the far distance, the carpenter can be seen streaking away down an exceedingly twisty road. (By the side of the road there is a gold-colored mushroom, smiling insipidly, for no discernible reason.)

In due time, says the next panel, the carpenter came to a very, very cross road. "Hmmm! Seems I smell something spice-like from this here radio." He sits down under a tree that is wearing a trunk-expression like a pregnant woman who has just been led on a guided tour through a slaughterhouse. "Well, I'll sit down to think . . . anyway, I'll sit down." From behind the tree suddenly appears a yellow foot and the word AHEM! "Uh, what's that?" asks the carpenter. And since he is alone, we must assume it is the radio to whom he is speaking.

In the next panel the visitor has stepped around the tree, and in a story-panel (on which is perched a weird-looking bird wearing a blue top hat) tacked to the tree, Carlson informs us: There stood a late weather report who had on hand all the best and cheapest brands of weather as he warned the carpenter. In big red letters: WAIT! (It behooves me, really, to describe this late weather report. He stands about six three, wearing a Mother Hubbard in blue, with pink pantaloons showing underneath. On a generally humanoid body rests his head, which is a large round circle in which the words "fair & warmer" are printed. The buttons on the Mother Hubbard say R-A-I-N. Like I said, I don't explain 'em, I only describe 'em.)

At this moment the walrus knew just what to do! (For a wonder.) Hustling down the twisty road past a way-sign reading "To the Very Royal Castle," the walrus looks like a hirsute Zero Mostel, and he's saying, "Yessir! I'm goin' right smack to th' king! There's no time t'lose. Any minute now that sneezin' stuff will get ripe and his concert will be sour!"

In the next panel, labeled: While the carpenter—, our secondary hero is being chased like a muthuh down the road toward the Very Royal Castle by the late weather report, still bearing the radio, and screaming, "No—I haven't time to wait for YOU! I must get to this nice dark gloomy castle an' SOON!"

BUT (says the next panel) at the very doorway a sign (reading: Rooms to Let—See Janitor), coming down on his head, stopped him. That was all he knew just then. CRACK!

Overleaf, a large wide guard picked up the drowsy carpenter. It was a grade A, but rough, welcome. "In y'come," says the guard. In the lower left corner of the panel, the radio also looks bonked.

In the next panel, the carpenter, clutching his head, is incarcerated in a cell that looks like the interior of a boiler (save that the barred window has curtains on it, and a lopsided stove in the corner sports a dripping old coffee pot). Through the barred door comes the voice of the large wide guard, "An' here's y'r cell. A lovely view an' three kinds of heat—steam, gas, an' midsummer!" The carpenter is groaning, "Ooo! Th' radio!" Which really seems dissociated, but then what can one expect when one has fled a late weather report, been conked by a rooms to let sign, and thrown up under a jail, all in the space of three panels? (The radio is saying, forlornly, "Lissen, boss, when do I get fed?")

Now the plot takes on a genuinely helter-skelter pace as we see in the next panel a Rube Goldberg locomotive pulling something that looks like a cast-iron baby's crib. The explanatory panel tells us: meantime, the walrus boarded a well-buttoned unlocal train headed direct to the castle. Hay was cheap, so the scenery was changed daily.

The late weather report (whose face now says "hot") is engineering the loco (which also has curtained windows . . . on the outside), and on the back deck of the baby crib, the walrus is staring out and intoning, "Oh me! Night is falling with nice neat patches, an' look who is the *engineer!* I don't like that guy! I'm leavin'!" From the sky, needless to add, there are nice neat patches falling.

Next panel, the report (with a face that says "rain") is saying, "Now's your chance," and the walrus has one leg over the rail, ready to dive, saying, "Okay, here I go!" As the loco dashes tracklessly away in the next panel, a delicate "tweet!" lofting back on the breeze, the walrus lands flat on his ass in the middle of a PLOP!

And in the castle the guard reported to the king, "Yep, he's in the guest cell AND he has a three-tune RADIO with him!" Before the king could answer—a loud whistle sounded outside. TWEET! (Accompanied by a C-note.)

The king stalks to the balcony, saying, "Can it be that UNLOCAL on time again? I'll go out on my 98 cent balcony and look." Two steps out, the balcony rips away from the outer wall, and the king plunges forward, screaming, "OOPS! This cheap balcony! It's loose —an' HERE I go!"

The king landed right on the little flat-car (right on his face). The late weather report—now reading "fair & hotter"—says, rather maliciously, I feel, "Hah! Th' king! Long may it reign! And it WILL rain tomorrow, too!"

After they had gone a few miles . . . the sneaky late weather report unhooks the loco, and chortling, "Guess I'll pull up the hook and leave you, ole bean!" he boils away, his face reading "snow."

Meanwhile, the walrus was now walking up to the royal front door. He spies the broken sign that clonked the carpenter. "Huh . . . a piece of a sign or something!"

(Held upside the down, the "rooms to let" reads: 137 01 51x10071.)

Reading the sign in pure arithmetic, he rang the bell at the same time, saying, "137-07+51xl00-71. 137-07+51x+97+7000000x0+1=?"

I particularly like the plus-or-minuses.

The heavy guard of course opened the door. He looks at the walrus holding the broken sign, and making reference to the pure arithmetic says, "It's a good thing you had the password. Where's th' rest of it?" "Over there," says the walrus, pointing with his cane. Did I mention the cane? Yeah, well, somewhere along the line he acquired a cane.

As the guard stepped out to look, the walrus sneaked in, slammed the door shut and turned the key, muttering "Stupid oaf!"

Next panel, a big round one, the wide heavy guard is blamming on the door with ten thousand fists, shouting, "Hey! Y'big hairy baboon! Whatsa idea of lockin' me OUT? Hey you, open up!"

Now . . . down a treacly staircase in the sub-basement of the very royal castle, the walrus approaches the door of the cell wherein the carpenter lies in durance vile. "Heh, heh, heh! I locked that sap out for good! Now I'm alone in here and I can find out where this smell comes from. It's just like my SNEEZE-STUFF! I'll open this door with its very correct doorknob an'—"

Then, suddenly, from within the cell comes an explosive, atomic AH-CHOO! and the door is blown outward, once again knocking the woggle-eyed walrus on his wooly west end. Out comes the carpenter, all smiles, holding the three-tune radio which now looks *much* healthier. The radio is sending and the candles have somehow become pink, phallus-like tubes. "Lookit," says the carpenter, holding the radio aloft, "it's FIXED! I found a grimmick in that—er—cell . . . and with that sneeze stuff it's sending out a BEAM, too!"

Then, in a long shot of the countryside, in which we see the *most* peculiar shape of the castle (with a nightshirt hanging out to dry and an' extremely satiated sun sinking in the East . . . the *East! ? !*) we read the panel that says: YES, a strange beam came out of the castle. And there it is, humble as little green peas, a jaggedy bolt of something or other that stretches across to the next panel where the legend reads, "Suddenly the king (alone on the flat car) felt something hit the high tip of his crown." It is, *naturellement,* the jaggedy bolt of castle-beam. "OW!" shouts the king, "what was that? And the car! It's beginning to move!" Yes, so it was! And soon it was moving fast, guided by the beam, and direct to the king's castle.

While, inside the castle, the walrus and the carpenter stride toward the front door. "I know what we will do," says the carpenter, reaching for the doorknob, "let's take it outside and see how it works!"

As he opened the door, the car, with the king on it, whizzed right inside. "Th' king!" ejaculated the carpenter. "Yep! Here I come!" said the king humbly. The walrus says nothing in that panel.

Now, only two panels from the end, the king leans over the flat-car rail, the lightning-rod in his crown still a-quiver, and as the carpenter presents him with the radio, he makes the longest speech of the story, a veritable *tour de force.* "WONDERFUL! You indeed have it! A radio with a super-schmaltz-beam! You should have a super-schmaltz reward—both of you—you, Mr. Walrus, will become my most royal TRIPE INSPECTOR at an almost salary! And *you,* my friend," addressing the carpenter, not the radio, "shall be my ROYAL CARPENTER . . . and clean up the mess around here."

And so, in the last panel, a silhouette square, they both had jobs to keep them busy ever after!

As for the guard and the weather report, they were certainly never heard of again!

THE END.

The epic poem died a lingering death when the form of the sonnet came into vogue. When the narrative style was introduced, poetry began a decline that is evident even today. And even before the poem can vanish, we see both the short story and the novel taking a back seat in importance to the kinetic forms of motion pictures and the other visual media. Comic books were the precursor of this change. And I find it not strange at all that a Carlson should have managed to spin his fantasy webs for so short a time. He was too far in advance of himself.

What he did was miraculous and happens only once in a particular art-form. We will never see his like again.

Thank God he passed this way at least once.

It was a richer world for George Carlson, from '43 to '49. And have you noticed . . . it's been a lot sadder since.

INDEX

Numerics

A

C

D

G

H

K

M

P

T

U

V

W